C000215548

A People Betrayed

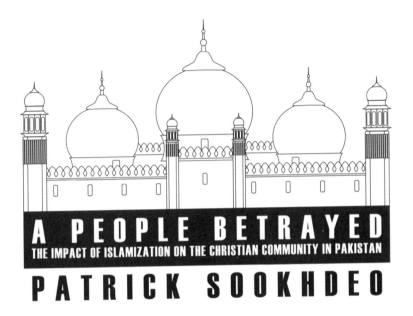

A PEOPLE BETRAYED

THE IMPACT OF ISLAMIZATION ON THE CHRISTIAN COMMUNITY IN PAKISTAN

PATRICK SOOKHDEO

Christian Focus Publications
and Isaac Publishing

ISBN 1 85792 785 0

Published in 2002 by
Christian Focus Publications, Geanies House,
Fearn, Ross-shire, IV20 1TW, Scotland
and
Isaac Publishing, The Old Rectory, River Street,
Pewsey, Wiltshire, SN9 5DB, England

www.christianfocus.com

Cover design by Alister MacInnes

Printed and bound by
WS Bookwell, Finland

Acknowledgements

I am indebted to Dr Kate Zebiri of London University's School of Oriental and African Studies for guiding me so knowledgeably, graciously and patiently in the writing of the doctoral thesis on which this book is based. Special thanks must also go to my dear Pakistani friends, Bishop Michael Nazir-Ali, Bishop Mano Rumalshah and Mr Zafar Ismail who have all given generously of their time and expertise to assist me in this work. I would also like to mention my gratitude to the staff of the Christian Study Centre, Rawalpindi, and the Institute for the Study of Islam and Christianity in the UK, as well as to Professor Lee Kam Hing of Malaysia. Others who have helped me are too numerous to mention individually, but I am conscious of my debt to them all.

Note on seperate electorates

Since completing this book, there has been an important change in the situation regarding separate electorates in Pakistan. On 16th January 2002 the Government of Pakistan announced that the system of separate electorates would be abolished. However, at the time of going to press (March 2002), there is still much dispute from both Christian and Muslim parties as to the best way forward.

CONTENTS

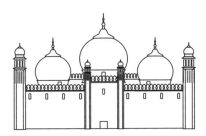

FOREWORD

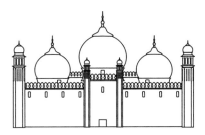

The origins of the Christian Community that exists in Pakistan today lie in the distant past. It is fitting that this book should start with a well-documented study of these, for the fact that Christianity has a long standing history in what is now Pakistan is a necessary basis for understanding the more recent developments since Pakistan came into existence as a state in which the Christian Community helped to achieve reasonable acceptance and security. The constitutional development of Pakistan as an Islamic State and the consequences, both constitutional and practical, for the Christian Community are examined in considerable detail with a very full range of supporting references. The author has thus made it possible for the reader who has the inclination to examine for himself the foundation of the statements made in the text.

This book is one that may daunt the general reader with its detail but for those who wish to study and learn from what has happened in Pakistan it is a fund of knowledge. The basic question as to whether there can be freedom for Christians in an Islamic state is the underlying theme of this book, and the results of the developments in Pakistan recorded here suggest a rather negative answer to that question. However, whether that negative answer is inevitable remains for the reader, in the light of all the information here, to consider.

Lord Mackay of Clashfern

PREFACE

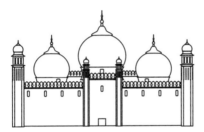

I write this preface less than a month since fifteen Pakistani Christians were shot dead at morning worship in St Dominic's Church, Bahawalpur, on Sunday 28th October 2001. The gunmen who burst into the service had come by motorcycle. They first locked the doors, singled out the priest and shot him, and then sprayed bullets from their automatic weapons into the crowd of worshippers, shouting, "Pakistan and Afghanistan – graveyard of Christians". Six of those who died were children.

This tragedy hit the headlines here in the UK for a day or two, and a spate of comments appeared in the press. Many of these attempted to set the event in context by describing the general situation of Christians in Pakistan.

The British *Daily Telegraph* stated that the number of

Christians in Pakistan is 750,000[1] though the true figure is around three million. The BBC stated that "Muslims and Christians have co-existed relatively peacefully in Pakistan since independence in 1947" – true in the sense that few Christians had been killed before 28th October, but not true if co-existence is taken to imply equality of rights and status. The BBC also alleged that any tensions that had developed between the two communities were due to the increasing amounts of land owned by Christians.[2] This is quite the opposite of the truth – it is the oppression of their powerful Muslim landlords that creates many of the difficulties experienced by rural Christians.

These are reputable authorities who are considered to be accurate and reliable, yet they made gross errors when writing about the Christian community of Pakistan. This ignorance may not be wilful, but it is nevertheless shameful.

It is probably not genuine ignorance that has produced the kind of bias against Christians seen in the standard Pakistani school text book by Muhammad Ikram Rabbani, *Introduction to Pakistan Studies*.[3] This subject is compulsory for Pakistani school children. The existence of Christians in Pakistan is hardly acknowledged in the book. A section on religion in India before the advent of Islam includes Buddhism, Jainism and Hinduism but completely

---

1. Laville, Sandra "Christians massacred at prayer" *The Daily Telegraph* (29 October 2001) p.1

2. Werge, Fiona "Analysis: Pakistan's Christian Minority" BBC World News website (28 October 2001)

3. Rabbani, M. Ikram *Introduction to Pakistan Studies: Secondary, Intermediate, 'A' & GCE 'O' Level* Lahore, Caravan Book House, 2001

4. ibid. p.8

ignores the existence of Christianity.[4] When Christianity is mentioned, it is described as something imposed by the British who tried to convert Indians by offering them various material inducements and when that failed, "attempts were made to convert the people by force".[5]

If any justification were needed for the publication of a book on the status of Christians in Pakistan, then these examples provide it. This community of three million people is unable to make its voice heard. The gradual encroachments on their liberties since 1947 appear to be of no interest to other Christians or to other Pakistanis. It was surely not to Pakistani Christians that *The Daily Telegraph* and the BBC turned when they wanted information on the Church in Pakistan. It is as if they do not exist – just as in the Pakistani school text book.

My hope is that this book will contribute to the process of understanding the Christian community in Pakistan.

Patrick Sookhdeo Ph.D., D.D.
Pewsey, Wiltshire
November 2001

---

5. ibid. p.36

INTRODUCTION

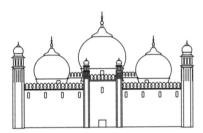

Pakistan came into being in 1947, a new nation with a new name. The word "Pakistan" had been coined in the 1930s by Choudhry Rahmat Ali, a student at Cambridge, who combined the initial letters of Punjab, Afghania (i.e. North West Frontier Province), Kashmir, Sind and the last three letters of Baluchistan. This name was later taken from the context that Rahmat Ali had had in mind and used for the proposed new state for Indian Muslims, which was also to include Bengalis. Perhaps the attraction of the not-wholly-appropriate[1] name was the fact that its literal meaning in Persian was "land of the pure" or "pure land".

---

1. at least from the point of view of East Pakistan which was not represented in the name.

Afzal Iqbal, a modernist and a former Pakistani ambassador to several countries, in his 1986 study of the Islamization of Pakistan, makes an interesting comment linking the process of Islamization with the very name of the country.

The people in their enthusiasm believed in 1947 that they had achieved a land which was pure – a concept associated with the early caliphate of Islam, an era of expansion, justice, equality, and social welfare, a period which covered the caliphates of Abu Bakr, Umar, Usman and Ali. Not only that, the people found a parallel in the migration of Muslims from India to Pakistan with the migration of Muslim Arabs from Mecca to Medina under the leadership of the Prophet of Islam.... [The leaders of the movement] readily made generous promises of ushering in a millennium, restoring the glory of Islam, converting Pakistan into a citadel of Islam, a laboratory of Islam, where experiments in statecraft would be conducted to show to the world that Islam could provide a panacea for all its ills....

Pakistan came into existence in spite of the opposition of the *ulama.* But once it came into existence the *ulama* thought they had an opportunity to play a role in changing its direction for they had serious reservations about the western educated elite. The *ulama* want to recreate, revive or reconstruct an Islamic state; they want to introduce the old Sharia Law, codifying all laws which were displaced by the British. This, then, is the process of converting the country into a real Pakistan, the land of the pure, the process of making it a good Muslim who abides by the laws of the Qur'an and the Sunnah. It is this process of Islamisation...[2]

It may be that Iqbal's link between the name "Pakistan" and the Islamization process is fanciful. Nevertheless Islamization is ongoing and indigenous Christians are increasingly finding themselves unwanted intruders in the land of the pure.

Pakistan was the first state in modern times to be created on the basis of religion. Much has been written of the events leading up to its creation for there was scarcely a more significant event for the British Empire in the twentieth century than the loss of India, the jewel in the crown, and its splitting into smaller gems. Much has been written of the ideological and political development of Pakistan after independence, as the place of Islam in the homeland created for Muslims of the sub-continent was slowly and painfully worked out. But comparatively little has been written of the situation of the millions of Christians in the Muslim homeland.

Generally speaking Pakistani Christians had high hopes of their new nation at partition in 1947. They rejoiced in the white stripe on the green national flag, which indicated that minorities had a place in the Muslim state. But these hopes have been gradually disappointed, as Islamization has taken place. Christians feel themselves betrayed on all sides.

Alone among the religions of the world, Islam has a defined set of rules in its Shari'ah for relationships with adherents of other faiths. These rules have been unaltered

2. Iqbal, Afzal *Islamisation of Pakistan* (Lahore: Vanguard Books Ltd, 1986) p.vi

since the tenth century A.D.[3] and assume a dominant role
for Muslims. Christians fall into the category of "People of
the Book", who have a privileged position relative to other
non-Muslims, though are of lower status than Muslims.
Nowhere in the modern Muslim world are Christians
treated exactly according to the Shari'ah, but almost
everywhere they are discriminated against to some extent.

The very fact that little has been written about the
situation of Christians (and indeed other non-Muslims,
excepting Ahmadiyyas) in Pakistan is itself a symptom of
their problems. Their existence is often ignored, and many
Muslim authors writing on the social, political and religious
situation of Pakistan make no reference to the presence of
non-Muslim citizens. Christian scholarship includes some
sociological studies by Westerners, mostly missionaries, and
the excellent work of the Christian Study Centre (CSC) in
Rawalpindi. But this material is limited in quantity. There
is a lack of Western academic sources on the practical
problems of daily existence faced by Pakistani Christians.

The lack of attention paid to their situation both by their
Muslim compatriots and by their co-religionists in the West
is one of the main grievances of Pakistani Christians. The
discrimination and injustice which they face go unnoticed
by others. "We are the voiceless," said the Church of
Pakistan Bishop of Peshawar, Munawar Rumalshah, about
the Pakistani Christian community, in an address that
repeatedly pointed to the inability of Christians in Pakistan
to make known their situation.[4]

---

3. Khadduri, Majid *War and Peace in the Law of Islam*
(Baltimore: The Johns Hopkins Press, 1955) p.36
4. Rumalshah, Munawar "Hear the cry – of the voiceless:
being a Christian in Pakistan" in Sheridan, Sharon *Hear the*

This study attempts to give the Christian of Pakistan a voice. It begins with a history of Christianity in Pakestan from its origins in pre-Islamic times. Some might argue that this is irrelevant to the concerns of the Christian community today, who have no particular genealogical continuity with the earlier Christians of the north-west part of the sub-continent. Pressure from Islam had resulted in the apparent eradication of Christianity by the middle of the fourteenth century and it was not introduced again until the sixteenth century. However, it is of enormous psychological importance to today's Christian community to know that their faith can validly be regarded as indigenous, not as a Western import. It could also be of political and social importance, lessening by one item the number of reasons for their rejection by the Muslim majority. Chapter 1 concludes with a survey of the Church in Pakistan today. Special consideration is given to the socio-economic status of the Christian community which is typically much lower than the average for the country as a whole. This poverty is one of the handicaps which the Christian community faces in asserting its rights as a minority. This first chapter forms a backdrop to the rest of the book and can be omitted by readers who prefer to move straight to the process of Islamization in Pakistan.

The second chapter examines the ideological development of Pakistan, with special reference to its effects on the Christian community. The ideals of equality for all citizens, irrespective of religion, as famously expressed

---

cry! *Standing in solidarity with the suffering Church* Report of a consultation organized by the Episcopal Council for Global Mission, New York, April 1998 (New York: Anglican and Global Relations, 1998) pp.39,44

by the revered founder of Pakistan, Muhammad Ali Jinnah, soon yielded to a superior place for Islam in the ideology of the state. A wide spectrum of Muslim opinion is overviewed, ranging from those who advocated a sacred state excluding human will to those in favour of a secular state excluding divine will. With each successive constitution, Islam was more firmly ensconced and the rights of non-Muslims subtly reduced. When Zia seized power in 1977 the process of Islamization escalated and began to be felt in a series of laws which had a negative impact on the lives of Christians.

Chapters 3, 4 and 5 examine in detail the kind of discrimination faced by Christians in Pakistan. This is compared with the classical Islamic concept of *dhimmi* status, which is discussed in chapter 3, along with how that has been worked out in practice in the history of Islam. Other possible Islamic categories to which the non-Muslims of Pakistan could be assigned are considered, for strictly speaking they cannot be *dhimmi*, because they were not conquered by the Muslims. Nevertheless *dhimmi* status is by far the best known category and the only one which has a detailed set of rules laid down for it within the Shari'ah. Chapter 3 therefore examines aspects of discriminatory practice experienced by Pakistani Christians which have a link with the traditional restrictions on *dhimmi*. Some of these forms of discrimination are enshrined in Pakistani law, for example the legal status of witnesses in a law court and marriage laws. Others arise out of the attitudes and actions of the Muslim majority, for example, lack of promotion to high office and the low social status and mistrust of Christians. This chapter also includes a summary of the legal and constitutional safeguards which currently exist to protect the rights of

Christians, whether or not they are enforced in practice.

Chapter 4 continues the survey of discrimination against Christians by considering the types of discrimination which are in no way linked to the traditional Islamic treatment of *dhimmi*. Some of these are illegal activities, such as bonded labour and crimes against women and property, which are nevertheless prevalent because the police are not motivated to try to protect the legal rights of Christians. Chief amongst the legal forms of discrimination is the separate electorates system, which effectively disenfranchises Christians and other non-Muslims[5]. Perhaps the next most important in this category is the "nationalization" of Christians schools in 1972 which has resulted in institutions set up to educate poor Christians being chiefly attended by wealthy Muslims. Lack of education prevents the majority of Christians from improving their socio-economic status and, arguably, also handicaps them in their attempts to seek better treatment for their community. Other issues covered are discrimination in employment and the media, and the relatively trivial but strongly symbolic belief of some Muslims that they cannot eat and drink with Christians.

Chapter 5 is logically a continuation of chapter 4, being a study of the so-called "blasphemy law" and its devastating effects on the Christian community. But this single issue is

---

5. Since completing this book, there has been an important change in the situation regarding separate electorates in Pakistan. On 16th January 2002 the Government of Pakistan announced that the system of separate electorates would be abolished. However, at the time of going to press (March 2002), there is still much dispute from both Christian and Muslim parties as to the best way forward.

of such great importance to Pakistani Christians that it has
been given a separate chapter. This is a relatively new issue,
resulting from the insertion of Section 295-C into the
Pakistan Penal Code in 1986 concerning defiling the name
of the Prophet Muhammad, which became much more
potent in 1991 when the death sentence was made
mandatory. Although the numbers of Christians affected
are relatively few, and none have yet been executed, the
existence of the law has resulted in the murder of four
Christians. It has created a definite increase in violence
and intolerance on the part of Muslims and enormous fear
in the Christian community. This chapter also looks at the
issue of apostasy from Islam, which is not a crime in
Pakistani law, although punishable in Islamic law. There is
some linkage between the ideas of blasphemy and apostasy
in Islam. This linkage also occurs in Pakistan where the
blasphemy law is sometimes invoked as a way of punishing
apostates.

Chapter 6 considers the various ways in which Christians
have responded to their situation. A recurring theme is the
disunity of the Christian community and the self-seeking
nature of many of their leaders leading to lost opportunities
to benefit the community as a whole. This disunity and a
historic apathy have hindered Christians from engagement
with the political arena, as has the system of separate
electorates. Other key issues are Pakistani Christian identity
and – somewhat related to this – whether or not they should
seek support and help from the West. Since the 1970s,
Christians have begun to stage protests and rallies to express
their feelings on particular issues and sometimes about their
situation in general. In 1998 a Roman Catholic bishop
committed suicide as a protest against the blasphemy law.

Christian human rights organisations and a Christian research centre are doing valuable work (as is the non-sectarian Human Rights Commission of Pakistan). In the last few years, appeals have been made – with some success – to engage the assistance of Western governments and Western-based organizations concerned with human rights and religious liberty. Closer links have also been developed with Muslims by means of some interfaith dialogue initiatives. Some individuals who could afford to so do have emigrated. Many long for an independent state for Pakistani Christians, but recognize that it is not feasible in practice.

The final chapter concludes by discussing the inevitability of non-Muslims having a lower status than Muslims in Pakistan, given that the state was founded on the basis of Islam. If a modernist interpretation of Islam had prevailed, this might not have been the case, but the conservatives are very much in the ascendancy and appear likely to continue to dominate for the foreseeable future. In such a context, discrimination and marginalization of non-Muslims is bound to occur, despite any ideals of equality with which the state may have begun. Christians in Pakistan are therefore wholly dependent on the laws and constitution safeguarding their interests, even though these are not properly enforced by the police and judiciary. The proposed fifteenth constitutional amendment would over-ride all the existing safeguards if it were to be passed. Even if it is never passed there seems little realistic hope that Christians could ever be completely equal with Muslims. Christians feel they have been betrayed by their Muslim compatriots and also by their co-religionists in other countries. The most feasible practical response to this situation might be for Christians to work within the Islamic paradigm to claim all the rights to which *dhimmi* are entitled rather than continuing to seek complete equality at the risk of ending up in a worse situation. Three possibilities that emerge from the study as a whole are highlighted: to seek the proper enforcement of the existing laws, to work for a change in the electoral system to give non-Muslims a political voice, and to overcome the disunity and passivity which have weakened the Christian community for many years.

This book is adapted from the author's doctoral thesis, which was completed in 1999. Soon after its completion, a bloodless coup occurred in Pakistan (12 October 1999), ousting the elected Prime Minister Nawaz Sharif and replacing him with General Pervez Musharraf. A very secular Muslim, Musharraf appeared intent on reversing the process of Islamization in Pakistan which has been described in this book. Although a military dictator his rule was therefore welcomed by liberal Pakistanis. He has been compared to Jinnah in his efforts to create equality for all citizens.[6]

Following the coup, Musharraf suspended the constitution and on 14 October 1999 issued his Provisional Constitutional Order in its place. But on 15 July 2000 he amended it by re-introducing the Islamic provisions of the constitution he suspended. This move had been demanded by the Islamic groups.[7]

Like Benazir Bhutto, he tried in vain to amend the

6. "The Saving of Pakistan?" *The Economist* (19 January 2002)

7. Centre for Legal Aid Assistance and Settlement *Update: Christians in Pakistan* (August 2000)

"blasphemy law" (see chapter 5) to make it less prone to abuse. He announced on 21 April 2001 that cases could only be registered after the veracity of the complaint had been established by a deputy commissioner of the police (i.e. a high ranking police officer). Less than a month later the vociferous opposition of various Islamist organisations had caused him to backtrack. He told a press conference on 16 May 2001: "As it was the unanimous demand of the *ulema, mashaikh*[8] and of the people, therefore I have decided to do away with the procedural change in registration of a First Information Report (FIR) under the blasphemy law."[9]

In August 2001 Musharraf's government tried to restrict and disarm the militant *jihadi* organisations which pervade Pakistan. But their leaders simply refused to surrender their weapons as ordered, and the government took no further action.[10]   Military dictator though he is, General Musharraf had appeared powerless to reverse the process of Islamization, until after September 11th 2001. Then, with American support he was able to be more effective and dealing with Islamic radicals and organizations.

---

8. By this he meant the heads of the Sufi (mystic) Islamic groups.

9. "Musharraf accepts ulema's demand on blasphemy law" *The News International* (18 May 2000); Rashid, Ahmed "Pakistan backs down over blasphemy law" *The Daily Telegraph* (18 May 2000)

10. Popham, Peter "Pakistan prepares to kill for blasphemy as Musharraf surrenders grip to the mullahs" *The Independent* (8 September 2001) p.14; "No plan to ban Jihadi groups: Minister" *Dawn* (24 August 2001)

Across the world today there is a proliferation of Islamic movements, seeking the Islamization of every country in which they are active. This was predicted by the noted author and scholar, Muhammad Asad (see chapter 2), who wrote in May 1947, three months before Pakistan came into existence, that

> the achievement of such an Islamic state [one governed according to the ideological imperatives of Islam] – the first in the modern world – would revolutionise Muslim political thought everywhere, and would probably inspire other Muslim peoples to strive towards similar ends; and so it might be become a prelude to an Islamic reorientation in many parts of the world.
>
> Thus the Pakistan movement contains a great promise for an Islamic revival.[11]

Some Islamic movements have made rapid strides in the most surprising contexts. Shari'ah is now established in eleven Nigerian states, although Nigeria's Christian population slightly outnumbers the Muslim population. Malaysia, a technologically advanced country with many Western leanings, has nevertheless been gradually moving towards a more Islamic position; at the time of writing there is energetic debate about whether it should become an Islamic state. Even Indonesia, the most populous Muslim nation but until recently also the paradigm of harmonious and equitable Christian-Muslim relations, appears poised

---

11. Asad, Muhammad "What do we mean by Pakistan?" (May 1947) reproduced in abridged form in *Impact International* (September 2001) p.7

to introduce Shari'ah in certain regions. Some years further down the line than these other countries, Pakistan can serve as a revealing model of how the process of Islamization may develop. Pakistan too, in its early days, seemed an unpromising context for Islamization, strongly influenced as it was by British law and structures. But as this book will seek to show, Islamization began early and largely unnoticed. Proceeding by small steps, mainly through democratic means and without violence, the advance was slow but steady. It remains to be seen whether President Musharraf can reverse the process.

ONE

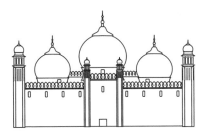

Historical and sociological factors affecting the Christian community in Pakistan

History of Christianity in Pakistan

The history of Christianity in Pakistan was until 1947 necessarily part of church history in India. It is possible, however, to trace something of the early contacts of Christianity within those regions which now constitute Pakistan. The north-west part of the Indian sub-continent was from the third century a province of the Sassanid Persian empire called India, bounded on the east by the Indus river, which also marked the eastern most boundary of the empire. But the word "India" was also used in ancient times to cover a broad range of geographical locations including the rest of the sub-continent, parts of the Arabian peninsula and even the Horn of Africa.

Thomas

The Mar Thoma church of South India has a strong and ancient tradition that it was the Apostle Thomas who brought Christianity to the Indian sub-continent in the first century. A Syriac source, written at Edessa in Mesopotamia (modern Urfa in Turkey) about 250, asserts:

> India and all its countries, and those bordering on it, even to the furthest sea, received the Apostles' hand of priesthood from Judas Thomas, who was Guide and Ruler in the Church which he built there, and ministered there.[1]

There is however, some doubt as to whether this Judas Thomas was the Apostle Thomas because he is listed on the same page separately from the Apostles.[2]

According to the "Thomas Christians" of south-west India, Thomas first arrived on the Malabar coast, near the port of Musiris, in about 50 or 52 A.D. Local Kerala traditions state that he founded seven churches, usually named as Cranganore, Quilon, Parur, Kokkamangalam, Nironam, Palayur and Chayal. In each of these towns he is said to have set up a cross, the seven crosses being known as "the crosses of St. Thomas". He preached in both east and west India, and many were converted – 6,850 of the Brahmin caste, 2,590 Kshatriyas, 3,780 Vaishyas, as well

1. *Epitome Canonum Apostolorum* p.32 in Cureton, W. "Doctrine of the Apostles" in *Ancient Syriac Documents* (London: 1864) p.33 quoted in Young, William G. *Handbook of Source Materials for Students of Church History*, (Madras: The Senate of Serampore College and the Christian Literature Society, 1969) p.26

2. Rooney, John "Exploring St Thomas" *Al-Mushir* vol.XXV nos. 1&2 (1983) p.80

as two kings and seven village chiefs whom he ordained as bishops and church leaders. His tomb at Mylapore, near Madras, is still held in reverence.[3]

Traditional songs, poems and other oral traditions from the Christian coummunities in South India refer to Thomas. *Thomas Rabban Pattu* [the song of Thomas] dates back scores of generations and gives a date of AD 50 for Thomas' arrival in India. Another song, *Margam Kali Pattu,* which was put into writing in 1732, records that Thomas built a king's palace in the kingdom of Chola, South India. The South Indian traditions state that Thomas' success was due not to his polemical ability but to his saintly life and his miracles. He is said to have suffered many false accusations and other forms of opposition. His martyrdom, according to a traditional poem, took place at Mylapore where Brahmin priests at the temple of Kali killed him after he refused to worship the goddess.[4] These traditions, being both strong and ancient, should not be dismissed lightly. In the words of one Metropolitan of the Mar Thoma Church:

> The History of the Christian Church in the first century does not depend entirely on historical documents. Tradition is often more true and more compelling than plain historical proof. In this sense St Peter's founding of the Roman Church and St Thomas' founding of the Malabar Church may be said to stand on the same

3. ibid. pp.81-82; Moffett, Samuel Hugh *A History of Christianity in Asia,* Vol. 1 *Beginnings to 1550* (San Francisco: HarperSanFrancisco, 1992), pp. 25-36

4. Thomas, P. *Christians and Christianity in India and Pakistan* (London: George Allen and Unwin Ltd, 1974) pp.12-28; Moffett op. cit. pp.25-36

footing. Both are supported by traditions which are sufficiently early and sufficiently strong.[5]

These South Indian songs and poems may be derived from the *Acts of Thomas*[6], an important early source – albeit apparently a fanciful adventure story – from which it has been inferred, however, that Thomas went first to the north-western part of the Indian sub-continent before going to the south. The *Acts* was written in Syriac between 180 and 230 probably at Edessa. It is thought to be a gnostic enlargement of an earlier work known as *Passio Thomae*.[7] It has been preserved in both Greek and Syriac, though the Syriac was "censored" more than the Greek version by orthodox scribes attempting to remove the gnostic elements.[8]

According to the *Acts*, the apostles in Jerusalem cast lots

---

5. Juhanon Mar Thoma quoted in Alexander Mar Thoma *The Mar Thoma Church: Heritage and Mission* (Tirvalla, 1985) p.3, cited in Nazir-Ali, Michael *From Everywhere to Everywhere* (London: Collins, 1991) p.25

6. English translations are found in James, M.R. *The Apocryphal New Testament* (Oxford: Clarendon Press? 1972) pp. 365-438 and Hennecke, E. *New Testament Apocrypha* (Philadelphia: Westminster Press, 1965) II pp.442-531, both based on Wright, W. *Apocryphal Acts of Apostles* (London, 1871, re-printed Amsterdam: Philo Press, 1968) cited in Rooney "Exploring St Thomas" p. 83

7. Rooney "Exploring St Thomas" p.84-5, who cites Medlycott, A.E. *India and the Apostle Thomas* (London: David Nutt, 1905) pp.269-73 and Schmidt, C. *Die Alten Petrussakten im Zussamenhang der Apocryphen Apostelliteraure* (Leipzig, 1903)

8. Nazir-Ali *From everywhere* p.26; Amjad-Ali, Christine "The Literary Evidence for Thomas in India" in Rooney, John (ed.) *St Thomas and Taxila: A Symposium on Saint Thomas* (Rawalpindi: Christian Study Centre, 1988) p.35

to decide which country each should preach in. India fell to the lot of Thomas, but he refused to go, despite a dream in which Christ appeared to him and promised him grace. Nevertheless he found himself taken to India anyway, as a slave of an Indian merchant named Habban, who had come to the Middle East in search of craftsmen and labourers to build a new palace for King Gundapharos.[9] Some time after their arrival at the King's court (probably at Sirkap, near Taxila, Pakistan) Thomas was summoned into the King's presence where he described himself as "a carpenter, the servant of a carpenter and an architect" who knew how to build "monuments and palaces for kings". The King was delighted, and entrusted him with money to build the new palace. Thomas, however, gave the money away to the poor and spent his time preaching Christianity in the villages. When challenged on this, Thomas told the King that he had built him a palace in heaven, an explanation which did nothing to mollify the King's wrath, until the King's brother Gad, who was very ill and close to death, had a vision of the heavenly mansions. Amongst them was a most beautiful palace which, an angel informed Gad, Thomas had built for King Gundapharos. As a result both Gundapharos and Gad were converted to Christianity. Thomas then went to another Indian kingdom whose ruler, Mazdai, had him speared to death by four soldiers.[10]

---

9. There are many forms of his name, e.g. Gundapharos (Greek), Gudnaphar (Syriac), Vindafarna (Persian). See Dar, Saifur Rahman "Gondophares and Taxila" in Rooney, John (ed.) *St Thomas and Taxila: A Symposium on Saint Thomas* (Rawalpindi: Christian Study Centre, 1988) p.19
10. *Acts of Thomas*, summarised by Farquhar, quoted in Young *Handbook of Source Materials*. pp.25-26, and by Rooney,

Although the *Acts* was written in distant Edessa, King Gundapharos was certainly a historical figure,[11] who ruled parts of Persia and Pakistan, from his capital at Taxila, also holding court at Kabul and Peshawar. According to coins discovered in the Kabul valley and the Punjab and other archaelogical evidence, he probably ruled from A.D. 21 to 50/60.[12] However, there is no independent evidence that he was converted to Christianity. His brother Gad may also have been historical,[13] but of course the introduction of historical figures does not prove a work to be factual rather than fictional. Mazdai seems to be legendary.[14] A number of descriptions of Indian culture are considered by some to point to the *Acts* being an authentic account of events in India[15], though others feel they carry little weight.[16] Thomas's visit to India was certainly believed by many of the early Church Fathers.[17] The fact of the existence of a Church in South India from very early times is concordant with an apostolic visit. The assertion that the apostle Thomas visited Pakistan thus seems reasonable and credible, but the case is far from proven.[18]

Local traditions in Sind maintain that Thomas also passed some time there. A small and secretive group known as

John *Shadows in the Dark* (Rawalpindi: Christian Study Centre, 1984) pp.29-31

11. Dar op. cit. passim
12. Rooney *Shadows in the Dark* pp 31-38; Rooney "Exploring St Thomas" pp. 83-86
13. Dar op. cit. pp.18,27
14. Young *Handbook of Source Materials* p.26
15. Rooney, "Exploring St Thomas" p.85
16. Amjad-Ali, Christine "The literary evidence" p.38
17. Rooney, "Exploring St Thomas" pp.80-81
18. Nazir-Ali *From Everywhere* p.25

theTatta Naga Fakirs claim to be descended from Christians baptized byThomas atThatta on the Indus. They claim to possess books (perhaps Matthew's Gospel) and relics which would prove this historical link, but these are not shown to outsiders. They are known to practise some Christian rites, but these could, of course, have been derived from later Christian missionaries and do not necessarily have to have been taught them byThomas.[19]

Christianity in India in the 2nd to 5th centuries
Whatever the truth of these traditions surrounding the coming of Christianity to India, there is strong evidence that Christianity had reached parts of the sub-continent by the third century A.D.[20] Certainly there appear to have been Indian Christians and Christians in India. Bardaisan, who converted to Christianity at Edessa in 179, mentions in his *Dialogue on Fate* (written in the same city about 196, either by himself or by one of his disciples) that there were Christians among the Kaishans who were then ruling a territory equivalent to modern Afghanistan and most of Pakistan.[21] The *Chronicle of Se'ert* is a document dating from either the 9th or the 13th century, which uses earlier sources to trace the history of the Patriarchs of the Church of the East up to about 640. It refers to Dudi [David], Bishop of Basra, who went to India where he evangelized many people. This visit would probably have been between

---

19. Rooney *Shadows in the Dark* p.45
20. Hoke, Donald *The Church in Asia* (Chicago: Moody Press, 1975) pp.475-99
21. Young *Handbook of Source Materials* p. 19
22. *Chronicle of Se'ert (Sa'ard)*1:8 quoted in Young *Handbook of Source Materials* p.27

295 and 300.[22] Writing in the ninth century, Ishu'-dad of
Merv, the bishop of Haditha in Assyria, commented that a
certain "Daniel, the Presbyter, the Indian" had helped to
translate the epistle to the Romans from Greek into Syriac.
This would have probably been in the early decades of the
fifth century.[23] The *Chronicle of Se'ert* mentions a Ma'na,
Metropolitan of Fars, who sent books of his own
translations of various Christian works to India. Ma'na's
translation work probably took place about 470. However,
it must be remembered "India" and "Indian" were very
broad categories.

Evidence that an Indian Church existed as such by the
early fourth century is suggested by the fact that one of the
church leaders who signed the Nicene creed in 325 was
John the Persian, who signed "on behalf of [the churches]
in the whole of Persia, and in the great India..."[24] There is
some uncertainty, however, as to what the term "India"
means in this context – it could be modern India or part of
Arabia or the Persian province of India [modern
Pakistan].[25] In the middle of the fourth century,
"Theophilus the Indian",[26] a zealous Arian, visited various

---

23. Ishu'-Dad of Merv *Commentary on Romans*, collophon,
quoted in Young *Handbook of Source Materials* p.28

24. Gelasius of Cyzicus *Ecclesiastical History* 2:17 quoted
in Young *Handbook of Source Materials* p.28

25. Stewart, John *Nestorian Missionary Enterprise: the story
of a Church on fire* (Trichur: Mar Narsai Press, 1961) pp.92-
93

26. According to B.J. Kidd's *History of the Church to AD
461*, Theophilus was from Sri Lanka. Assemani, however,
believes that he came from the island of Divu [modern Diu]
which was then at the mouth of the Indus. See Stewart op. cit.
pp.53-54,92

parts of India and "reformed many things which were not rightly done among them, for they heard the reading of the gospel in a sitting posture and did other things repugnant to the divine law". Stewart deduces from this that there were resident congregations, with regular church services and a resident clergy which he believes "show beyond any reasonable doubt that the Christian community in India in AD354 was an indigenous community".[27] Some of the hymns of the Syrian writer St Ephraem Syrus (c.306-373)[28] contain references to Christianity in India and suggest, by their racist metaphors, that it is Indian Christians, rather than fairer-skinned immigrants, which the saint had in mind.[29] Ardashir Pharihd in Baluchistan had a bishop or metropolitan as did other parts of Baluchistan.[30] Baith Lapat [later Gundeshapur, now Shahabad, North India] had a bishop from at least 225. One scholar comments on the Christian community in North India in early times:

"The majority of these were undoubtedly Indians by blood and ancestry who had embraced the new faith for its own sake, as proselytes of Christian missionaries from Persia and Mesopotamia."[31]

---

27. Philostorgius, referred to in Stewart op. cit. pp.88-89

28. The hymns (*Carmina Nisibena*) are quoted in Medlycott op cit. pp. 22-31

29. For example, "In India are thy miracles, O Thomas", "The sun-burnt India thou hast made fair, the tainted mind of dark people thou hast purified", "The cross of light has obliterated India's darkened shades", quoted in Stewart op. cit. p.88

30. Stewart op. cit. p.86

31. Mingana, A. "The Early Spread of Christianity in India" in *Bulletin of the John Rylands Library Library* Vol. X, no. 2, (1926) p.437 quoted in Stewart op. cit. p.87

The Taxila Cross

In 1935 a small cross was discovered in a field near the site of the ancient city of Sirkap, near Taxila. It is now housed at the Anglican Cathedral in Lahore. This cross has become an object of great significance to Pakistani Christians, who see in it tangible proof that Christianity is part of the heritage of Pakistan. It was adopted as the symbol of the Church of Pakistan at its inauguration on 1 November 1970, which declared:

> Adopting the Taxila Cross as our Symbol, we want to establish the fact that the Christian Church is not a recent addition in this country. Its heritage and past go back to the early centuries of the Christian era.[32]

In fact, archaeologists are uncertain as to whether the cross really dates from the second century, as the Church of Pakistan claims, and even as to whether it is in fact a Christian symbol. It is a cross with arms all of equal length, and equilateral crosses like this are not uncommon in pre-Christian and Buddhist artefacts.[33]

Assyrian Church of the East[34]

Cosmas Indicopleustes [the India-sailor], a well-travelled Alexandrian merchant, writing about 525, reported that there were churches in Malabar and in Kalyan, near Bombay. He also mentioned Christians in the Ganges

32. *The Pakistan Times* (1 November 1970)
33. Rooney *Shadows in the Dark* pp.42-45
34. This is the modern name for the ancient "Church of the East". Other names used at various times include "East Syrian", "Church of Persia", "Chaldean" and "Nestorian". The latter occurs commonly in much of the literature and was used

valley, as well as churches and Christian communities amongst "the rest of the Indians", a phrase which in context almost certainly means the people of present-day Pakistan. Furthermore he reported that there was a church with clergy in Sri Lanka, but that it was composed entirely of immigrant Persians, not of the indigenous people.[35] According to Cosmas Indicopleustes (himself an Assyrian Christian), Christians in the sub-continent were served by clergy and bishops appointed from Persia, so from the sixth century at least the Church in India must be reckoned part of the Assyrian Church of the East.[36]

After the Muslim Arab conquest of Persia in the middle of the seventh century, the Assyrians became a *rayah* (protected people, *dhimmi*) on the usual terms according to which Christians under the Caliph's rule were treated, that is, somewhat better than they had been treated under the Sassanid monarchy in Persia.[37]

They were able to continue developing their tremendous missionary effort across Asia. As already noted, they had sent missions to the west coast of India and Sri Lanka, churches being established in these areas by the first quarter of the sixth century. In Hindu areas the Assyrian missionaries seem to have faced a very determined counter-

by the Church of the East itself for many centuries but is now regarded by them as pejorative. See Horner, Norman A. *A guide to Christian Churches in the Middle East* (Elkhart, Indiana: Mission Focus Publications, 1989) pp.20-22

35. Cosmas Indicopleustes *Topographia Christiana* Books 3 and 11 quoted in Young *Handbook of Source Materials* pp.29-30

36. ibid. loc. cit.

37. Fortescue, Adrian *The Orthodox Eastern Church* 3rd edition (London, Catholic Truth Society, 1911) pp.92-93

offensive from Brahmins, which, according to some historians, included the rapid fabrication of various Hindu legends. This followed what may have been earlier efforts by Brahmins (perhaps working in collaboration with Buddhists) in the third century A.D. to halt the progress of Christianity by forging "ancient" pillar and rock inscriptions ascribed to Asoka in the third century BC.[38]

Despite this opposition, the Assyrian Church appears to have become well established in the sub-continent. Because the part of Pakistan which lies west of the Indus was within the Persian empire, it was automatically included in the structures of the Assyrian Church of the East. But many sources indicate that much or all of the rest of the sub-continent was also included. In the middle of the seventh century the Assyrian Patriarch Isho-Yahb III rebuked the metropolitan of Riwardashir for actions which had caused the interruption of the episcopal succession in India. The Patriarch defined this India as stretching from the borders of the Persian empire (the Indus) to Kalah, which is sometimes identified as Galla in Sri Lanka and sometimes as Quilon in South India. Whatever the southern boundary of the Assyrian bishoprics was, this source indicates that their ecclesiastical structures covered most or all of the sub-continent.[39] This is confirmed later by Morinus who speaks of the Assyrian Patriarchs sending bishops and archbishops all over India, as the Catholic Pope does for Catholic countries.[40] Another Assyrian Patriarch, Timothy I (779-823), also refers to "the Indians" as a province under his jurisdiction.[41]

---

38. Stewart, op. cit. pp.236-252
39. Mingana op. cit. pp.90-91
40. ibid. p.91

Assyrian metropolitans of India are referred to in the ninth century and later, for example by Patriarch Theodore (852-858).[42]   Gundeshapur [modern Shahabad, North India] is mentioned as the seat of an Assyrian metropolitan by Elijah of Damascus in 893. At this time there was also a metropolitan of India.[43]   Patna was the seat of a metropolitan in 1222.[44]   Gundeshapur is also included in the list of Assyrian metropolitans given by 'Amr ibn Matta in 1349. (Indeed it had had a bishop since at least 225, as mentioned above, and a metropolitan since at least 410, i.e. since before the development of the Assyrian church as a separate entity.)[45]

In the course of time, various traditions began to circulate concerning good relations between Muslims and Assyrian Christians in the earliest days of Islam. Consequently, Assyrians came to be given more favourable treatment than other *dhimmis*. This was especially the case while the Caliphate was based at Baghdad (750-1258), although there were intervals of intense persecution. During most of this time the Assyrian Patriarch was also

---

41. Stewart op. cit. p.91

42. ibid., loc. cit.

43. Young, William G. *Patriarch, Shah and Caliph: A study of the relationships of the Church of the East with the Sassanid Empire and the early Caliphates up to 820A.D. with special reference to available translated Syriac sources* (Rawalpindi: Christian Study Centre, 1974) p.41

44. Wiltsch *Geography and Statistics of the Church* pp.163-168 quoted in Stewart op. cit. p.93

45. Stewart op. cit. pp 77-102; 'Amr *History of the Nestorian Patriarchs* p.126 quoted in Young *Handbook of Source Materials* p.22; Mashiha-Zakhka *Chronicle of Arbil*, and *Synodicon Orientale [Records of Eastern Synods]*, quoted in Young *Handbook of Source Materials* p.23

based at Baghdad. Assyrians were treated by the Caliphs as the senior Christian community, and their Patriarch had, at least at times, civil authority over all Christians under the Caliph's rule. Assyrians, by virtue of their great scholarship inherited from Greek culture in Syriac translation, had much influence at the Caliph's court. Their learning was contributed to Arab civilization, which in turn passed it on to Spain and thus to medieval Europe.[46]

However, Christians in the northern part of India began to face severe difficulties as successive bloody Muslim invasions occurred from 1001 onwards. Gradually more and more territory was conquered. When Marco Polo visited central India around the end of the thirteenth century, he reported not only three Christian kingdoms, but also three "Saracen" kingdoms.[47] By 1330 the whole of India down to the Vindhya mountains was under Muslim domination. In 1344 the southward movement of the Muslim forces was halted by an alliance of Hindu states – the empire of Vijayanagar – but by this time Christianity had in all likelihood been more or less eliminated from the whole of India north of the Vindhya mountains and also from much of the Deccan to their south.[48] Stewart comments:

> That the decay of Christianity in central and northern India was due largely to subversion by the Muhammadans is confirmed by the fact that as late as A.D. 1784 Tippu Sultan, the Muhammadan ruler of Mysore, forcibly circumcised thirty thousand Christians

---

46. Fortescue op. cit. pp.91ff
47. Cordier *Marco Polo*, Vol. II p.427 quoted in Stewart op. cit. p.93
48. Stewart op. cit. pp.232-234

(some writers say fifty thousand) and removed them, and presumably their families with them, to the country above the Western Ghauts. He harassed the Christians in their hiding places and compelled them, under pain of having their ears and nose cut off, to abjure their religion and embrace Islam. How many of the forebears of the more than a million Mapilla (Moplah) and other Muslims in the Malabar and South Canara districts of the west coast of India today were originally Christians, who similarly became Muhammadans under compulsion, we have no means of knowing.[49]

Following the virtual elimination of the Assyrian Church in the late fourteenth century by Timur Leng's Tartar forces, the only Assyrians who remained – that is, alive and unconverted to Islam – were in South India[50] and Kurdistan.[51] Nicolo Conti, visiting India in the fifteenth century reported a thousand Assyrian Christians in Malepur [Madras] and added that Assyrians "are scattered all over India as the Jews are among us".[52] In 1442 the vizier of Vijayanagar was a Christian called Nimeh-pezir.[53] In the eighteenth century there was a numerous and

---

49. ibid. pp.235-236

50. including those in Mysore referred to in the quotation by Stewart above

51. It is interesting to note that as late as 1503 Assyrian patriarch Elijah V ordained three metropolitans and sent them to India, China and Java. Stewart op. cit. p.91

52. Nicolo Conti *India in the Fifteenth Century* p.7 quoted in Stewart op. cit. pp.93-94

53. Report by Abd-er-Razzak *Hakluyt Library*, 1st Series, Vol. XXII p.41 quoted in Stewart op. cit. p.93

devout Christian coummunity amongst the Marathas.[54]
Some Hindu Marathas had family names which indicated
that their forebears had been Christian.[55] The Nabob of
Arcot had many Christians amongst his troops, and there
were also many Christians in a Sudra caste called the ill'
ellani Kamavarus.[56]

The large Roman Catholic communities which exist in
South India today are probably the descendants of Assyrian
Christians who were absorbed into Roman Catholicism
after the advent of Catholic missionaries to India.[57] This
absorption process was far from smooth and easy, involving
even guns and the threat of bloodshed, as the Assyrians,
proud of their race and ancient traditions, reluctantly
submitted to the imposition of a Catholic hierarchy from
Europe. A critical event occurred at Mattanchery in 1653
when a huge mob of Indian Christians, eager to welcome
a Syrian Orthodox Patriarch from Antioch and to free
themselves from the domination of the Portuguese in Goa,
swore on the cross at Mattanchery Church that they would
not accept the authority of Goa. It is interesting to note
that this revolt was against the authority of the Portuguese
rulers of Goa and the Jesuits rather than against the
authority of the Pope, and that most of the former Assyrians

---

54. *Lettres Edifiantes et Curieuses* quoted in *History of
(R.C.) Telugu Christians* (Trichinopoly, 1928). See Stewart
op. cit. p.96

55. Hunter, Sir W.W. *The Indian Empire* p.240 referring to
Gazetteer of the Kanara district of the Bombay Presidency Vol.
XV p.397. See Stewart op. cit. p.96

56. *History of (R.C.) Telugu Christians* (Trichinopoly, 1928)
pp.258,294 referred to in Stewart op. cit. p.97

57. Stewart op. cit. pp.291-300

continued as Catholics calling themselves Syrian Catholics or Catholic Chaldeans.[58]

There is, however, one nominally Assyrian group in India known as the Church of Trichur or, informally, the Mellusians, which has about fifteen thousand adherents. They are a schismatic sect which arose in the second half of the nineteenth century from Catholic Chaldeans in Malabar, and are led by the Metropolitan of Malabar and the Indies, who is based at Trichur.[59]

Catholic

Vasco da Gama, who sailed into the Indian Ocean in 1498, was probably the first Roman Catholic to reach the sub-continent. He was closely followed by the first Catholic missionaries, Franciscan brothers, who arrived from Portugal in 1500.[60] In 1542 the first Jesuit missionary to India, Francis Xavier, arrived in Goa. Meanwhile Portuguese enclaves were being set up along the Indian coasts. The Mughal emperor Akbar had a fascination with religions of all kinds, and abolished the *jizya* imposed by his predecessors, thus creating a common citizenship for all his subjects, Hindus and Muslims alike.[61] In 1579 he

---

58. Thomas op. cit. pp.76-104,224

59. Attwater, Donald *The Dissident Eastern Churches*, (Milwaukee: The Bruce Publishing Company, 1937) pp 221, 231-232; Fortescue op. cit. pp.108-109; Janin, Père Raymond *The Separated Eastern Churches* translated by P. Boylan (London: Sands & Co., 1933) pp.209-210

60. W.W. Hunter *The Indian Empire* p.244 referred to in Stewart op. cit. p.98

61. Sharma, Sri Ram *The Religious Policy of the Mughal Emperors* (first published Calcutta, 1940, reprinted Lahore: Panco Press, 1975) p.23

sent an ambassador to Goa with a letter to the Jesuits requesting that they "send me two learned priests who should bring with them the chief books of the Law and the Gospel, for I wish to study and learn the law and what is best and most perfect in it". It seems that his choice of Jesuits rather than any other kind of Christian could have been prompted by a report he had heard three years earlier of two Jesuit priests in Bengal who had refused absolution to some Portuguese merchants who had defrauded the Mughal officials of taxes which were legitimately due to the Mughal government. A group of Jesuit missionaries was duly sent, and arrived at Akbar's court at Fatehpur Sikri in February 1580. Akbar allowed them to preach and make conversions; he even donated funds for the construction of the first church in Lahore in 1600. Akbar's interest in Christianity waxed and waned. At one point (1590) he ordered that all minarets in Lahore be demolished and that the mosques be turned into grain stores and stables. In 1601 he finally agreed to issue a written firman granting freedom of worship and the right to preach publicly and make converts, thus making official his earlier verbal statement. However, he never converted to Christianity, and died in 1605, his own personal beliefs still a mystery to the rest of the world.[62]

Akbar's son, Salim, who changed his name to Jehangir when he acceded to the throne, paid lip service to Islamic

---

62. Barrett, David (ed.) *World Christian Encyclopedia* (Oxford: Oxford University Press, 1982) p.543; Hoke op. cit. p. 493; Stock, Frederick and Margaret *People Movements in the Punjab* (1975) pp.309-26; Rooney, John *The Hesitant Dawn* (Rawalpindi: Christian Study Centre, 1984) pp.21,26,34-5,40,49,54; Thomas op. cit. p.106

orthodoxy, in a way his father had not done, and one of his first edicts was to prohibit the sale of alcohol.[63] Nevertheless he seemed at first even more favourable to Christianity than his father had been. He gave generous gifts for the building and maintenance of churches in Lahore and Agra. He surrounded himself with religious pictures, most of which were Christian, and always wore a golden crucifix around his neck. He was friendly to the missionaries and seemed pleased when they out-argued the Muslim *ulema* in debates. However, he also restored the mosques which his father had desecrated and sometimes attempted to force Christians to apostasize.[64]

In 1608 and 1612 the first English ambassadors arrived at Jehangir's court. The Portuguese Goans, resenting the attention paid by the Mughals to the English, seized a Mughal galleon in 1613.[65] Jehangir immediately severed trade and diplomatic relations with them, and ceased to be so tolerant towards Christianity. He cut off his allowances to the Jesuit priests, and closed the churches at Lahore and Agra. Life continued to be so difficult for the Christians in Lahore that the following year the entire Christian community of Lahore moved to Agra. By 1615, however, good relations were restored between Jehangir and the Portuguese, and in 1624 the church in Lahore was opened

---

63. Edwardes, S.M. and Garrett, H.L.O. *Mughal Rule in India* (New Delhi: Asian Publication Services, 1979) pp.54-5

64. ibid. p.62; Guerreiro, F. and Payne, G.H. *Jahangir and the Jesuits* (London, 1930) p.47 ff. cited in Rooney *The Hesitant Dawn* pp.57-60

65. *Calendar of State Papers*, Colonial Series, East Indies (1862) 1513-1616 No. 659 p.258 cited in Rooney *The Hesitant Dawn* p.63

again, but it does not seem that an indigenous Christian community developed there again, nor that the refugees ever returned from Agra. In his later years, Jehangir became even more open to Christianity, but never actually converted.[66]

Meanwhile other Catholic orders were active in other parts of what is now Pakistan. An Augustinian friar is known to have died in Sind in 1598, and in 1613 the Carmelites Fr Louis Francis and Brother John Baptist arrived in Thatta [near Karachi], a large and important city whose population was mainly Hindu, with a small number of Portuguese. Circumstances called Fr Louis away after six months, but in 1618 he returned and quickly built a church and a small convent. The church, beautifully decorated for its opening, was an object of great fascination to the local people but after a fortnight of constant visitors, local Muslims threatened to burn it down and murder the priest. The Mughal governor stepped in to prevent this, but Fr Louis decided to restrict access to the church somewhat. Fr Louis also opened a chapel at the port of Lahri Bandar, two days journey away. He made only three converts – one Hindu and two Muslims – whom he baptized the day before he died. In 1624 Augustinian friars arrived at Thatta and Lahri Bandar. There was great rivalry between them and the Carmelites, but neither group managed to win many converts.[67] Jesuit missionaries were also active in Kashmir. During a severe famine in 1607-8 many starving children were abandoned on the streets. The Jesuits

---

66. Edwardes and Garrett op. cit. p.67; Rooney *The Hesitant Dawn* pp.63-64; Thomas op. cit. p.114
67. Rooney *The Hesitant Dawn* pp.65-70

gathered as many as they could, baptized them, and tried
to nurse them back to health, but all died.[68]

Muslims in the sub-continent at this time were much
more tolerant towards the preaching of other religions than
were Muslims further west. For example, an English
traveller named Coryate who acted as muezzin in a
mosque, calling the faithful to prayer with the words "There
is no God but God, and Hazrat Isa [Prophet Jesus] is the
Son of God", lived to tell the tale.[69]

Jehangir's son, Prince Khurram, succeeded to the
imperial throne in 1626 under the title Shah Jehan. The
Portuguese Jesuits, who had already antagonized him by
refusing to support his rebellion against Jehangir in 1622,
were immediately deprived of their imperial pensions and
lost their influence at court. Having ruthlessly dealt with
various other enemies, Shah Jehan then turned on the Jesuit
missionaries in earnest and in 1632 ordered that the
Portuguese settlement at Hugli in Bengal be destroyed. A
Mughal army of 150,000 was sent to besiege Hugli, which
was defended by a garrison of only a thousand – 300
European troops and 700 Indian Christian troops. The
town fell after a siege of three months, and more than 4,000
Christians were captured and taken to Shah Jehan in Agra.
Many were killed, some were sold as slaves, some escaped
death by converting to Islam, and some were forcibly
converted. Their religious images were broken up and
thrown into the river.[70]   In 1633 (or perhaps 1634) Shah
Jehan ordered the closure and destruction of all Christian
places of worship. The church at Lahore and its bell tower

68. ibid. pp.47,70
69. Thomas op. cit. pp.121-2
70. Edwardes and Garrett op. cit. pp.74-5

were duly destroyed, so was the church at Thatta. By 1655 the Augustinians had left Thatta. It is not known what happened to the buildings at Lahri Bandar, but the mission there was soon abandoned. Buildings at Agra were also destroyed. Some time between 1632 and 1634 Shah Jehan also issued a decree forbidding conversions from Islam, but this was not rigorously enforced. Public Christian worship was also forbidden.

Although Shah Jehan later permitted some re-building (e.g. at Agra) and in 1641 even gave permission for the re-opening of the missions in Sind, the Catholic work in Pakistan was much reduced. At the end of his reign there was still a Jesuit presence in Lahore, but this was now seen by the Jesuits mainly as a convenient staging post on the way to their new missons in Tibet. Meanwhile, the Carmelite priests at Thatta did little more than perform church services for the shrinking Portuguese community.[71]

In 1658 Aurangzeb rebelled against his father Shah Jehan, and seized the empire from him. In 1668 he began to introduce a series of Islamic reforms. The first of these ordered stricter standards of behaviour at court, the destruction of Hindu temples, and forbade non-Muslim public religious displays. In 1669 he ordered the closure of schools at Thatta and Multan where Hindus were reported to be teaching from "unholy books" and banned "the teaching and infidel practices of the unbelievers".

It appears that these decrees had little effect on the Christians at Lahore, but at Thatta the Mughal authorities interrogated the Carmelite priests and confiscated their library. One of the accusations against them was that they

---

71. Rooney *The Hesitant Dawn* pp.85-91; Stock op. cit. pp.309-26

had been instructing Muslim children and sending them to Goa for baptism. In addition, popular anti-Portuguese sentiments resulted in further harassment of the priests by the Muslims whenever the Portuguese seized a local ship. Some time before November 1672 the mission was closed.

The Christian presence in Lahore continued into the eighteenth century, by which time there was a signficiant Dutch presence. Fr E. de Figueiredo wrote in 1735 about Lahore as follows:

> Here is generally stationed the elite of the Mughal army, composed for the greater part of Christian officers, who by their fidelity and courage in all dangerous attacks on the enemy prepare the way for the Emperor's felicitous victories. They carry on their banners the holy cross, fulfil during their military service their Christian duties, and make themselves more redoubtable to the enemy by their piety than by their military tactics. Since the time of Fr Jerome Xavier ... no permanent resident priest was stationed there. For the spiritual consolation of these officers and other Christians who are in great numbers, Lahore is visited twice a year by a priest, who extends his apostolic zeal also further northwards, visiting the Provinces of Multan, Backar, Kabul and even Candar or Candahar.[72]

Jesuit work in the northern part of the sub-continent effectively finished in 1760, as a result of the suppression of their order in all Portuguese territories by the Marquis

---

72. Weldbott, band 31, p.1 quoted in Rooney *The Hesitant Dawn* p.94

de Pombal, who had become dictator in Portugal in 1755. Some Jesuits continued to live and work in Goa, which was beyond the jurisdiction of Portugal. In 1783 the whole of north India was assigned to the Italian Capuchin mission to Tibet, but they did not have the resources to cope with such a large area. Sind and Baluchistan remained the responsibility of the Carmelites in Bombay. This divison of responsiblity was largely academic since Catholic work in Pakistan was in abeyance until the conquest of Sind by the British in 1842.[73]

Immediately the Carmelites became active in Sind, setting up a centre in Hyderabad and a school in Karachi. Ten years later the Jesuits took over the work. Early work in the Sind concentrated on Goans, South Indians, Anglo-Indians and Europeans rather than indigenous people, but in the 1860s there were some conversions of Sindis. In the succeeding decades Catholic work blossomed and flourished all over Pakistan. By 1880 Lahore had a missionary centre and an orphanage for girls. By 1889 Sialkot had become an important missionary centre, with six missionaries. In 1892 work began in the canal colonies. The latter two locations were very significant in the Chuhra movement which began in 1884.

The first decades of the twentieth century saw considerable growth in the numbers of Catholics. For example, in the Punjab, an estimated 1,500 Catholics in 1901 had increased to 45,641 by 1931. Many of these converts were from other Christian denominations, but others were from the Chuhras (basically Hindus but strongly influenced by Islam). In the 1930s and 1940s there

73. Rooney *The Hesitant Dawn* pp.91-96

were also numbers of conversions from other scheduled castes,[74] for example Bhils and Kohlis. Growth of the Catholic Church continued after the Chuhra movement had waned, and between 1949 and 1972 the number of Roman Catholics in Pakistan almost tripled to 341,231. The vast majority of these new converts came from Protestant denominations.[75]

Protestant[76]

Apart from the presence of British army chaplains, Protestant Christianity in Pakistan began with the visit of John Lowrie, an American Presbyterian missionary based at Ludhiana, to Lahore on 8 December 1835. The Sikh ruler of Lahore invited him to open a school there, but ill-health forced him to return to the US. His successors, John Newton and Charles Forman, arrived in 1849, the year after the second Sikh war had brought the Punjab under British rule. Forman spent more than 40 years in the

---

74. The Indian terminology "scheduled castes" is used here because the normal modern Pakistani terms – that is, "minorities" or "backward classes" – seem respectively confusing in this context and unsuitable for an academic study. The term "scheduled castes" was included in the title of a political party as late as 1949. See Tinker, Hugh *India and Pakistan: a political analysis* 2nd ed., revised, (London: Pall Mall Press Ltd, 1967) p.74. It was also used by Khurshid Ahmad in 1955. See Ahmad, Khurshid's editorial footnote in Maududi, S. Abul A'la *The Islamic Law and Constitution* translated and edited by Khurshid Ahmad 7th edition (Lahore: Islamic Publications Ltd, 1980) p.70

75. Stock op. cit. pp.309-26

76. Barrett op. cit. pp 542-5; Campbell op. cit. pp.9-15; Hoke op. cit. pp 475-99; Stock op. cit. pp 17-32, 57-139, 280-1; Webster op. cit. passim

Punjab and founded the college in Lahore which is still known by his name. From this work developed the Lahore Church Council.

In 1850 Anglican British missionaries with the Church Missionary Society (CMS) settled in Karachi. In a few years they had moved into all four provinces of modern Pakistan, often at the request of British civil officers. CMS missionaries were more widely spread over Pakistan than any those of any other group.

The Associate Presbyterian Church of North America – soon to become the United Presbyterian Church of North America and not to be confused with the American Presbyterian Church mentioned above – started misson work in the Punjab in 1855. The work was initially centred on Sialkot. From this developed the United Presbyterian (UP) Church of Pakistan, which grew to be the largest Protestant denomination in Pakistan.

Yet more Presbyterians, this time the Church of Scotland, arrived in Pakistan in 1856. The work began in Sialkot but got off to a very shaky start with the murder of the missionary, his wife and baby son by an escaped prisoner during the Indian Mutiny the following year. The Scottish mission resumed in 1861.

In 1873 American Methodists began work in Karachi. The Salvation Army entered in 1883 and the Brethren in 1892. Lutheran work was begun on the north-west frontier by the Danish Pathan Mission in 1903. Adventists, Baptists and Pentecostals have also been involved in work in Pakistan.

In the early decades of Protestant mission, progress in winning converts was very slow. The Church of Scotland mission had fewer than 200 after 20 years of labour. After a similar period of time, the American UP missionaries had 153 adult communicants. The British CMS missionaries were much the same. During this period, missionary work was mainly directed towards the educated and high castes. In some cases this was a deliberate policy. For example, the German missionary, Pfander, who opened a CMS mission station in Peshawar in 1854, saw a number of learned Muslims converted through his writings and public disputations. In other cases it was quite unwitting. For example, the first UP missionaries spent a lot of time preaching in Urdu in the city bazaars and distributing tracts. Their audience was limited because only educated people spoke Urdu, only men went to the bazaar, only 1% of Muslim, Hindu and Sikh people could read, and the rural population had no opportunity to hear the Gospel at all. Schools, orphanages and medical work were also established. Individuals who did become Christians were usually rejected by their families and thus became dependent on the missionaries, many of them living in the mission compound.

However, all this changed with the Chuhra movement (see above). The Chuhras formed the largest of the scheduled castes in the Punjab. Occupying an inferior position even among scheduled castes[77] they were amongst society's lowest and most despised people. They carried out dirty and menial jobs. Their religion was a kind of "islamized Hinduism" which included belief in a mediator and the need for sacrifices.

---

77. Streefland, Pieter H. *The Christian Punjabi sweepers: their history and their position in present day Pakistan* (Rawalpindi: Christian Study Centre, 1974) p.1

The mass conversions to Christianity, which became known as the Chuhra movement, began in 1873 with an illiterate elderly Chuhra man called Ditt. Ditt was converted to Christianity by a young Hindu convert. He went to the Presbyterian mission in Sialkot requesting baptism. This the missionaries reluctantly agreed to, after much pleading from Ditt. Against the missionaries' wishes, Ditt returned to his village where he faced ostracism and rejection. Nevertheless he stayed there, and before long his wife, daughter and two neighbours had become Christians. They were baptized by the missionaries. In 1874, Ditt's uncle and three other men converted. Gradually the number of Chuhra Christians in the Sialkot area grew. Many heard the Christian message from Ditt himself as he travelled from village to village selling hides.[78]

Meanwhile, Chuhras in other areas were also converted. In 1873 a Chuhra from Gujranwala was baptized, and soon afterwards two others from Gurdaspur area were baptized. The movement grew. Like the UP, the Anglicans and American Presbyterian missionaries also began to turn their attention to rural people. The Church of Scotland grew 40-fold in a decade, to number 8,000 by 1892. By 1904 the UP Church had 10,000 communicant members. The first Sialkot convention, held in 1904, was another milestone, and in the following decade a further 22,000 communicant members were added to the UP Church. Between 1902 and 1915 Methodists increased in number from 1,200 to 15,000. The Salvation Army, who always chose to be involved with the poor rather than the wealthy

---

78. Pickett, J. Waskom *Christian Mass Movements in India* (New York: The Abingdon Press, 1933) p.23

elite, were also active amongst the Chuhras in evangelism and with schools and clinics. Growth in Salvation Army numbers was steady but unspectacular until 1906 when it rose to a rate of nearly 1,000 new members a year. The 1911 census reported that in the Punjab alone (meaning both Pakistan's Punjab and modern India's Punjab) there were 163,994 Christians,[79] which included 92,739 Presbyterians, 29,051 Anglicans, 18,007 Salvation Army, 11,723 Methodists, 8,497 Roman Catholics and 1,117 Baptists. Christians were most heavily concentrated in the mass movement areas.[80] In the following decade the number of Christians in the Punjab almost doubled again to reach 315,031.[81] By 1935 almost all the Chuhras had become Christians.

Modern Period

Partition
The creation of Pakistan in 1947 profoundly affected Christians living there. The number of Christians in Pakistan (West and East) at this time was estimated to be

---

79. The rapid growth can be seen by comparison with the corresponding figures for the three preceding censuses were: 3,823 in 1881, 19,547 in 1891, 37,980 in 1901 – quoted in Campbell, Ernest Y. *The Church in the Punjab* (place of publication not stated, perhaps Nagpur: National Christian Council of India, 1961) p.11

80. Kaul, Harikishan Punjab. *Part II Tables, Census of India, 1911*, vol. XIV, pp.444-51 quoted in Webster, John C. *The Christian Community and Change in Nineteenth Century North India* (Delhi: The Macmillan Company of India Limited, 1976) pp.227-8

81. 1921 census, quoted in Webster op. cit. p.247

516,000.[82]   Large numbers of Muslims from India moved into Pakistan and their co-religionists felt obliged to provide them with work. This often meant that agricultural jobs formerly done by Christians were given to the newly arrived Muslims. The Christians were forced into the towns to seek work, for example, sweeping, often displacing scheduled caste Hindus from these jobs (see chapter 4).[83] They settled in squalid *bastis*, but were frequently moved on as their homes were demolished to make room for new buildings. This moving had extra complications for Protestant Christians owing to the policy of "comity" which had evolved at the Edinburgh missionary conference of 1905. For if they moved far they were likely to find themselves in an area assigned to a different Protestant denomination from that in which they had lived before. Their former pastor was unable to visit them, and they, as rural poor, were not necessarily welcomed by the "respectable" town Christians of the other denomination. Catholics, on the other hand, having no system of comity, found Catholic churches wherever they went, which welcomed them. Many Protestants converted to Catholicism.

Independence also triggered two mass movements of conversion to Christianity in the Lahore area. One was the Balmiki Hindus, who, some Christians believed, feared persecution after independence and turned to Catholicism in the hope of escaping this. The other was the Mazhabi Sikhs, many of whom converted to Islam while others converted to Christianity, perhaps also in the hope of avoiding persecution.[84]

---

82. Streefland op. cit. p.26

83. Nazir-Ali, Michael "Pakistani Christians" 21 October 1991 p.2

Socio-economic status of Christians

The socio-economic profile of the Pakistani church is a matter of some controversy, since few precise figures are available. Undoubtedly a large proportion of Pakistani Christians today are descendants of scheduled castes such as the Chuhras. But this is not a unique characteristic of Christianity. Islam, Buddhism and Sikhism have all attracted converts from among lower caste Hindus, who have naturally been eager to escape from their marginalized and oppressed status within Hinduism.

Christians who have come from the scheduled castes have been compared, in their psychology as a suppressed people, with the black community of the USA.[85] While it is true that many Christians are "sweepers" and many sweepers are Christians, there are also Christians in every area of business and professional life (especially teaching and nursing) and there are also sweepers who are Hindu and even Muslim (*musalli*, the descendants of scheduled caste Hindus who converted to Islam).[86]

Early converts to Christianity in Pakistan were often from Muslim and caste-Hindu backgrounds and their descendants are a part of the Church today. Many of the most famous church leaders in Pakistan came from these backgrounds. The mass movements amongst the scheduled castes began, as described above, in the late nineteenth century. Although missionaries feared that these

---

84. Rooney, John *Into Deserts: A History of the Catholic Diocese of Lahore, 1886-1986* (Rawalpindi: Christian Study Centre, 1986) pp.99-101

85. Heinrich, J.C. *The psychology of a suppressed people* (London: George, Allen and Unwin, 1937) passim

86. Nazir-Ali, Michael "Pakistani Christians" op. cit.; Streefland op. cit. pp.29-30

movements would have a detrimental effect on the work amongst Muslims and caste-Hindus who despised the scheduled castes, this did not prove to be the case. It should also be noted that some mass movements took place amongst Muslim groups, for example, the Narowal Khojas.

The Pakistani Christian community can be divided into five groups:

(i)   Christian dynasties originating from affluent families belonging to one of the South Indian churches who had moved to the North some time in the past

(ii)   Converts from Muslim or caste-Hindu backgrounds

(iii) Goans, from the former Portuguese colony in India

(iv) Anglo-Indians i.e mixed race

(v)   Christians with a background in the mass movements amongst the scheduled castes of Sind and the Punjab, included formerly nomadic groups[87]

Surveys in the 1930s and 1950s indicated that the Christian community was on the whole severely deprived economically and socially. A 1938 study of certain Christian communities in the Sialkot district of the Punjab concluded that "until the economic level of this entire group is very substantially raised, very little progress beyond that already made can be attained".[88] A 1955 survey of Christian education in Pakistan, particularly the Lahore

87. The main nomadic groups were the Bhil, Kohali and Marwaries and were sometimes known collectively as "tribal peoples".

88. Lucas, E.D. and Thakur Das, F. *The Rural church in the Punjab* (Lahore: Forman Christian College, 1938) p.52

area, organised by the American Presbyterian Mission in West Pakistan, recommended that education be given a high priority, in particular elementary education.[89] A 1956 study and report for a conference on "The Economic Life of the Church" held in Lahore that year found that it was essential for Christians to be enabled to increase their incomes, and various recommendations about education, training, agriculture and cottage industries were made.[90] A survey was conducted from November 1956 to February 1957 of 61 village churches, mainly around Lahore, Multan and Rawalpindi, which used a questionnaire including a question asking the nature of the major problems of the Church and the community. The two most frequently listed problems of the Church were illiteracy and poverty, seen as linked, and the two most frequently listed problems of the community were unemployment and the inability to get land to farm, also seen as linked to each other.[91]

Probably the most detailed research on the socio-economic status of Christians in Pakistan was a survey conducted by the Research and Social Action Committee of the West Pakistan Christian Council between December 1954 and December 1959. The 1951 census had recorded 541,000 Christians in Pakistan,[92] of whom 434,000 were

---

89. DeYoung, Chris *The Pakistan Educational Survey* (1955)

90. Vaugh, Mr and Mrs Mason *A study of Economic Development in West Pakistan, Report and Recommendations* (unpublished paper, 1956)

91. Comfort, Richard O. *The village church in West Pakistan: Report of a consultation held under the auspices of the West Pakistan Christian Council, November 10, 1956 to April 1, 1957* (printed for private use, no date given) pp.39,172

92. Streefland op. cit. p.26

in West Pakistan.[93]   For the survey, 28,520 families
(totalling 152,789 individuals) were questioned. More than
90% of these were Protestants, and thus the survey was in
this respect unrepresentative of the Pakistani Christian
population as a whole. The survey report summarized
some of the findings as follows:

(a) We have noticed that the per capita income is very
low (Rs9/- $2.00 per month) and that probably is due to
the fact that a major section of the community are
unskilled labour. A larger section of the community do
not own property of any description. There is quite a
good deal of unemployment and a great deal more of
under employment. 40% of the people interviewed were
under-employed. The number of people in Business and
Industry is practically negligible.

(b) The situation of literacy in the community is also
disappointing. It perhaps may sound strange to some
who have a feeling that the Christian community is well
up in literacy and education. It was found that excluding
those under 5 years of age the literacy percentage for
Christians is 14.5 whereas for the whole country it is 18.1
and for the majority community 18.3. A more
discouraging factor is regarding the school going
children. The percentage of children of school going age
who actually are in schools is 20.3 whereas the
perecentage for the country is 43%... It was also noticed
that there is a sharp decline in the percentage after the
primary stage from 14% primary, to 4% at the middle

stage, and in the college stage it drops down to 0.4%. That means that out of 203 of the community which go to school, only 4 reach the college level...

(c) A third disappointing factor is in the sphere of social life. It was found that debt has been the one great scourge of the social life of the community. The figures of debt were found out to be 33 per capita, i.e. to say that a family of 6 members with limited means of income was under a debt of Rs180/- or $40.00 which certainly is no ease (*sic*) to the family.[94]

With regard to the above, the survey also noted that in 1921 Christians had had a substantially higher literacy rate than the national average. Only 0.1% of the Christians questioned in the 1950s survey had to beg for their living.[95]

A survey of Christians in the North West Frontier Province (NWFP) was conducted by Laurits Vemmelund from February to September 1972, examining 44 different Christian communities. With reference to the overcrowding and limited access to facilities such as latrines, water and electricity, Vemmelund comments: "More than 80% of all Christians domiciled in the N.W.F.P. live under conditions not congenial for any kind of family life."[96] Child mortality

---

94. West Pakistan Christian Council *Survey Report of the Chuch in West Pakistan: A Study of the Economic, Educational and Religious Condition of the Church 1955-1959* (Lahore: West Pakistan Christian Council, 1960) pp 39-40

95. West Pakistan Christian Council, *Survey Report 1955-1959* p.41

96. Vemmelund, Laurits "The Christian Minority in the North West Frontier Province of Pakistan" *Al-Mushir* Vol XV Nos. 4-6 (April-June 1973) pp.117-119

is well over 15%.[97]   Of all employed Christians, 72% worked as sweepers.[98] The number of children aged between 6 and 18 who were not receiving any kind of edcuation was 48%.[99] Among married adults, 64% of men were illiterate and 84% of women were illiterate.[100]

Urbanization

In the early days of the nineteenth century missionary work, most converts to Christianity were city-dwellers. However, the mass movements which began in the last quarter of that century changed the Christian community to a predominantly rural community, as confirmed by the occupations of Christians listed in the 1911 census.[101] Webster states by 1914 the composition of the Christian community of North India (by which he meant Pakistan's Punjab and a large part of North India on the modern map) was "about ten per cent urban high caste and about ninety per cent rural outcaste".[102] As noted already, after partition Christians began to drift towards the cities in a search for better conditions and for work, many of their jobs having been taken by the Muslim immigrants from India.[103] By 1961, 15% of Christians in the Punjab lived in cities.[104]

---

97. ibid. p.103 The uncertainty of this figure reflects the fact that most women were very reluctant to admit that any of their children had died, feeling that it brought shame on them (see p.99)

98. ibid. p.130

99. ibid. p.141

100. ibid. p.146

101. Webster op. cit. p.228

102. Webster op. cit. p.229

103. Campbell op. cit. pp.4-5,17,35,62

104. Campbell op. cit. p.74

Twenty years later 55% of the Christian population had become urban,[105] in comparison with a Muslim population that was only 29% urban.[106] While it is hard to say whether working life is better as an agricultural labourer or as a street-sweeper, it is certain that Christians living in urban contexts are safer from violence and injustice than are rural Christians. The tyrannical *zamindar* system (see chapter 4) – apparently an immovable feature of rural life[107] – does not function in the cities, and the security forces and judiciary are more in evidence. While police may often not exert themselves on behalf of Christians, especially if the Christians are poor, it is still true as a general rule that lawlessness is less prevalent in urban situations than in the country and this in itself improves the security of Christians. This is particularly interesting given the fact that rural Christians consider themselves superior to urban Christians.

Church structure

The Pakistan Christian Council was formed in the 1920s, and loosely links together the Protestant denominations.

The 1960s saw a growing self-government within the Pakistani Church. In 1960 the Diocese of Karachi was

---

105. Addleton, Jonathan "A demographic note on the distribution of minorities in Pakistan" *Al-Mushir* Vol. XXVII No. 1 (Spring 1985) gives tables (pp.41-43) from the 1981 census, which are summarised in McClintock, Wayne "A sociological profile of the Christian minority in Pakistan" *Missiology : An International Review* Vol. XX No.3 (July 1992) p.346

106. The author's own calculations using data from Addleton op. cit. pp.41-3

107. Malik, Iftikhar H. *State and civil society in Pakistan: politics of authority, ideology and ethnicity* (Basingstoke: MacMillan Press, 1997) p.85

formed under the first Pakistani Anglican bishop, Chandu Ray.[108] In 1961 the UP Church gained independence from its American mother-church.[109] At this time the total number of Christians in Pakistan was 733,000 of whom 584,000 lived in West Pakistan.[110] As the 60s went on, various factions developed. Since Christians in Pakistan have little opportunity for leadership in politics or community affairs, leadership positions within the Church assume a great importance and the competition for them is intense.[111] Eventually these factions led to schisms in the UP Church, the Lahore Church Council, the Methodists and Anglicans in 1968.[112]

Soon afterwards the trend reversed. Following India's example where several major denominations united to form just two groupings – the Church of North India and the Church of South India – the Church of Pakistan was formed in 1970 by a merger of the Anglicans (110,000), United Methodists (60,000), Presbyterians of the Sialkot Church Council i.e. Church of Scotland (20,000) and Lutherans (2,000). Its four original dioceses have now been expanded to eight: Karachi, Lahore, Sialkot, Faisalabad, Peshawar, Multan, Hyderabad and Raiwind. The Church of Pakistan now numbers 460,000, and is the largest Protestant denomination. Some elements of the bodies involved in this union chose to remain separate, and thus several small new groups were formed, such as the National

---

108. Barrett op. cit. p.543
109. Stock op. cit. p.185
110. 1961 census quoted in Streefland op. cit. p.26
111. McClintock op. cit. p.344
112. Barrett op. cit. p.543; Webster, Warren in Hoke, op. cit. p 477; Stock op. cit. pp.185-187

Virgin Church of Pakistan, the Orthodox Church of Pakistan (Anglican), and the Methodist Church of Pakistan.

In the 1920s the Pakistan Christian Council had been formed, which loosely links together some of the Protestant denominations including the Church of Pakistan, the United Presbyterians, Presbyterians of the Lahore Church Council, the Associate Reformed Presbyterians (110,000) and the Salvation Army (42,000).[113]

Protestant groups outside the Pakistan Christian Council include the United Church in Pakistan (40,000), the National Methodist Church (38,000), the Christian Brethren (32,000), the Seventh Day Adventists (18,800), the Full Gospel Assembly (16,100), the Indus Christian Fellowship (3,020), International Missions (3,000), Pakistan Christian Fellowship (1,590) and Evangelical Alliance Churches (1,200), as well as many smaller groups. The total number of Protestants is estimated at 1.3 million. Larger than any single Protestant denomination are the Roman Catholics, who number 720,000.[114]

Demographics

The 1981 census
The following analysis is based on the 1981 census. Of course, the situation will have changed considerably since then, not only because of natural growth of the Christian community (Pakistan has one of the highest population growth rates in the world), but also because of other factors,

---

113. Webster, Warren in Hoke op. cit. p 476; Johnstone, Patrick *Operation World*, 5th edition (Bulstrode: WEC Publishing, 1993) pp.432-433

114. Johnstone op. cit. pp 432-433

for example, the current mass movement among tribal groups in the Sind.[115] The 1981 census gave a figure of 1.3 million (1.6%) for the Christian community, but Pakistani Christians themselves believe this to be a gross underestimate. Some believe the figure today may be as high as 3.5 million, which amounts to nearly 3% of the population. A more accurate figure may be approximately 3 million.

Almost 97% of the population of Pakistan is Muslim. But the Christian community of 1.3 million (1.6%) is the largest religious minority (closely followed by the Hindu community). Four-fifths of Pakistani Christians live in the Punjab, but Christians are found in each of the country's more than 60 districts. Most of the Christians who live outside the Punjab are of Punjabi origin.

An analysis by province reveals the following:

Punjab

The district with the largest number of Christians is Lahore, which has a Christian community of about 190,000 (5.4% of the district's total population). Faisalabad, Sialkot, Gujranwala and Sheikhpura also have Christian communities of over 100,000. Of Punjab Christians as a whole, 38% live in urban areas.

Sind

Two-thirds of the Christians in Sind live in Karachi, which is the only division to have more than 100,000 Christians. The second greatest concentration of Christians is in the Hyderabad area. More than 82% of Sind's Christian community are city dwellers.

---

115. Nazir-Ali, Michael "Pakistani Christians" op. cit. p.2

Baluchistan
There are only about 20,000 Christians in Baluchistan, half of whom live in Quetta. The rest are thinly scattered across the remaining districts. Baluchistan is an overwhelmingly rural province, yet two-thirds of the Christians live in urban areas. Institutional church structures are probably very rare outside of Quetta.

North West Frontier Province
The Christians in this province number 38,500, of whom almost half live in Peshawar. More than half the Christian population live in urban areas, which is a far higher proportion than for the province's population as a whole. Many of the districts have very small and isolated Christian populations.[116]

Barrett's estimates
Barrett gives the following figures in his *World Christian Encyclopedia*:[117]

---

116. Addleton op. cit. pp 32-45
117. Barrett op. cit. p 542
118. Crypto-Christians are defined by Barrett as "secret believers in Christ not professing publicly nor enumerated or known in government census or public-opinion poll, hence

	mid 1980 Adherents	%	2000 (estimated) Adherents	%
all Christians	1,475,500	1.8	2,909,000	2.0
crypto-Christians[118]	310,500	0.4	679,000	0.5
professing	1,165,000	1.4	2,230,000	1.5
Protestants	696,000	0.8	1,330,000	0.9
Roman Catholics	386,000	0.5	750,000	0.5
Pakistani indigenous	83,000	0.1	150,000	0.1
affiliated	1,475,500	1.8	2,909,000	2.0
total practising	1,032,850 (70% of affil.)		1,890,900 (65% of affil.)	
non-practising	442,650 (30% of affil.)		1,018,100 (35% of affil.)	
Protestants	805,000	1.0	1,470,000	1.0
Evangelicals	396,000	0.5	725,000	0.5
Neo-pentecostals	5,000	0.0	20,000	0.0
Roman Catholics	480,000	0.6	1,028,000	0.7
Catholic Pentecostals	6,000	0.0	30,000	0.0
Pakistani Indigenous	190,000	0.2	410,000	0.3
Marginal Protestants	500	0.0	1,000	0.0

unknown to the state or the public or society (but usually affiliated and known to churches)".

Conclusion

Although accurate up-to-date figures are not available, the present Christian community of Pakistan probably numbers about three million, and forms the largest religious minority (something over 2%), though official figures are lower. Almost all are ethnically Punjabi, most of them still living within the Punjab. Protestants form the majority, and were divided into many denominations until the formation of the Church of Pakistan in 1970 merged some of these denominations together. Catholics outnumber any single Protestant denomination. Compared with the population as a whole, the Christian community is more urbanized, more impoverished and comprised of a larger proportion of lower caste.

It is of great pyschological significance to Christians in modern Pakistan to know that their faith was present in their country before the advent of Islam, and even before the birth of Islam. Although Christianity was apparently eliminated in the fourteenth century so that it had to be re-introduced again by Europeans, Christians are encouraged by reminding themselves that they follow a faith which is neither new to Pakistan nor (originally) a Western import. They also set great store by the fact that they are indigenous "sons of the soil", not immigrants.

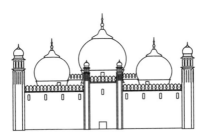

TWO

The ideological development of the state of Pakistan and its ramifications for the Christian community

Muhammad Ali Jinnah

Muhammad Ali Jinnah (1876-1948), the undisputed founder of Pakistan, brought into being a country whose purpose was to serve as a homeland for Indian Muslims. The "two-nation theory", on which Jinnah based his argument for a separate Muslim-majority state after India's independence from Britain, was first hinted at by Sir Syed Ahmed Khan (1817-1898), the Muslim reformer who "successfully wrested the leadership of the Muslims from the hold of the orthodox divines and sent them on the road to modernism".[1] Sir Syed spoke of "two races" or "two

---

1. Hyder, Khurshid "Pakistan under Bhutto" *Current History* Vol. 63 No. 375 (November 1972) p. 202

eyes", between which a rift might open or be closed.[2]
Seven hundred years of Muslim rule over Indian Hindus,
followed by Hindu ascendancy under the British, had
created a strong antagonism between the two faith-
communities, reinforced by their radically different cultural
and societal norms.[3]

A brief survey of the events which led to the creation of
Pakistan indicates that a significant preliminary was the
founding of the All-India Muslim league in 1906 which
pressed successfully for separate electorates for Muslims,[4]
considered by many a telling indication of the separateness
of the Muslim and Hindu peoples.[5] The two-nation line
of argument was revived and focused by the poet-
philosopher, Sir Muhammad Iqbal (1876-1938), who
proposed in a speech to the Muslim League in 1930 the
establishment of a unified Muslim state in the north-west.[6]
In 1940 the Muslim League under Jinnah passed the
Lahore Resolution calling for independence for the
Muslim-majority states in the north-west and east of India.[7]
This Resolution contained in its third paragraph a

---

2. Tinker op. cit. pp.12-13

3. This analysis is given by authors from as widely differing
stances as the arch-secularist Muhammad Munir [*From Jinnah
to Zia* 2nd ed.(Lahore: Vanguard Books, Ltd, 1980) pp.19-20]
and the pro-Jamaat-i-Islami Z.A. Suleri ["Counter-revolution
in Pakistan" *The News International* (14 August 1996) p.12].

4. Wheeler, Richard S. *The politics of Pakistan: a
constitutional quest* (Ithaca and London: Cornell University
Press, 1970) pp.9-11

5. Munir *From Jinnah to Zia* p.6

6. Wheeler op. cit.p.26

7. Wheeler op. cit. p.28; Richter,W.L. "Political Dynamics of
Islamic Resurgence in Pakistan" *Asian Survey* (June 1979)
pp.547-557

commitment to the protection of the rights of minorities which ran:

That adequate, effective and mandatory safeguards should be specifically provided in the Constitution for minorities in these units and in the regions for the protection of their religious, cultural, economic, political, administrative and other rights and interests in consultation with them...[8]

An alternative way of viewing the desire of Muslims for their own nation was their unwillingness to be a minority in a Hindu-majority context, particularly having experienced rule by the Indian National Congress in several provinces for a few years prior to 1940. Jinnah himself declared: "Pakistan started the moment the first non-Muslim converted to Islam in India long before Muslims established their rule ... As for a Muslim it was a duty imposed on him by Islam not to merge his identity and individuality in any alien society."[9] The highly respected left-wing journalist M.A. Niazi asserts: "It was not a paradox, but inevitable, that the Muslims of minority areas felt this competitive pressure [between Hindus and

---

8. quoted in William, Javed "What role have the political parties played regarding the identity of religious minorities in Pakistan?" – a paper given at a seminar on "Religious Minorities in Pakistan: struggle for identity" (July 1996) reproduced in a book of the same title ed. Moghal, Dominic and Jivan, Jennifer (Rawalpindi: Christian Study Centre, 1996) p.64

9. quoted in Burke, S.M. and Quraishi, Salim Al-Din *Quaid-i-Azam Mohammad Ali Jinnah: His personality and his politics* (Karachi: Oxford University Press, 1997) p.252

Muslims] more, and thus were more convinced by the arguments in favour of a separate Muslim nation, which required a state of its own, than their co-religionists who were in majorities in their provinces."[10] G.W. Choudhury, who later became professor at the University of Dacca and federal Minister for Communications, described the concern felt by the Muslims of India to safeguard their rights and concluded "Pakistan was, in a sense, itself the product of minority problems."[11] Iqbal believed, in Mangha's summary, that "Muslims had deteriorated because they were no more in power".[12] This all fits with traditional attitudes, for as Zebiri points out, "Classical Islamic jurisprudence as formulated from the ninth century onwards pre-supposed a situation where Muslims enjoyed political hegemony."[13] It is relevant here to remark how rarely debated is the subject of how Muslims should live if they are a minority in a non-Muslim state.[14] Hakim is one of the few Muslim writers to discuss this subject,[15] and Al-

10. Niazi, M.A. "In the name of Islam" *The News International* (25 August 1996).

11. Choudhury, G.W. "Religious Minorities in Pakistan" *The Muslim World* Vol. XLVI No. 4 (1956) p.315

12. Mangha, Raphael "Iqbal and the Reinterperation of Islam: A Ground and Guide for the Theological Task" *Al-Mushir* Vol. 38 No. 2 (1996) p. 37

13. Zebiri, Kate "Relations between Muslims and Non-Muslims in the Thought of Western-Educated Muslim Intellectuals" *Islam and Christian-Muslim Relations* Vol. 6 No. 2 (1995) p. 257

14. The *Hedaya* has 4 pages on this [*The Hedaya: Commentary on the Islamic Laws*, transl. by Charles Hamilton, Vol. II, 1791 (New Delhi: Kitab Bhavan, reprinted 1985) pp.192-196] out of a total of 1,849.

15. Hakim, Khalifa Abdul *Islamic Ideology: the fundamental*

Faruqi makes a passing reference to it.[16]

What then of those who would be minorities in a Muslim-majority state? These were a substantial size in East Pakistan (approximately 25%, mainly Hindus)[17] and would have been an even greater proportion of West Pakistan (some estimate 26%, others 30%) if the enormous cross-migration at independence had not occurred.[18]

Jinnah famously declared, just days before independence, that the religion of Pakistani citizens should be immaterial from the state's point of view.

> You are free, you are free to go to your temples. You are free to go to your mosques or any other place of worship in this State of Pakistan. You may belong to any religion or caste or creed – that has nothing to do with the business of the State....We are starting in days when there is no discrimination, no distinction between one community and another, no discrimination between one caste or creed or another. We are starting with the fundamental principle that we are all citizens and equal citizens of one State.[19]

---

beliefs and principles of Islam and their application to practical life, 8th edition (Lahore: Institute of Islamic Culture, 1994) pp.251-3

16. Al-Faruqi, Ismail "Rights of Non-Muslims Under Islam: Social and Cultural Aspects" *Journal of the Institute of Muslim Minority Affairs* Vol. 1 No. 1 (1979) pp.99-100

17. Richter op. cit. pp.547-557

18. Munir *From Jinnah to Zia* p.33

19. Speech as president of the Constituent Assembly, 11 August 1947, quoted in Munir *From Jinnah to Zia* p.30

This was not a new stance, adopted for the benefit of international onlookers as partition drew near. It was preceded and followed by similar statements about the equality of all citizens.[20]

Christian aspirations

Unlike Muslims, Indian Christians could not look forward to a state in which they would be a majority, but they did face the prospect of a choice between being a minority within a Muslim majority or being a minority within a Hindu majority. This choice was particularly relevant for Punjabi Christians whose homeland straddled the national boundary that was eventually created.

A minority of Christians, headed by Mr E. Bannerji, of the Nationalist Christian Association (an organisation derided by its opponents for being very new and very small), emphasised the homogeneity of Christians throughout the sub-continent and expressed fears that Christians in Pakistan would not be able to have contact with Christians in India. They therefore argued for Christians to remain in India after partition.[21]

The opposite view was taken by the Joint Christian Board, an organization formed in 1947 by the All India Christian Association, Punjab, the All India Christian League, Punjab, the All India Anglo-Indian Association, Punjab and the Catholic Association, in order to present

---

20. Munir *From Jinnah to Zia* p.29-32
21. E. Bannerji in "Proceedings of the Punjab Boundary Commission Lahore, 21-31 July 1947" in Sadullah, Mian Muhammad (compiler) *The Partition of the Punjab 1947* Vol. II (Lahore: National Documentation Centre, 1983) p.190-198 especially p.196

the case of Christians to the Boundary Commission. Emphasizing that he spoke for a mass organisation with wide support,[22] the Joint Christian Board's representative, Dewan Bahadur S.P. Singha, expressed the Punjabi Christians' feeling of affinity and solidarity with Muslims rather than with Hindus:

> Our people have been living with the Muslims for a long time and they have become Muslimised more or less in culture and outlook. They trust the Muslims more. They dress like them... They are economically as poor as the Muslims. With Muslims they have a religious affinity.[23]

As well as similarities in culture and religion, Singha explained, the Christians felt more comfortable with Muslims than with Hindus because the Hindu caste system excluded and stigmatized them, and summarized, "Because they have been living with Muslims, a Christian in the village is of the same type as his Muslim neighbour. He prefers to be in Pakistan."[24] Conscious of their poverty and powerlessness as a community, they were also aware that their percentage would be greater in Pakistan than it was currently in the Punjab as a whole.[25]

Punjabi Christians expressed their desire for the whole of the Punjab to become part of Pakistan, rather than the

---

22. Evidence for broad support, including lists of members, given by Singha in Sadullah, Mian Muhammad op. cit. pp. 221 ff.

23. Singha, Dewan Bahadur S.P. in "Proceedings of the Punjab Boundary Commission Lahore, 21-31 July 1947" in Sadullah, Mian Muhammad op. cit. p.225

24. ibid., loc cit.

25. ibid. p.233

eastern part to remain in India, as preferred by the Sikhs. Apart from maintaining the unity of the Punjab, this would have had the distinct advantage of increasing the number of non-Muslims in Pakistan as a whole. Expressing in passing his confidence in the democratic nature of the future Pakistan, Singha offered as a compromise "Eastern Punjab could rejoin Hindustan if Pakistan really proves to be a non-democratic state, which some fear it is going to be. We ourselves have no such apprehensions."[26] If the eastern part was not to join Pakistan, then the Christians of eastern Punjab should be allowed to move to West Punjab and be part of Pakistan.[27]

Another reason why most Punjabi Christians wished to be part of Pakistan rather than India, was the strongly felt issue of electoral representation. Separate electorates had been introduced in India for Muslims in 1909 and for Christians and Sikhs in 1935, but they would be removed when India gained independence and a joint electorate system was established. It was expected, however, that Pakistan would grant a separate electorate to Christians. Christians very much wanted to have a separate electorate to ensure a minimum number of Christians elected.[28] In due course Pakistani Christians discovered the disadvantages of separate electorates (see chapter 4) but at this stage it was one of their greatest aspirations.

Having once made public their preference for Pakistan, the urgency was redoubled by the fear of retaliation if they

---

26. ibid. p.228
27. ibid. p.235
28. Memorandum of the Joint Christian Board to the Viceroy and other submissions in "Proceedings of the Punjab Boundary Commission Lahore, 21-31 July 1947" in Sadullah, Mian Muhammad op. cit. p.228-232

had after all to remain in India. Singha reported that some Christians had already begun to experience persecution in the villages.[29] Thus, Punjabi Christians became Pakistanis at partition on 14 August 1947 enthusiastically and with high hopes of increased freedom, political power and social acceptability in their new state.

The place of Islam in the fledgling Pakistan

The widely difffering aspirations for the new state of Pakistan are summed up by Ishtiaq Ahmed:

> Pakistan meant different things to different people. To the landlords it meant continued leadership; to the doctrinal-minded Muslims, a unique opportunity to create an Islamic state in the light of their ideas; to the Muslim intelligentsia and the poorer classes, a state where social and economic justice would prevail and their dignity established, according to Iqbalite teachings; to the peasants, freedom from the yoke of the Hindu money-lender; to the regional leaders, greater autonomy than was expcected in a united India dominated by the Congress; to the Muslim bourgeoisie, the necessary environment where they could develop their potential, which seemed choked in a united India due to the many times greater strength of Hindu and Parsee capital based in Bombay and Calcutta; to the bureaucrats and the military, an excellent opportunity to secure quick promotions; and to the military establishment it brought a central role in a country where civilian political process

---

29. Singha, Dewan Bahadur S.P. in "Proceedings of the Punjab Boundary Commission Lahore, 21-31 July 1947" in Sadullah, Mian Muhammad op. cit. p.235

was dependent from the very beginning upon its support and active participation.[30]

The relationship of the Indian Muslims' homeland to the religion of Islam has been ambiguous and hence much debated from the very start.[31] According to Niazi, "one of the major problems confronting Pakistan, and the Pakistani people, since the new country came into existence, has been its relationship with Islam. There has always been a strange ambivalence, which has its roots in how proto-Pakistanis defined themselves..."[32] As Niazi points out, the leadership of the movement for the creation of Pakistan was in the hands "of those who could fight the British with their own tools, that is, the hands of those who were thoroughly steeped in the Western intellectual tradition of the time, and who had indeed reduced the presence of Islam in their own lives to personal observance and a loose ethical code, which did not have much to do with the running of the state." Thus there was an inbuilt bias towards a Western view of the relationship between religion and state, and of the role of religion in nationalism. This was of course the way in which contemporary Christianity in Europe related to the state and to nationalism – a far looser, less structured, more personal way than Islam teaches. According to Niazi, to relegate Islam to a religion which is part of the national culture but does not impact on daily life "leaves both the people and rulers of Pakistan in a somewhat hypocritical

30. Ahmed, Ishtiaq *The Concept of an Islamic State in Pakistan* (Lahore: Vanguard Books Ltd, 1991) pp.80-81

31. Dil, S.F. "The myth of Islamic resurgence in South Asia" *Current History* (April 1980) pp. 167-178

32. Niazi, M.A. loc. cit.

position, for unlike Christianity, Islam does not take kindly to being ignored by the state."[33]

The *ulema* naturally sought a traditional Islamic state.[34] For example, the All India Jam'iyyat Ulama-i-Islam adopted at their founding session in 1945 in Calcutta a resolution for the establishment of a worldwide Islamic caliphate, and reintroduction of Shari'ah-based law. The following year the All India Sunni Conference declared their commitment to the establishment of Islamic government based on Qur'an, Muhammad's teachings and the principles of Islamic jurisprudence.[35]   It was their belief that the proposed state would not be sufficiently Islamic which led some of the religious parties to oppose the calls for the formation of Pakistan, for example Mawdudi's Jama'at-i-Islami and the Jam'iyyatul Ulama-e-Hind under Madni.[36]

Jinnah's words have been quoted as support for the mutually exclusive assertions that he intended to found a secular state[37] and that he intended to found an Islamic state.[38]   Amjad-Ali believes that as Islam gained an

---

33. ibid.

34. The range of opinion amongst the *ulema* is surveyed in Choudhury, Golam W. *Islam and the Modern Muslim World* (Kuala Lumpur: WHS Publications Sdn Bhd, 1993) pp. 53-60

35. Pirzada, Sayyid A.S. "The oppositional role of ulama in Pakistani politics" *Monthly Current Affairs Digest* 49 (September 1998) pp.29-30

36. Iqbal, Afzal op. cit. p.54; Pirzada op. cit. p.30

37. for example, Munir *From Jinnah to Zia* pp.30-33; Amjad-Ali, Charles "Islamisation and Christian-Muslim Relations in Pakistan" *Al-Mushir* Vol. 29 No. 3 (Autumn 1987) p.75

38. for example, Burke and Quraishi op. cit. p.368 ; Perwez, Ghulam Ahmed cited in Ahmed, Ishtiaq op. cit. p.131; Pirzada,

increasingly dominant role in the state this was reflected in retrospective writings about the movement for the creation of Pakistan, in which the role of secularists was increasingly down-played.[39] What is in no doubt is that following Jinnah's death in September 1948 a process of official Islamization began, traceable in the framing of successive constitutions as well as new specific legislation. This process was at first gradual and fairly subtle, but received a great impetus under General Zia ul-Haq (president 1977-88).

Those in favour of an Islamic state tend to claim that the process of Islamization goes right back to the origins of Pakistan, for example, the assertion of Justice Lodhi, a judge in the Baluchistan High Court, that:

"Fortunately for us, we are one such country which has never overlooked the necessity of ordering lives of its people strictly in accordance with Islam, eversince (*sic*) emancipation from foreign rule, though the pace of progress has been slow till recently, when some serious efforts were made to speed up such efforts. In fact the creation of Pakistan itself was for the purpose to establish a truly Islamic State..."[40]

Syed Sharifuddin interviewed in Faruqi, M.H. "Jinnah's Pakistan: Islamic or secular?" *Impact International* (August 1995) p.21

39. Amjad-Ali, Charles "Islamisation and Christian-Muslim Relations" p.76

40. Lodhi, Justice Zakaullah "Ijtehad in the process of Islamization of laws" address at the seminar on the "Application of the Shari'ah" held at Islamabad October 9-11, 1979, reprinted in *All Pakistan Legal Decisions*, Vol. XXXII (1980) Journal 21

According to Lodhi, an Islamic state such as Pakistan should use a "relaxed, liberal and realistic interpretation" of Islam which is to be achieved by *ijtihad*.[41]   He also declared that the Islamization of laws and punishments was not sufficient on its own to achieve an Islamic state, but rather it was necessary to introduce Islamic education and training and to lay down "a definite Islamic system in all walks of life". He recommended that "real emphasis should be on the laying down of principles in different walks of life and then to resort to laws to ensure that such principles were enforced *stricto senso* (*sic*)".[42]

Objectives Resolution

In contrast to Lodhi's assertion, the process of the Islamization of Pakistan is generally considered to have started with the adoption of the "Objectives Resolution" by the Constituent Assembly on 12 March 1949, less than six months after the death of Jinnah.

A statement about the nature of the state of Pakistan to be embodied in a future constitution, the Objectives Resolution was a very significant document, given that the Constituent Assembly (1947-1954) failed in its seven years of existence to accomplish its task of formulating a constitution for Pakistan. The minorities thus remained

---

41. *Ijtihad* is the use of independent reasoning in interpreting the Qur'an and Sunna. Around the tenth century, leading scholars felt that all essential questions had been answered and therefore there should be no more *ijtihad*, but only an unquestioning acceptance of the opinions of earlier scholars. In modern times some reformers are calling for "the door of *ijtihad*" to be re-opened.

42. Lodhi, op cit. 22-3

without constitutional protection until 1956. It is important to note that the members of the Constituent Assembly were chosen by Jinnah from the elected members of the provincial assemblies. There were 17 Hindus and 2 Sikhs, but no Christians, in a total assembly of 72. There is little evidence as to the reason for this omission but it seems more likely that he simply did not see them as being significant rather than indicative of a mistrust of Christians. He did nominate two Christians, C.E. Gibbon and S.P. Singha, to be on the Constituent Assembly's sub-committee on "basic rights of minorities". Perhaps he saw this as appropriate to their status as a weak and virtually voiceless minority within the non-Muslims, but this is conjecture.

The Objectives Resolution affirmed principles such as equality, justice, and freedom of thought, expression, belief, faith, worship and association. It also declared that provision must be made for religious minorities "freely to profess and practise" their faiths and that their "legitimate interests" should be safeguarded. Democracy, freedom, equality, tolerance and social justice were affirmed, with the proviso "as enunciated by Islam". But the key wording, which came to have so much significance in the future as a justification for many of the stages of Islamization, stated of the constitution:

... the Muslims shall be enabled to order their lives in the individual and collective spheres in accordance with the teachings and requirements of Islam as set out in the Holy Quran and the Sunna.[43]

---

43. Quoted in Mehdi, Rubya *The Islamization of the Law in Pakistan*, Nordic Institute of Asian Studies, Monograph Series No. 60 (Richmond: Curzon Press Ltd, 1994) p.73. Full text is

The fact that there are many variations of Islamic law, each based on the Qur'an and *Sunnah*, created the possibility of numerous different interpretations of the Objectives Resolution. For example, the Jama'at-i-Islami claimed that the Objectives Resolution incorporated the four principles necessary for an Islamic constitution, which their leader Mawdudi (see below) had demanded in a speech the previous month. The vagueness and ambiguity of the Objectives Resolution has made it a far more powerful tool in the hands of the Islamic religious groups than most people envisaged at the time it was first passed.[44] In the words of Bishop Michael Nazir-Ali it was "a Trojan horse" in that the legislators at the time did not realise the implications.[45]

The main concern of non-Muslims at the time of the passing of the Objectives Resolution was the clause which stated that "sovereignty over the entire universe belongs to God Almighty alone, and the authority which He has delegated to the State of Pakistan through its people for being exercised within the limits prescribed by Him is a sacred trust". These words were interpreted by the Islamic groupings as a political and constitutional statement indicative of a theocratic rather than a democratic state i.e. a state governed by the Shari'ah. This is what alarmed some non-Muslim members of the constituent assembly,

---

found in Constituent Assembly of Pakistan Debates, Vol V, No. 1 (7 March 1949) p.1 or in Iqbal, Afzal op. cit. pp. 42-3

44. Mehdi, Rubya op. cit. pp.21-24; Dawood, Jan Mohammed *The religious and political dilemma of Pakistan* (Karachi: Hasan Publisher, 1993) pp.32-3

45. Rt Rev. Dr Michael Nazir-Ali, Bishop of Rochester, interview with the author (11 May 1998)

such as B.K. Datta and S.C. Chattopad (both Hindus).[46] By others the words were interpreted as merely a spiritual principle of no relevance to practical politics.[47] Joshua Fazl-ud-Din, a Christian advocate in the Lahore High Court who later became Deputy Minister for Law, Finance and Parliamentary Affairs for West Pakistan, saw that without constitutional safeguards this phrase could be used to justify the relegation of non-Muslims to *dhimmi* status as well as particular problems for Christian converts from Islam.[48] The phrase was in fact a compromise devised to satisfy different opinions by a wording which permitted varying interpretations.[49] It was ruthlessly analysed – indeed, ridiculed – by Fazlur Rahman, a member of the Council of Islamic Ideology in the Ayub Khan era, who considered it an absurdity resulting from the traditionalists' lack of understanding and the modernists' pragmatism.[50]

Another section of the Objectives Resolution which was criticized by non-Muslim members of the Constituent Assembly was the statement in the fourth paragraph that

---

46. Mehdi, Rubya op. cit. pp.74-5

47. For example, Iftikharuddin, Mian in *Constituent Assembly of Pakistan Debates* Vol. V No. 4 (10 March 1949) p.51

48. Fazl-ud-Din, Joshua *Future of Christians in Pakistan* (Lahore: The Punjabi Darbar Publishing House, 1949) pp.114-5, 120, 122

49. Ahmed, Manzooruddin "Sovereignty of God in the Constitution of Pakistan: A study in the Conflict of Traditionalism and Modernism" *Islamic Studies* Vol. IV, No. 2 p.210 Rashiduzzaman, M. *Pakistan: A Study of Government and Politics* (Dacca: Ideal Library, 1967) p.86

50. Rahman, Fazlur "Islam and the Constitutional Problem of Pakistan" *Studia Islamica* Vol. XXXII No. 4 (Dec 1970) pp. 277-9

"principles of democracy, freedom, equality, tolerance and social justice, as enunciated by Islam shall be fully observed". B.K. Datta asserted that if these principles were "as enunciated by Islam" non-Muslims would enjoy very little of them, being condemned "forever to an inferior status".[51]

Despite the reassurances of the Prime Minister Liaquat Ali Khan and other ministers, the non-Muslims remained uneasy about the Objectives Resolution. This feeling was doubtless reinforced by statements by the Islamic traditionalists that the resolution placed too much emphasis on the rights of minorities.[52]

The constitutions

One of the main reasons for the lengthy period of nine years spent formulating the first constitution was the debate about what Fazlur Rahman, calls the "Islamicity" of the constitution.[53] The *ulema*, though not directly involved in formulating the constitution, were able, through the medium of the Board of Talimat-e-Islamiyyah (Board of Islamic Teachings) established by the Constituent Assembly, to call for a constitutional requirement for all laws to be in line with the requirements of the Shari'ah.[54] When the Constituent Assembly did not appear to be taking sufficient notice of their recommendation, the *ulema* followed this

---

51. *Constituent Assembly of Pakistan Debates,* Vol. V No. 2 (8 March 1949) p.13
52. Mehdi, Rubya op. cit. p.78
53. Rahman, Fazlur "Islam and the Constitutional Problem" p.275. The other main reason, according to Rahman, was the difficult relationship between East and West Pakistan.
54. Pirzada op. cit. pp.30-1

up in 1951 with a charter of 22 fundamental principles of the Islamic state on which the constitution should be based.[55]

Many authors have traced the Islamic provisions in the various constitutions of Pakistan,[56] the main points of which will be outlined below. Writing after two constitutions had been in turn enacted and abrogated, Rahman claims a lack of logic in the scattering of references to Islam throughout the text. He is "startled" to find that, rather than having the principles, values and goals of Islam embodied in the every part of the Constitution, "Islam appears as an item among a host of other matters of goals and policy".[57] He calls the constitution an "Islamic fetish: a mere *ad hoc* and mechanical application of the term 'Islamic' to certain concepts to the exclusion of others."[58] It is the appearance and disappearance of these references to Islam in various parts of the Constitution which have been so closely traced by traditionalist Muslims, modernist Muslims and non-Muslims, as an indication of the progress of Islamization.

1956 constitution (abrogated 1958)[59]

This, the first constitution of Pakistan, was a compromise designed to appease both the traditionalists and the modernists.[60] The Objectives Resolution was made the preamble (to the satisfaction of the *ulema*[61]), with the

---

55. ibid. p.34

56. A detailed version is given in Mehdi, Rubya chapter 2

57. Rahman, Fazlur "Islam and the Constitutional Problem" pp.276, 279-80

58. ibid. p.285

59. Government of Pakistan Ministry of Law *The Constitution of the Islamic Republic of Pakistan* (Karachi, Manager of Publications, the Government of Pakistan, 1956)

60. Choudhury, G.W. *Constitutional Development in*

insertion of a new clause stating that Jinnah had founded Pakistan to be a democratic state "based on Islamic principles of social justice" – a phrase that was not clarified. As Rahman points out, it was a phrase interpreted by different groups according to their own wishes, and in the eyes of revivalists would imply the Muslim community's special status as distinguished from non-Muslims.[62] Rahman also cites the addition of the word "Islamic" to the concept of "social justice" as one example of what he considers the senseless sprinkling of references to Islam in a document which he believes should, by virtue of its Islamic nature throughout, not have needed to refer to Islam at all.[63]

Part I Article 1(1) named Pakistan as the "Islamic Republic of Pakistan" but this was not held to imply that Islam was the state religion. Part II – on fundamental rights – assured religious minorities of equal treatment (Articles 5(1), 13, 14(1), 17(1), 21) and the freedom to profess, practise and propagate their faith (Article (18). The President was to be a Muslim (Article 32(2)), but there was no such condition attached to Speaker of the National Assembly who was to exercise the functions of President in the President's absence or illness or between Presidents (Article 36(1)).

Various articles promoted Islamic teaching and practice

Pakistan (London: Lowe and Brydone, 1971) p.103; Esposito, John L. "Pakistan: Quest for Islamic Identity" in Esposito, John L. (ed.) *Islam and Development* (Syracuse: Syracuse University Press, 1980) p.143; Huq, Mahfuzul "Some reflections on Islam and Constitution-making in Pakistan 1947-56" *Islamic Studies*, Vol. V, No. 2 (1966) pp.209-10

61. Pirzada op. cit. p.35
62. Rahman, Fazlur "Islam and the constitutional problem" p.283
63. ibid. p. 279

following the principle that the state should "enable the Muslims of Pakistan individually and collectively to order their lives in accordance with the Qur'an and *Sunna*" (Article 25(1)). In a similar vein, article 198(1) stated that "No law shall be enacted which is repugnant to the Injunctions of Islam as laid down in the Holy Qur'an and *Sunna*... and existing law shall be brought into conformity with such Injunctions." This wording later came to be of great importance in the Islamization process. Article 198(4) affirmed that nothing in the article should affect the status of non-Muslims as citizens. Provision was made to set up an organization "for Islamic research and instruction to assist in the reconstruction of Muslim society on a truly Islamic basis" (Article 197(1)).

Amidst all the ambiguities, checks and balances, the only clearly discriminatory provision was the ban on non-Muslims as head of state. The word "Shari'ah" was conspicuous by its absence. The articles intended to increase the Islamic character of the country were not enforced – the Islamic Research Institute was not set up until after the constitution had been abrogated and no steps were taken to bring laws into line with the Qur'an and *Sunnah*.[64] In the words of Afzal Iqbal, "The Constitution had an Islamic façade, but the hard core was missing."[65]

1962 constitution (abrogated 1969)[66]
The 1962 constitution was formulated under President Mohammad Ayub Khan, who had seized power in a military coup in 1958. In its early days the new regime

64. Mehdi, Rubya pp.80-87
65. Iqbal, Afzal op. cit. p.65
66. original in Mahmood, Shaukat *The Constitution of*

appeared to favour a secular state, reasoning that Islam could not serve as the basis of the state in Pakistan because of the variety and divergence of Islamic sects. But before long the government's attitude changed and emphasis was placed on the primacy of Islam in Pakistan.[67] Ayub Khan favoured a progressive and liberal interpretation of Islam, and this was reflected in some of the differences seen in the 1962 constitution when compared with the 1956 constitution.[68] However, many of these changes were reversed in amendments, particularly those made in the Constitution (First Amendment) Act of 1963, which came into force in 1964.[69]

The Objectives Resolution retained its place in the preamble to the 1962 constitution, but with some modifications which prepared the way for a more liberal interpretation. For example, the 1956 version required that Muslims should be enabled to "live their lives in accordance with the teachings and requirements of Islam, as set out in the Holy Qur'an and the *Sunna*". The inclusion of the *Sunna,* and the exclusion of *ijma* and *qiyas,* was the most restrictive combination which could be chosen of the four sources of Islamic law.[70] By contrast the 1962 constitution's preamble omitted "the Holy Qur'an and *Sunna*" and in

---

Pakistan 1962 (Lahore: Pakistan Law Times Publications, 1962), amended version in Mahmood, Shaukat *The Constitution of Pakistan (as amended upto date)* (Lahore: The Pakistan Law Times Publications, 1965)

67. Rahman, Fazlur "Some Islamic Issues" p.284

68. Ahmed, Manzooruddin "Islamic aspects of the new constitution " pp.249-77

69. Text of this Act given in Mahmood, Safdar *Constitutional Foundations of Pakistan* pp.596-605

70. Rahman, Fazlur "Some Islamic Issues" pp. 284-302;

the constitution itself replaced "the Holy Qur'an and *Sunna*" with "the fundamental principles and basic concepts of Islam" (Article 8(2) principle 1.1) – a much broader definition. Rahman states that this change "led to general suspicion that this had been done in order to eliminate the *Sunna* of the Prophet as the second binding Islamic source besides the Qur'an", probably under the influence of Ghulam Ahmed Parwez (see below).[71] However, this change and most of the others were reversed by the amendments passed under pressure from the traditionalists, which came into effect in 1964, restoring references to the "Holy Qur'an and *Sunna*".[72] Similarly, the 1962 constitution renamed Pakistan as "the Republic of Pakistan" (Article 1(1)) but in 1964 this was amended to the 1956 name, "the Islamic Republic of Pakistan".[73]

Another liberalization was made in Part II with respect to the ban on the enacting of laws "repugnant" to Islam (Article 6 principle 1). As in the preamble, the qualifying phrase of 1956 referring to the Qur'an and *Sunna* – "as laid down in the Qur'an and Sunna" – was omitted. Unlike the equivalent article in 1956 (i.e. Article 198(1) quoted above) this ban was not enforceable in a court of law.[74] Also unlike the 1956 constitution, there was no requirement for existing laws to be brought into conformity with the

---

Anderson, J.N.D. "Pakistan: an Islamic state?" in Code Holland, R.H. and Schwarzenberger G. (eds.) *Law, Justice and Equality* (London: Sir Isaac Pitman & Sons, Ltd, 1967) pp.129-30

71. Rahman, Fazlur "Some Islamic Issues" p.286
72. Constitution (First Amendment) Act, 1963, sections 2 and 4
73. Constitution (First Amendment) Act, 1963, section 3
74. Mehdi, Rubya op. cit. p.90

injunctions of Islam. But the amendments which came into effect in 1964 restored the wording of 1956 in both respects.[75] In all other fundamental rights non-Muslims were guaranteed equal treatment (e.g. Article 6 principle 2).

The rights of non-Muslims were also safeguarded by Article 6 principle 7 and Article 8 principles 3, 14; this included the provision that no law would prevent a religious community from professing, practising and propagating their religion (Article 6 principle 7 (a)) and no law would compel anyone to any religious practice other than their own (Article 6, principle 7(b)). For Pakistani Muslims, a number of principles were laid down to promote Islamic morals and practices (Article 8 principles 1, 18, 19, 20) and to strengthen links with Muslim countries (Article 8 principle 21). As in the 1956 constitution, the only directly discriminatory clause was that the president must be a Muslim (Article 10).

The most significant lasting innovations of the 1962 constitution were the provisions for the establishment of two new institutions, the Advisory Council of Islamic Ideology (Article 199) and the Islamic Research Institute (Article 207). The function of the Council was to make recommendations to the government on methods to enable Muslims "to order their lives in all respects in accordance with the principles and concepts of Islam". The Council could also be consulted about the Islamic soundness of specific pieces of legislation. But its decisions were not to be binding on the government or any other authority. When the significantly absent phrase referring to the Qur'an and

---

75. Constitution (First Amendment) Act, 1963, section 4

Sunnah was inserted by an amendment of 1963,[76] this gave the Council freedom to interpret from these sources for themselves rather than adhering to the traditional schools of law (*madhahib*).[77] The members of the Council formed under the 1962 constitution were constantly criticized by the traditionalists for being too modernist in their interpretation of Islam, but the Council recommended the de-liberalizing constitutional amendments which came into effect in 1964.[78]

As mentioned, the Islamic Research Institute, originally provided for in the 1956 constitution, had not been established until 1959. According to the 1962 constitution its function was to "undertake Islamic research and instruction in Islam for the purposes of assisting in the reconstruction of Muslim society on a truly Islamic basis". Like the Council of Islamic Ideology, the Institute's recommendations were not binding on the government, as Ayub Khan was at pains to make clear.[79]

1973 constitution[80]

If the 1962 constitution – at least before amendment – was coloured by Ayub Khan's desire to liberalize, the 1973

---

76. Article 204(1) as amended by Constitution (First Amendment) Act, 1963, section 8

77. The judiciary tends to refer to the Qur'an and *Sunnah* whereas the legislature has to take *madhhab* into account, due to tensions with the Shi'as.

78. Mehdi, Rubya op. cit. pp.92-3,206-7

79. Khel, Muhammad Nazeer Kaka "The role of ideology in constitutional development in Pakistan" J*ournal of Law and Society* Vol. I No. 1 (1982) pp.67-77

80. Full text in Butt, M. Rafiq *The Constitution of the Islamic Republic of Pakistan, 1973* (Lahore: Mansoor Book House, 1991)

constitution reflected President Z.A. Bhutto's socialism but also his concern to appease traditionalist critics. He came to power in December 1971, just after the loss of Bangladesh. Pakistan without its eastern wing was much more homogeneous in terms of religion (a quarter of the population of East Pakistan had been non-Muslim) and felt itself more closely linked with the Middle East which was beginning a period of dramatic increase in power and prestige.[81] Interestingly Caroe, writing long before eastern Pakistan began to seek independence, asserts that this more westward focus had been a characteristic of the area of West Pakistan in pre-Muslim times and that "below the conscious level of thinking though it be, is one of the emotional bases of the patriotism of West Pakistan today."[82] Whatever the truth of this, the loss of the eastern half of the country resulted in a renewed emphasis on Pakistan's Islamic identity. Professor Waheed-uz-Zahman asserted:

If we let go the ideology of Islam, we cannot hold together as a nation by any other means... If the Arabs, the Turks, the Iranians, God forbid, give up Islam, the Arabs yet remain Arabs, the Turks remain Turks, the Iranians remain Iranians, but what do we remain if we give up Islam?[83]

---

81. Richter op. cit. pp.547-557; Dil op. cit. pp.167-178

82. Caroe, Sir Olaf *The Pathans* (Karachi: Oxford University Press, 1958) p.257

83. uz-Zahman, Waheed "Editor's Note" in *The Quest for Identity* (Proceedings of the First Congress on the History and Culture of Pakistani held at the University of Islamabad, April 1973. Islamabad: University of Islamabad Press, 1974) p. iv

In this context the 1973 constitution was framed. The ambiguous wording of the earlier preambles was expanded with a paragraph on preserving democracy and creating an egalitarian society through a new order. To the disappointment of some modernists the term "Islamic socialism" was absent from the constitution,[84] but scattered throughout were provisions concerned directly or indirectly with the economic system, nationalisation, the provision of basic necessities and preventing the concentration of wealth and the means of production and distribution in the hands of the few.[85]

As regards the place of Islam in the 1973 constitution, Pakistan continued to be described as an Islamic Republic, not a Socialist Republic (Article 1(1)), and the requirement for the President to be a Muslim continued (Article 41(2)). To this was added the provision that Islam was to be the state religion (Article 2), and that the Prime Minister also must be a Muslim (Article 91(2)).

As in the 1962 constitution, Pakistani Muslims were to be enabled to live their lives in accordance with Islam and to "understand the meaning of life according to the Holy Qur'an and *Sunna*" (Article 31). There was also the familiar prohibition of laws – future and existing – repugnant to the "injunctions of Islam as laid down in the Holy Qur'an and *Sunna*" (Article 227). The fundamental rights of non-Muslims were safeguarded in a similar way to the previous constitution.

A difference from the earlier constitutions was seen with

---

84. Rahman, Fazlur "Islam and the new constitution of Pakistan" in Korson, Henry (ed.) *Contemporary problems of Pakistan* (Leiden: E.J. Brill, 1974) pp.31.33
85. Mehdi, Rubya, op. cit. pp.101-2

respect to the two advisory bodies. The Council of Islamic Ideology was retained from the 1962 constitution (Articles 228-231), whereas the Islamic Research Institute, which had been in both the earlier constitutions, was omitted.[86] Significantly, the Council was by now composed of conservatives while the Institute was modernist.[87] Thus the government would receive more conservative and reactionary recommendations. Indeed, the constitution as a whole was not only more socialist but also more Islamic than earlier constitutions. Still, the position of non-Muslims was little affected in practice until the last months of Bhutto's presidency (April-July 1977) during which a number of laws were passed enforcing Islamic practice on such matters as alcohol, gambling and the weekly day of rest, and the introduction of Shari'ah promised for later in the year. These moves were apparently a response to the nine-party oppostion grouping, the Pakistan National Alliance, which challenged Bhutto in the March 1977 elections. They included the Jamaat-i-Islami and other extreme Islamic parties, and their common rallying call was *nizam-e-Mustafa*, literally "order of the Prophet" but freely translated as "Islamic system".[88]

The 1985 amendments to the 1973 constitution[89]
Prior to the presidency of General Zia ul-Haq (1977-88), the constitutions were inconsistent in that Islamic provisions

---

86. The Islamic Research Institute lost its status as a consultative body on Islamization and became an autonomous research institute.
87. Rahman, Fazlur "Islam and the new constitution " p.41
88. Richter, op. cit. pp.547-557
89. Full text of amended constitution in Butt op. cit.

were written in but not put into practice. The intention appeared to be to satisfy both traditionalists (by the wording) and modernists (by the lack of implementation). Christians and other non-Muslims were largely unaffected, except in the matter of being prohibited from the highest political offices.[90]

Under Zia, who seized power from Bhutto in a coup on 5 July 1977, the Islamization of Pakistan moved from rhetoric to reality. *Nizam-e-Mustafa* was proclaimed as a political, social and economic panacea.[91] The Revival of the Constitution of 1973 (Presidential Order 14 of 1985) was promulgated with the aim of radically Islamizing the 1973 constitution. A very widely debated change made by this Order concerned the Objectives Resolution which according to a newly inserted Article 2A, was to "form part of the substantive provisions ... and shall have effect accordingly". Zia commented:

> Now that the Objectives Resolution has been made a part of the Constitution, rights flowing from the Resolution shall be justiciable *(sic)*. You have secular human rights given in the first part together with Islamic rights defined in the Objectives Resolution. Thus liberties and privileges given by religion will be enjoyed by citizens as much as their other human rights of a secular nature.[92]

While still unspecific as to practice, this constitutional sanction for Islamic human rights was widely perceived as a turning point in the Islamization process. The intention

90. Mehdi, Rubya op. cit. p.107
91. Richter op. cit. pp.547-557
92. General Zia ul-Haq in an interview published in the *Pakistan Times* (5 March 1985)

to promote Islamic human rights had clear repercussions for non-Muslims. Furthermore, a slightly different version of the Objectives Resolution was substituted, which omitted the word "freely" from the clause about religious minorities professing and practising their faiths. Thus, the new version, contained in an annexe to the constitution ran:

Wherein adequate provision shall be made for the minorities to profess and practise their religions and develop their cultures;[93]

The previous version had said the minorities would be able "freely to profess and practise their religions ..."[94] Alarmed Christians protested about the possible implications of the omission of "freely".[95] Similar hints of a changing status for non-Muslims were given by other small changes, such as the requirement for National Assembly members to be Muslims (Articles 51(1)), indeed practising Muslims (Article 62) – apart from those in the seats reserved for minorities (Article 51).[96]

---

93. Butt op. cit. p.190

94. ibid.p.1

95. for example, Amjad-Ali, Charles "Islamisation and Christian-Muslim Relations" pp.76-7; a delegation of bishops to the parliamentary committee reviewing the Shariat Bill, reported in Malick, Nasir "Religious Minorities provided protection, says Niazi" *Dawn* (6 January 1991); Shahani, M.L. (Advocate in the Supreme Court) *Constitution, Law and Status of Minorities* (unpublished paper, 26 April 1992) p.4

96. The practical effects of these Articles are limited to preventing non-Muslims from contesting seats other than their reserved seats. No challenge has ever been issued to a Muslim candidate or Muslim sitting MNA on the basis of not being a *practising* Muslim.

Legislation

As the 1985 amendments were drafted and came into effect, creating a constitutional framework for Islamization, practical changes to the law – which very much affected Christians and other non-Muslims – were passed in the years before and after 1985. The main innovations concerned the creation of Shariat benches in the superior courts (1979) and then a Federal Shariat Court (1980), the passing of a number of laws putting into practice the *hudood* punishments of Islam (1979), a more Islamic Law of Evidence (1984), and the Enforcement of Shariah Act (1991). These are dealt with in detail in chapter 3. A landmark decision in the Supreme Court in 1993 ruled that the fundamental rights guaranteed in the constitution were limited by whether they conformed to "the injunctions of Islam as contained in the Qur'an and Sunnah" (see chapter 3).

Competing ideologies

We have outlined above the evolution of the constitution of Pakistan, which before Zia reflected presidential preference tempered by more or less vague Islamic formulations to appease the traditionalists. Zia changed the pattern by his enthusiasm for the Islamic provisions. However, there was a prolonged and vociferous debate about the appropriate framework for a Muslim state such as Pakistan. Many have attempted to classify the thinkers of this period by various systems. Wilfred Cantewell Smith, writing just before independence, separated intellectual movements, political movements and theological groups, each category being further subdivided.[97] The spectrum of opinion is analysed by Ishtiaq Ahmed into four main approaches: The sacred state excluding human will, the sacred state admitting human will, the secular state admitting divine will, the secular state excluding divine will.[98]

The difficulty here is that of identifying the demarcation lines between one category and the next. The common three-fold subdivision often applied to analyses of Islam in general – that is, radical, conservative and modernist – is too simplistic to apply to theories of the Islamic state as applied to Pakistan, and in particular with reference to attitudes to Christian minorities.[99] The following studies of leading groups and thinkers therefore are arranged according to their different understandings, beginning with the most traditional and conservative and concluding with the most liberal and secular.

The Tanzim Islah-i-Pakistan

The first approach, the absolutist position seeking a revival of traditional Islam and the full implementation of Shari'ah,

---

97. Cantwell Smith, Wilfred *Modern Islam in India*, 2nd Indian edition (London: Victor Gollancz Ltd, 1946) passim
98. Ahmed, Ishtiaq op. cit. p.31
99. Iftikhar H. Malik follows Hamza Alavi's division into eight categories of Muslim elite groups in British India which went on to have an enduring and reinvigorated influence in post-partition Pakistan: (i) Islamic traditionalists – the Deobandis (ii) Islamic traditionalists – the Brelvis and Pirs (iii) Islamic fundamentalists (iv) Islamic modernists (v) Secular and nationalist Muslims (vi) Secular / trans-communal rightist provincial politics (vii) Secular non-communal provincial politics (viii) Secular non-communal nationalists. See Alavi, Hamza "Pakistan and Islam: Ethnicity and Ideology" in Halliday, Fred and Alavi, Hamza (eds.) *State and Ideology in the Middle East and Pakistan* (London: Macmillan, 1988) p.79, quoted in Malik, Iftikhar H. op. cit. p.45

would, according to the majority of the *ulema*,[100] have given non-Muslims the status of *dhimmi*, without the right to participate in politics.[101] Converts from Islam to another faith would be punished by death. Typical of this position was the Tanzim Islah-i-Pakistan, which asserted that Pakistan should be a model Islamic state, governed by sacred law alone without manmade laws.[102] Where interpretation of divine injunctions was found to be required only qualified experts in Islamic law could make the necessary *ijtihad*.[103] Democracy of any kind was anathema.[104] The Tanzim expressed bitter disappointment that Pakistan fell so far short of the ideal of the pious caliphs.[105]

Abul Ala Mawdudi

Somewhat less extreme was the position of Abul Ala Mawdudi (1903-1979), an immensely influential writer and

---

100. Maulana Abul Hasanant, who held that *dhimmi* may not even hold public office, Maulana Ahmad Ali, who held that *dhimmi* could hold public office but not make or administer the law, Mian Tufail Muhammad who stated that minorities should not have the same rights as Muslims, all in *the Report of the Court of Inquiry constituted under Punjab Act II of 1954 to enquire into the Punjab disturbances of 1953* (Lahore: Government Printing, Punjab, 1954), often called the "Munir Report" after its chairman, Muhammad Munir, pp.212-4 . See chapter 3.

101. but see the arguments in chapter 3, that non-Muslims who were not a conquered people were *mu'ahids* rather than *dhimmi*.

102. *Report of the Court of Inquiry* p.25.

103. *Report of the Court of Inquiry* pp.24-8

104. ibid. p.57

105. ibid. pp.5-6

thinker who founded the Jamaat-i-Islami in 1941 and during his lifetime produced over 120 books and pamphlets and over 1,000 speeches and press statements.[106] Mawdudi believed that an Islamic state should be free of all traces of nationalism,[107] its purpose being to uphold and enforce the sovereignty of God.[108] Three other conditions were necessary for such a state to exist: acceptance by the government of the limitation that it would exercise its powers within the bounds laid down by God, the repeal of all existing laws contrary to the Shari'ah, and that all new laws would be "in consonance with the real spirit of Islam and its general principles".[109] He believed that by its very nature an Islamic state distinguishes between Muslims and non-Muslims living within its jurisdiction.[110]

Unlike the Tanzim, Mawdudi envisaged an elected

---

106. Hussain, Asaf *Islamic Movements in Egypt, Pakistan and Iran: an annotated bibliography* (London: Mansell Publishing Ltd, 1983) p.47-8

107. Mawdudi, S. Abul A'la *The process of Islamic revolution* (Lahore: Islamic Publications Ltd, 1970) quoted in Hussain op. cit. p.48. Z.A. Suleri, a pro-Jamaat-i-Islami commentator, and at one time chief editor of the *Pakistan Times*, wrote that the birth of Pakistan was "a flagrant breach of the western notion [of nationhood] based on race, language and geography..." ("Counter-revolution in Pakistan" *The News International*, 14 August 1996 p. 12)

108. Maududi, S. Abul Ala *The Islamic Law and Constitution* translated and edited by Khurshid Ahmad, 7th edition (Lahore: Islamic Publications Ltd, 1980) p.212-9

109. Mawdudi, S. Abul A'la "Twenty-nine years of the Jamaat-e-Islami" *The Criterion* (Karachi) Vol. 6 No. 1 (Jan-Feb 1971) p. 29 Maududi *The Islamic Law and Constitution* pp.75-6

110. Maududi, S. Abul A'la *Rights of Non Muslims in Islamic State*, 7th edition (Lahore: Islamic Publications Ltd, 1982) pp.1-3

government, in which non-Muslims could participate indirectly by means of a separate representative Assembly for non-Muslims through which demands for their collective needs could be submitted to the (Muslim) Parliament.[111] Only Muslims would be allowed to fill posts related to state policy.[112] Non-Muslims would be in a separate category of citizenship, distinct from Muslim citizens, either as conquered *dhimmi* paying *jizya* or as those who voluntarily accept the hegemony of an Islamic state and enter into a contact with it, *mu'ahids*.[113] They would have the same criminal and civil law as Muslims, though in personal matters they could follow their own law.[114] For reasons of general public welfare and self-defence, there should be a prohibition of "such cultural activities as may be permissible in non-Muslim creeds, but which, from the point of view of Islam are corrosive of moral fibres and fatal".[115] A Muslim woman was not permitted to marry a non-Muslim man.[116] Though non-Muslims were free to propagate their faith and win converts from amongst other non-Muslims,[117] Muslims who converted to another faith were to be punished by death.[118]

---

111. Maududi *The Islamic Law and Constitution* p.296

112. ibid. pp.188-9

113. ibid pp. 278-80. See also Maududi *Rights of Non Muslims* passim

114. Maududi *The Islamic Law and Constitution* pp.147, 282-286

115. Maududi, Abul A'la *Jihad in Islam* (Kuwait: International Islamic Federation of Student Organisations, no date) being a version of a speech delivered on Iqbal Day (April 13) 1939 at Lahore Town Hall

116. Maududi, S. Abul Ala *Purdah* (Lahore: Islamic Publications Ltd, 1981) p. 241

117. Maududi *The Islamic Law and Constitution* p. 297

Muhammad Asad

From Mawdudi's scheme for a traditional Islamic state, it is not a great leap to the type of state envisaged by Muhammad Asad (1900-92), despite the fact that the latter is generally characterised as a modern state. Asad, a European convert to Islam formerly called Leopold Weiss, was director of the Department of Islamic Reconstruction from 1948 to 1961. He presented his views to the Constituent Assembly in his thesis "Islamic Constitution Making" under the auspices of the government of the Punjab in March 1948. Dismissing as naïve and unrealistic the purist traditionalists, he still sought something more Islamic than a Western-style parliamentary democracy, something that "would be Islamic in the full sense of the word and would also take the practical requirements of our time into consideration". He developed his concept of a modern Islamic state by returning to the basis of the Qur'an and *Sunnah*, finding clear-cut political principles from the former and details and methods of application from the latter.[119]

Asad differed significantly from Mawdudi and the absolutists in considering that only the small part of the Shari'ah derived directly from the Qur'an and *Sunnah* remained valid permanently. Other parts had been derived by *ijtihad* and this could be done afresh by each generation. Although Mawdudi believed in the possibility of human

---

118. *Report of the Court of Inquiry* p.218

119. Asad, Muhammad *The principles of state and government in Islam*, new edition (Gibraltar: Dar Al-Andalus Limited, 1980), a development of Asad's essay *Islamic Constitution-Making*, published in 1948, when he was director of the Department of Islamic Reconstruction, pp. ix-xi

legislation in areas not covered by earlier *ijtihad*, he limited the scope of this to a much smaller range of issues than did Asad.[120]

The result Asad arrived at from this process was a political system which consisted of a government elected by Muslims only, and headed by a president.[121] He felt strongly that Islam must be more than simply the religion which happened to belong to a people who were struggling for independence. Rather, the justification for Pakistan's existence was the establishment of an Islamic polity and the adherence of its people to the teachings of Islam.[122] It was neither race nor culture which bound Pakistanis together but their common Islamic faith. Thus he believed "only a good Muslim can be a good Pakistani".[123]

Non-Muslims were to be a separate nation from the Muslim community and were not to be "entrusted with any key position of leadership".[124] Non-Muslims who wished to serve in the armed forces would be permitted to do so, and would on that account be exempt from paying *jizya*.[125] Asad explicitly insisted that non-Muslims should not be discriminated against "in ordinary spheres of life".[126] He believed that "an Islamic polity denotes justice for all" and that the best way to reassure the apprehensive non-Muslims about their position in Pakistan would be to

120. Asad op. cit. pp.14-17; Ahmed, Ishtiaq op. cit. p.190
121. Ahmed, Ishtiaq op. cit. p.123
122. Asad, Muhammad "What do we mean by Pakistan?" (May 1947) reproduced in abridged form in *Impact International* (September 2001) pp.6-10
123. Asad "What do we mean by Pakistan?" p.9
124. Asad *The principles of state.* p.40
125. ibid. p.74
126. ibid. p.40, see also p.87

convince them of the truth of this.[127]

Ghulam Ahmed Parwez
Another very influential scholar whose concept of an Islamic state, like Asad's, falls into Ahmed's category "sacred state admitting human will" was Ghulam Ahmed Parwez (1903-1985). Parwez was a keen follower and exponent of the Iqbalian school, and a progressive thinker. One of his recurring themes was that of *din* – Islam as a "code of life", with detailed instructions for behaviour in every situation. He argued that Islam can only become a living reality when Qur'anic laws can be enforced upon a definite geographical territory. This then was the purpose for which Pakistan was created, he asserted.[128]

Parwez differed significantly from Asad in that he believed the constitution of an Islamic state should be based on the Qur'an alone, not on the *Sunnah*.[129] According to Rahman, Parwez was following a trend in the sub-continent, which began with Syed Ahmed Khan in the late nineteenth century, of historically discrediting the *hadith*.[130] Ignoring the *Sunnah* was indeed revolutionary, since the vast majority of Muslims have always looked on the prophet's example as an essential part of Islam; Parwez thus earned

---

127. Asad "What do we mean by Pakistan?" pp.8-9

128. Parwez, Ghulam Ahmed *Quaid-i-Azam Aur Do Quomi Nazaria* (Lahore: Idara-Tulu-e-Islam) pp.2-3 cited in Ahmed, Ishtiaq op. cit. p.129

129. Parwez, Ghulam Ahmed *Qurani Aein Kay Bunyadi Khat-o-Khal* (Lahore: Idara-Tulu-e-Islam) pp.2-3 cited in Ahmed, Ishtiaq op. cit. p.130

130. Rahman, Fazlur "Some Islamic Issues" p.286. See also Faruqi, M.H. "Integral to Islam" *Impact International* (February 1998) p.44

himself a *fatwa* issued in 1962 by more than a thousand *ulema* which declared him to be an unbeliever for this heretical teaching.[131] The political structure which Parwez believed to be Qur'anic was that of a "controlled democracy", that is, the people exercising their freedoms within the limits prescribed by the Qur'an.[132] Like Asad, he believed that the Islamic state must make a distinction between Muslims and non-Muslims, although only in the political arena.[133] Like Asad, he believed in complete religious freedom – Muslims should be permitted to change their faith and non-Muslims should not be forced to embrace Islam.[134]

Khalifa Abdul Hakim

One step closer to secularism than Asad was the teaching of Dr Khalifa Abdul Hakim, a renowned thinker regarded as an authority on the Iqbalian philosophy. He emphasised that Islam was a religion of peace, surrender, harmony and good deeds, and that all theistic religions should be united in a Brotherhood of Faith.[135]

He asserted that "The Muslim State shall be a Socialist Republic... It shall be a theocratic democracy with no priesthood and no Church. It shall be a theocracy only in the sense that it derives its authority from God. God shall

---

131. Ahmed, Aziz *Islamic Modernism in India and Pakistan 1857-1968* (London: Oxford University Press, 1967) p.233; Rahman, Fazlur "Some Islamic Issues" p.286

132. Parwez, Ghulam Ahmed *Qurani Aein Kay Bunyadi Khat-o-Khal* (Lahore: Idara-Tulu-e-Islam) pp.4-8 cited in Ahmed, Ishtiaq p.130

133. Parwez, Ghulam Ahmed *Islam: a challenge to religion*, 3rd edition (Lahore: Asmat Alam Press, 1996) p.271,276-7

134. ibid. p.275

135. Hakim op. cit. pp.ix-x, 11, 13

be the symbol for universal social justice."[136]

Despite acknowledging both the Qur'an and *Sunnah* as sources,[137] Hakim placed greatest emphasis on the Qur'an.[138]   Although non-Muslims were still a separate nation and obliged to pay *jizya*[139] they could hold key posts and should have "complete liberty of religious belief".[140] A Qur'anic distinction was to be drawn between "People of the Book" (Jews, Christians and Sabeans, according to the Qur'an) and polytheists (Hindus) the latter being viewed far more severely, but Muslims and non-Muslims were guaranteed equal civil rights,[141] with non-Muslims having their own personal law.[142]

Javid Iqbal

Unlike the scholars mentioned above, Dr Javid Iqbal, the son of Sir Muhammad Iqbal and a senator and supreme court judge, saw value in secularism, which he considered to be "an integral part of Islam" in the sense that Islam does not distinguish between the spiritual and the profane. He therefore asserted that "the Islamic state assimilates the qualities of an ideal 'Secular State'."[143]   He also placed emphasis on the concept that the Muslim state existed before Pakistan was created, in Indian Muslims' consciousness of their distinct identity. The creation of the

---

136. ibid. p.247
137. ibid. p.265; Ahmed, Ishtiaq op. cit. p.191
138. Hakim op. cit. p.264
139. ibid. p.246
140. ibid. loc. cit.
141. ibid. pp. ix-x
142. ibid. p.247
143. Iqbal, Javid *Ideology of Pakistan* (Lahore: Ferozsons Ltd., 1971) p.4

state of Pakistan was required to implement the pre-existing "ideology of Pakistan".[144]

This state, he asserted, was an ideal secular state, at least as envisaged by Jinnah. "In the political sense, irrespective of their religion or race, all Pakistanis are citizens of the State of Pakistan on equal terms."[145] Yet, at the same time he states that "Pakistani nationhood is not the real basis for the unity of the state of Pakistan; it is merely an apparent basis". The primary consideration, he says, is "Islam, which cements us as a nation and also provides the basis for the unity of the State".[146] Any loyalty to or love for the geographical territory of Pakistan he condemns, thus eliminating the basis for non-Muslim patriotism.[147] This seems to completely undermine his use of the term "secular state" to describe the kind of state he envisaged. He also affirms that the head of state must be a Muslim and non-Muslims cannot be part of the elected Muslim assembly. Legislation must be based on the Qur'an and *Sunnah*, although the *ijma* of the past was not binding.[148] The Muslim assembly could even withhold the application of Qur'anic laws in certain circumstances.[149] An Islamic state should provide maximum freedom for its citizens, including freedom of religion.[150]

---

144. ibid. pp.1-3
145. ibid. p.4
146. ibid. p.2
147. Ahmed, Ishtiaq op. cit. pp.145-6
148. Iqbal, Javid op. cit. pp.51-2
149. Ahmed, Ishtiaq op. cit. p.146
150. Iqbal, Javid op. cit. pp.64,72-7

Syed Muhammad Zafar

If Javid Iqbal's concept of Pakistan was secular more in name than in practice, Syed Muhammad Zafar advocated a truly secular state in the modern sense, albeit seeking continuity with the political spirit of Islam – Ishtiaq Ahmed's "secular state admitting divine will". Zafar was law minister and constitutional adviser in various Muslim League governments and is chairman of the Human Rights Society of Pakistan. In his 1980 work *Awam, Parliament, Islam,* he argued that government through consultation was a principle of Islam, and therefore concluded that a Western-style parliamentary democracy fitted well with the teachings of Islam.[151] He believed that past *ijma* need not be adhered to now, and that elected representatives had the right of *ijtihad,* not just religious scholars. His secularism, however, did not extend to disregarding specific Qur'anic laws, such as those of inheritance and the *hudood* punishments, which must still be followed.[152] How this affected non-Muslims he did not discuss, but freedom of religion would follow from his reasoning. He recognized territorial nationalism as not contrary to Islam[153] which indicates a less precarious position for non-Muslims than in Javid Iqbal's version of a "secular state".

Muhammad Usman

Prof. Muhammad Usman, socialist writer and thinker, also favoured a democracy as the appropriate political system for Pakistan, with Islamic socialism as the economic basis.

---

151. Zafar, S.M. *Awam, Parliament, Islam* (Lahore: Aeina-i-Adab, 1980) pp.15-17,19-20
152. ibid. pp.24, 289-90,312-18
153. ibid. pp.300-310

In contrast to Zafar he did not believe that a democracy would always and automatically be the way in which the Qur'anic principle of consultation was best put into practice. But for the contemporary context he held that a modern democracy was the best system. He did not examine the position of non-Muslims, but religious freedom can be assumed from what he says on other subjects. Despite his assertion that Islam does not specify any particular type of government, he still adhered to clear Qur'anic legislation where that exists, mentioning, for example, inheritance and marriage laws. He did not comment on the *hudood* laws.[154]

Muhammad Munir

Muhammad Munir, who was a highly respected lawyer and eventually Chief Justice of Pakistan, took his place at the extreme end of the spectrum of opinion, described by Ishtiaq Ahmed as "the secular state excluding divine will". He dismissed any idea of an "ideology of Islam"[155] and advocated a straightforwardly secular democratic state, whose legislation would be unaffected by the fact that most of its citizens were Muslim. This he believed was what Jinnah had intended. In this state non-Muslims would have complete equality with Muslims.[156] He criticized the Objectives Resolution for stating that sovereignty rests with Allah (it should rest with the people) for referring to the protection of religious minorities (there should be no distinction between religious majorities and minorities) and for the provision relating to enabling Muslims to lead their lives in accordance with Islam (contradictory to the concept

154. Usman, Muhammad *Islam Pakistan Mein* (Lahore: Maktab-i-Jadid, 1969)
155. Munir *From Jinnah to Zia* pp.25-8
156. ibid. p.33

of secular state).[157]   He condemned the death penalty for apostasy,[158] and cast doubt on the levying of *jizya* from non-Muslims[159] and the concept of separate electorates for non-Muslims.[160]

Conclusion

In the main, Christians had chosen freely to remain in Pakistan and not to join the mass emigration of Hindus at partition because of the greater empathy they felt with Muslims. They had looked forward to a free and equal existence in the new nation-state. Perhaps a hint of the way things would develop could have been seen in the fact that the Constituent Assembly formed to guide Pakistan through independence and in its first years had no Christians among its members, although there were 19 non-Muslims of other faiths amongst the total of 72 members.

Despite the ambiguities of the various constitutions and the variety of arguments debated in the public arena, the Christian community have felt themselves increasingly weakened and marginalised by the process of Islamization. Writing in 1987, after ten years of Zia's Islamization, Amjad-Ali asserted that the problems of non-Muslim minorities were caused by Pakistan's ideological framework "since there is no place in it for pluralism of belief and existence. In fact we are experiencing a concerted attempt to produce a more entrenched homogeneity within the country, inspite of major differences within Islam itself."[161]

The issue of religious minorities is a two-edged weapon

---

157. ibid. p.36
158. ibid. p.133; *Report of the Court of Inquiry* p.220
159. Munir *From Jinnah to Zia* p.107
160. ibid. pp.115-6

in the Christian community's experience. Firstly, it was the reluctance of Muslims to exist as a minority within a Hindu majority which resulted in the creation of Pakistan. From there the rapid evolution of ideology following Jinnah's death soon led to the argument that a Muslim-majority nation must function as a traditional Islamic state. Despite a vigorous public debate (in which, however, the voice of Christians was seldom heard), the traditionalists began gradually to gain ground. First the texts of the constitutions were adapted to allow a more conservative interpretation. Modifications here and there began increasingly to imply that minorities were not full and equal citizens of the nation. Eventually the constitutional wordings were given practical force by a series of laws, beginning in Z.A. Bhutto's last months and then continuing with greater impetus under Zia. Again the concept of the inferiority of minorities, which appears inherent to traditional Islamic view, reappears, and this time with a direct effect on Christians.

The protest suicide of John Joseph, Catholic bishop of Faisalabad, on 6 May 1998, in response to the helplessness of Christians in the face of the "blasphemy laws" (see chapter 5) prompted a comment from Zia-ul-Qasmi, leader of the Sipah-e-Sahaba:

Nobody has forced Christians to live in Pakistan and if they have to live in Pakistan then they have to live in respect of the constitution and law of the land.[162]

---

161. Amjad-Ali, Charles "Islamisation and Christian-Muslim Relations p.73

162. "Tense Faisalabad prepares for bishop's funeral today" *The News International* (10 May 1998)

This would suggest that traditionalists are almost as reluctant to *have* minorities in the "Pure Land" as to *be* a minority themselves.

THREE

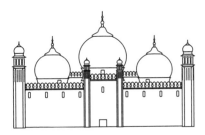

The relevance of the concept of *dhimmi* in theory and practice

Dhimmi in classical Islam

An examination of Qur'anic texts in the order of their revelation[1] shows that initially Jews and Christians – *ahl al-kitab* (people of the book i.e. who had their own revealed scriptures) – are considered favoured by God (unlike the pagans) though not of equal status with Muslims. Also in this category are the mysterious Sabeans whose identity is uncertain (mentioned only three times). To this some would add the Magians (mentioned in S.22:17) usually considered to be Zoroastrians.[2] The early references to Jews and Christians are peaceable and commendatory; they are

---

1. a task complicated by the fact that there is no unanimity on the exact chronological order of the revelations

2. Zebiri op. cit. p.256

virtually embraced within the fold of Islam as honorary Muslims. For example:

> Those who believe (in the Qur'an), and those who follow the Jewish (scriptures), and the Christians and the Sabians, – any who believe in God and the Last Day, and work righteousness, shall have their reward with their Lord: on them shall be no fear, nor shall they grieve.[3]

This distinguished them from other non-Muslims who were called *kafirun* (unbelievers) and who, as polytheists, were unequivocally condemned. For example,

"O ye who believe: truly the Pagans are unclean"[4] and the famous "sword verse" commanding Muslims to "fight and slay the pagans wherever ye find them."[5]

Later texts, however, present the *ahl al-kitab* as refusing to accept Muhammad's teaching. An interesting verse in Sura 5 commends Christians and condemns Jews and polytheists.

---

3. S.2:62, an early Medinan surah. This and other quotations from the Qur'an are taken from A. Yusuf Ali's *The Holy Qur'an: Text, Translation and Commentary* (Leicester: The Islamic Foundation, 1975), except where otherwise stated. Another good example is the Meccan S.29:46 forbidding disputes with the People of the Book (apart from evil-doers) and acknowledging "our God and your God is one". A very late Medinan surah contains a similar sentence though without the promise of heavenly reward (S.5:72) but is followed very soon after with explicit condemnation of those who believe Christ is God and believe in the Trinity i.e. Christians (S.5:75,76).

4. S.9:28

5. S.9:5

Strongest among men in enmity to the Believers wilt thou find the Jews and Pagans; and nearest among them in love to the Believers wilt thou find those who say, 'We are Christians': because amongst these are men devoted to learning and men who have renounced the world, and they are not arrogant.[6]

Jews and Christians are then criticised and condemned together,[7] though some scholars believe that the references to Christians were added later to passages which were originally hostile only to Jews.[8] Sura 9, one of the last suras, makes a definite separation[9] between Muslims on the one hand and Jews and Christians on the other.[10]

Some scholars consider this apparently progressive hardening of attitude towards the *ahl al-kitab* to be the result of the deterioration in relations between Muslims and Jews in Medina and later the military conflict with the Byzantine

---

6. S.5:85 Also, the sin of polytheists will never be pardoned according to S.4:116.

7. For example, S.5:54 prohibits Muslims from friendship with Jews and Christians and S.2:135-141 attacks the religion of Jews and Christians

8. Watt, W. Montgomery *Muhammad at Medina* (Karachi: Oxford University Press, 1981) pp.317-8

9. For example S.9:29, quoted below, which commands that people of the Book must be fought if they do not follow Muhammad's teaching

10. Reviews of the gradually changing Qur'anic attitudes are found in Arkoun, Mohammed "The Notion of Revelation" in Havemann, Axel and Johansen, Baber (eds.) *Gegenwart als Geschichte: Islamwissenschaftliche Studien* (Leiden: Brill, 1988) pp.82-3 and Sherif, Faruq *A guide to the contents of the Qur'an* (London: Ithaca Press, 1985) pp.91-4

Christians.[11] Whatever the reason, by the time the
revelations of the Qur'an ceased, there were three
categories of people – Muslims, *ahl al-kitab* and *kafirun*. It
was the *ahl al-kitab* who were eligible to become *dhimmi*,
if conquered by Muslims. *Kafirun* were supposed to be
eliminated altogether by conversion or killing, though this
became impracticable when the Muslim armies
encountered them in large numbers and they tended to be
treated as *ahl al-kitab*.[12]

The *hadith* mainly take a similar stance to the People of
the Book as do the later Qur'anic verses i.e. they are *dhimmi*
– protected people, paying *jizya* and submitting to a number
of restrictions.[13] With regard to the status of Christians
specifically, Wijoyo describes varying attitudes according
to the geographical location of the Christians concerned.
Egyptian Christians were most favourably regarded,
because one had given Muhammad his only male
descendant. Second in favour were the Abyssinian
Christians who had offered hospitality to the persecuted
Meccan Muslim refugees. The Byzantine Christians –
against whom many wars were fought during the Islamic
conquests – receive the most unfavourable accounts in the
hadith, being considered treacherous and unreliable.[14]

---

11. Zebiri op. cit. p.256

12. Cahen, C. "Dhimma" in *Encyclopaedia of Islam* Vol. II
(Leiden: Brill, 1983) p.227

13. Discussed in detail by Fattal, Antoine *Le Statut Légal
des Non-Musulmans en Pays d'Islam* (Beyrouth: Imprimerie
Catholique, 1958)

14. Wijoyo, Alex Soesilo "The Christians as religious
community according to the hadit" *Islamochristiana* Vol. 8
(1982) pp.84-5

Jews and the Constitution of Medina

The first *dhimmi* were the Jews of Khaybar, near Medina, a disparate group among whom the most prominent were the Banu 'n-Nadir who had fled there after their expulsion from Medina in 625. They were attacked and besieged by Muhammad in 628, eventually surrendering under the terms of a treaty by which the Jews were permitted to continue cultivating their land there but had to hand over half the produce to the Muslim conquerors. About the same time similar treaties were forced on the Jewish colonies at Fadak and Wadi 'l-Qura. In another treaty made at this time with the Jews of Tayma, the tribute levied was called *jizya*.[15]

Such treaties were a novelty in Muhammad's dealings with Jews, since previous military engagements (with the three main Jewish tribes of Medina itself – the Qaynuqa in 624, the Banu 'n-Nadir in 625 and the Qurayzah in 627) had resulted in the expulsion or death of the Jews concerned until there were no important groups of Jews left in Medina. There had been no option of remaining *in situ* and paying tribute.[16]

An ancient document known as the Constitution of Medina[17] includes much material about the rights and duties of Jews in Medina. The exact date of the document, preserved by Ibn Ishaq, is uncertain, though agreed to be authentically from Muhammad's period in Medina (622-632).[18] The three main Jewish groups of Medina are not

---

15. Watt op. cit. p.218

16. ibid. pp.209-214,216

17. translation in Watt op. cit. pp.221-5

18. The reasons for its authenticity are given by Wellhausen, Julius "Muhammads Gemeindeordnung von Medina" *Skizzen und Vorarbeiten* (Berlin: G. Reimer, 1884-99) Vol. IV (1889) pp.65-83, especially p.80, who dates it to 622 or 623. They are

mentioned by name, although many other Jewish groups
are listed, which might suggest that the document post-
dates the expulsion of the Qurayzah. There are reasons for
thinking that it is a collection of documents of different
dates.[19] The most significant feature of the Constution in
the context of treatment of non-Muslims is the fact that
nine Jewish groups are listed as being part of the *umma*,
the Muslim community.[20] Membership of the *umma* is
precisely what *dhimmi* do not have in later Islamic
legislation. Yet the Jews, though members of the *umma*, do
not seem to be of exactly equal status with the Muslim
members of the *umma*. They are apparently subordinate
and somewhat mistrusted.[21]

Much debate surrounds the definition of "*umma*" in the
Constitution, for on this hangs, it can be argued,
Muhammad's original intention for non-Muslim minorities
in an Islamic state. Clearly it is not religiously defined, but
does involve political and military loyalties. Humphreys
discusses various arguments, including Gil's egregious
assertion that the Jews were obliged to convert to Islam.
Other scholars, however, agree that the Jews were allowed
to retain their old religion and law.[22] Matters were clearly
different by the time of Umar II (717-720) who considered
himself primarily a Muslim, secondarily an Umayyad and
an Arab. He aimed to hold the fragile Umayyad Arab

summarised by Humphreys, R. Stephen *Islamic History*
(London: I.B. Tauris, 1991) pp.92-8

19. Watt op. cit. pp.225-8
20. sections 25-33 in Watt's translation. This fact is one of
the arguments for an early date for the Constitution.
21. Humphreys op. cit. p.97
22. ibid. pp.95-8

empire together by transforming it into a Muslim empire. His first step was, naturally, to try to persuade the non-Muslim subjects to become Muslims, offering them a lifting of *jizya* and equal citizenship with Muslims, irrespective of their tribe, in other words membership of the *umma* depended only on religion.[23] The rescript he circulated to all his governors for this purpose "carries every indication of genuineness" according to Gibb.[24] Some Pakistani Christians are arguing from the Constitution of Medina to assert their rights as non-Muslims.[25]

Christians and the Covenant of Umar
With regard to Christians the first detailed document purports to be an agreement with the Christians of Najran, to the south of Mecca, who sent a deputation to Muhammad in 630. A peace treaty was made according to which Muhammad would not interfere with ecclesiastical affairs or property and would protect the people of Najran. In return he was to receive an annual payment of 2,000 garments of a stipulated value, and in time of war armour, horses and camels were to be lent to the Muslims, though the Christians themselves did not have to fight.[26] Some scholars believe the alleged copies of this

---

23. Shaban. M.A. *The 'Abbasid Revolution* (Cambridge: Cambridge University Press, 1970) p.89

24. Gibb, H.A.R. 'The Fiscal Rescript of "Umar II" *Arabica* Vo. II no. 1 (Leiden, January 1955) quoted in Shaban op. cit. p.89 who also quotes Gibb's translation of the rescript.

25. Nazir, Noreen "The Concept of Ummah in the Medina Pact and its Implications on Pakistani non-Muslims" *Al-Mushir* Vol. 41 No. 4 (1999) passim

26. Watt op. cit. pp.127-8 (translations of Muhammad's letters are given on pp.359-60)

treaty to be a fabrication.[27] Around this time Muhammad began to demand also that the Christian tribes to the north of Mecca either convert to Islam or pay tribute.[28] Christians are not mentioned in the Constitution of Medina. They are however, the subject of the so-called Covenant of Umar.[29] This key document is attributed by Arab historians to Caliph Umar I (634-644) – or sometimes to Umar II (717-720) – but is generally considered by Western scholars to date from the period of Abbasid rule (750-1258), perhaps around 1100.[30] Whatever its origin the Covenant of Umar became the pattern for the definition and codification of the status of *dhimmis*, but was rarely enforced in its entirety.

The *dhimmi* were considered to be beneficiaries of a treaty or *dhimma*, by which the Muslim community granted them hospitality and protection in return for their submission. In the *Hedaya*, the authoritative text-book of Hanafi law, particularly used in Pakistan and also Turkey, India, Bangladesh and parts of Central Asia, this treaty is described as a "contract of subjection".[31] In the early years various regulations were imposed, differing according to local conditions, many of which appeared to be designed either to secure supplies for the victorious Muslim troops or to guard against espionage by the non-Muslims (e.g. maintaining a distinctive dress code).[32] But the most characteristic and lasting stipulation was the imposition of

---

27. Young *Patriarch, Shah and Caliph* p.159
28. Watt op. cit. pp.115-6,126
29. Discussed in Tritton, A.S. *The Caliphs and their non-Muslim Subjects: A Critical Study of the Covenant of Umar* (London: Oxford University Press, 1930)
30. Lambton, Ann K.S. *State and government in medieval Islam* (Oxford: Oxford University Press, 1981) p.203
31. The *Hedaya* Vol. 2 Book IX, pp.221-2

a poll-tax on adult males known as *jizya*. This was intended to cover the costs incurred by the Muslims in protecting the *dhimmi*,[33] or in lieu of the military service which they were not allowed, as non-Muslims, to perform[34] or both.[35] If a Muslim ruler failed to protect the life and property of non-Muslim citizens, he was obliged to return the *jizya*.[36] (Muslims still recall with pride an example of this happening, when the Muslim army in the eighth century had to withdraw from various nearby cities for a campaign at a certain place in Syria thus leaving the *dhimmis* unprotected.)[37]

Despite this reasoning, *jizya* was recognised by both Muslims and non-Muslims as a humiliating sign of submission.[38] According to Klein it was sometimes called "captivity-tax".[39] In the words of the Qur'an:

Fight those who believe not in God nor the Last Day, nor hold that forbidden which hath been forbidden by God and His Apostle, nor acknowledge the religion of truth (even if they are) of the People of the Book, until they pay the jizya with willing submission, and feel themselves subdued.[40]

---

32. Cahen op. cit. p.227

33. Khuri, Fuad I. *Imams and Emirs: State, Religion and Sects in Islam* (London: Saqi Books, 1990) p.83

34. The *Hedaya* vol. II Book IX p.212

35. Doi, Abdul Rahman I. *Non-Muslims under Shari'ah* (Maryland: International Graphics, 1979) p.55

36. ibid. loc cit.

37. Baig, Khalid "Moral World Order" *Impact International* (September 1998) p.4. See also Maududi, *Rights of Non Muslims* pp.23-4

38. Doi op. cit. p.59

39. Klein, F.A. *The Religion of Islam*, (London: Curzon Press Ltd, 1979) p.176

According to some jurists, the *jizya* was to be paid in a public ceremony in which the one paying was struck on the head or neck.[41] Because of the subservient position implied by payment of *jizya*, the Banu Taghlib (a tribe of Christian Arabs who fought on the side of the Muslims) preferred to pay four times as much tax, provided it was called *zakat* (obligatory alms, required of Muslims according the Qur'an) and not *jizya*.[42] Bat Ye'or summarises the symbolism of the *jizya* as follows:

> The vanquished had to pay the victor for the right to survive in his homeland, and the product of his labour was not merely paid to the state, but was intended to finance the *jihad* and consolidate its acquisitions. Thus the *dhimmi* worked for the benefit of the power that oppressed him, and for the community from which he was excluded.[43]

The later-developed rules for *dhimmi* were stricter and mainly emphasised their inferiority, including restrictions on their buildings and mounts. The erection of new places of worship was forbidden and some outward expressions of worship, such as processions and bells, were also limited. A *dhimmi* man could not marry a Muslim woman although a Muslim man could marry a *dhimmi* woman. Children of a mixed marriage were Muslims. A *dhimmi* could not own

---

40. S. 9:29

41. Ibn 'Abidin iii.294, quoted in Klein op. cit. p.176

42. Khuri op. cit. p.83. See also the *Hedaya* Vol. II Book IX pp.222-3

43. Bat Ye'or *The Dhimmi: Jews and Christians Under Islam* revised and enlarged English edition (London: Associated University Presses, 1985) p.144

a Muslim slave although the converse was permitted. *Dhimmi* merchants had to pay higher customs duties. According to most schools of law, the blood-money for a *dhimmi* was less than that for a Muslim.[44]

It is significant to note that the tightening of regulations concerning *dhimmis* in the late Middle Ages accompanied the growing numerical dominance of the Muslim population, who at the time of the original conquests, at least beyond Arabia, were a minority in relation to their subject peoples. Cahen points out that this was accompanied by a growing distinction between the treatment of Christians and the treatment of Jews. Christians were considered to be "friends of foreign powers" and thus were treated more harshly than Jews, who could not be so considered at that time.[45] Bat Ye'or writes of a '*dhimmi* syndrome' being the 'combined psychological effects of vulnerability and humiliation. Reduced in extreme cases to a precarious survival, evaluated in monetary terms, the *dhimmi* perceives himself and accepts himself as a dehumanized being.'[46] While such language may be considered emotive it nevertheless indicates the detrimental effect on self-image which non-Muslim minorities commonly experience.

Perhaps unexpectedly, *dhimmis* were not excluded from government bureaucracy. Despite hints of prohibition in

---

44. Lists of the rules are given in many sources, for example the *Hedaya* Vol II Book IX pp. 219-222, Klein op. cit. p.176, Khuri op. cit. pp. 84-6, Cahen op. cit. pp.227-8

45. Cahen op. cit. p.228-9

46. Bat Ye'or *The Decline of Eastern Christianity Under Islam: From Jihad to Dhimmitude* (London: Associated University Presses, 1996) pp. 235-9

the Qur'an[47] and explicit prohibition by rulers such as Umar II (717-720),[48] the help of non-Muslim administrators was indispensible to the Muslim rulers of the newly conquered lands. But this practice continued for centuries, for example the Assyrian Christians of Iraq and the Copts of Egypt held important positions in the administration of their respective countries.[49] From time to time during the Middle Ages there were public outcries against the presence of *dhimmi* in high administrative positions, and a number of *dhimmis* converted to Islam in order to keep their positions.[50] The issue of how much authority and power a non-Muslim can have in a Muslim state is one which continues to be debated, not least amongst Pakistani scholars discussing their country's mode of government. (See chapter 2.)

Indeed, the whole issue of the rights, restrictions, role and status appropriate for *dhimmis* continues to be discussed by contemporary Muslim scholars. The Palestinian Ismail al-Faruqi (1921-1986), though Western educated, added to the traditional limitations on political influence, further restrictions in the areas of education, culture, social and moral issues, whose necessity arises from the assumption that modern *dhimmis* mix daily with Muslims, rather than living in their own fairly closed communities; thus strict regulations about public behaviour were deemed necessary by al-Faruqi to preserve the Islamic character of society.[51] A contrasting Pakistani view

---

47. For example S.3:28 and 5:54
48. Lambton op. cit. p.206
49. Cahen op. cit. p.228-9
50. ibid. p.229
51. Al-Faruqi op. cit.) pp. 90-102; see also discussion in Zebiri op. cit. pp.258-262

is that of Fazlur Rahman (1919-1988) who believed that the modern situation calls for a relaxation of the rules imposed on *dhimmi* rather than increasing the restrictions.[52] A wide range of other views exist, some even more radical than that of Fazlur Rahman, but one characteristic of modern thinkers is that the classical distinction between *ahl al-kitab* and other non-Muslims has been abandoned by most so that the word *dhimmi* is usually synonymous with "non-Muslim minorities".[53] It is interesting to note how the word 'minority' has acquired in some contexts the same stigma which '*dhimmi*' used to have.[54] Two examples of the defence of Christians indicate clearly how "minority" is sometimes used by Muslims in the sense of "second-class citizen". Thus Benazir Bhutto, as leader of the opposition and former Prime Minister, when speaking of Christian minorities in Pakistan said "I do not like referring to minorities, I believe that we are all Pakistanis".[55] Similarly, Asma Jehangir, a leading lawyer with the Human Rights Commission of Pakistan, said of a Pakistani Christian, "I do not think that the fact he is a Christian makes him a minority... Today we announce that there are no minorities in our country, all are citizens of

---

52. His thinking on the subject is reviewed in Zebiri op. cit. pp.262-4

53. Zebiri op. cit. pp.270-1

54. The Christians of Malaysia and Egypt strenuously resist the use of the term "minority" to describe themselves, though they are numerically well below 50% of the population

55. Her speech at a Seminar on the Constitutional Rights of Minorities and Women in Pakistan, held in Lahore, on October 21, 1991, is published as Bhutto, Benazir "Minorities, Women and the Political Processes" *Al-Mushir* Vol. 33 No. 4 (Autumn 1991) p.110

Pakistan."[56] Christians themselves, on the other hand, make free use of the word[57] and are keen to be considered a minority as this carries with it the implication that they deserve preferential treatment like the lowest castes. For example, they would like to have fixed quotas in jobs, education etc.

Mu'ahids

In contrast to *dhimmi*, who are non-Muslims conquered by Muslims, there is another class of non-Muslim within an Islamic state, the *mu'ahids*. They are non-Muslim minorities living within an Islamic state who were **not conquered** by the Muslims. They are considered to have voluntarily chosen to live in the Islamic state and to have made an agreement with the state. They are not liable to pay *jizya*.[58] Some *ulema* and others argued that Christians and other non-Muslims living in Pakistan fall into this category[59] but others stated that they could not be *mu'ahids* since no agreement had been made with them.[60] Christians themselves have often argued that they are "sons of the soil", native inhabitants of Pakistan whose ancestors had

---

56. Speaking at the same seminar, and published as Jehangir, Asma "Minorities and women in Pakistan" *Al-Mushir* Vol. 33 No. 4 (Autumn 1991) p.125

57. For example, the National Commission for Justice and Peace entitles its human rights monitor 97 "A Report on the Religious Minorities in Pakistan".

58. Maududi *Rights of Non Muslims* pp.7-9.

59. Ahmed, Ishtiaq op. cit. p.87; Shehab, Rafi Ullah "Status of Non-Muslims under Holy Prophet's administration" *Pakistan Times* (April 12, 1979) p. 4

60. Maulana Abdul Haamid Badayuni, president of the Jami'at-ul-Ulama-i-Pakistan in *Report of the Court of Inquiry* p.213

lived there as far back as they could trace, unlike many Pakistani Muslims who migrated to Pakistan from other parts of India at independence.[61] In the words of Michael Nazir-Ali, speaking soon after his appointment as Bishop of Rochester, "The Christians of Pakistan have nowhere else to go. They are not from anywhere else."[62] Joshua Fazl-ud-Din points out that Christian Pakistanis had not been conquered by Muslim Pakistanis, indeed had struggled side by side with them for liberty from the British, so *dhimmi* status is inappropriate.[63] However, the *mu'ahid* argument is relatively rare, and is not often cited in the discussion of the status of Christians.

A third category of non-Muslims

If Pakistani Christians have neither been conquered (*dhimmi*) nor made an agreement with the state (*mu'ahids*) then there must be a third category of non-Muslims to which they belong. Mawdudi lists the non-*dhimmi* non-*mu'ahid* non-Muslims as "those who are in the Islamic State in any other way" although he appears at a loss as to how they should be treated.[64] This may also be the

---

61. For example, Group Captain Cecil Choudhury, Pakistan Air Force, in a radio report on *The World Tonight* (BBC Radio 4, 10 June 1998); also, Moghal, Dominic "The right of dual vote for non-Muslim Pakistanis and the anxieties of the religious groups: A moment of reflection for inter-faith harmony in Pakistan" Urdu version in *Al-Mushir* Vol. 38 No.2 (1996), English version in *Al-Mushir* Vol. 39 No. 2 (1997) p.64 [of English version]; Rumalshah "Hear the cry" p.40

62. quoted by Shahed Sadullah in "From Raiwind to Rochester" *Daily Jang*, August 26, 1994

63. Fazl-ud-Din *Future of Christians* p.108

64. Maududi *Rights of Non Muslims* pp.6-7

argument of Maulana Abdul Haamid Badayuni, formerly
president of the Jami'at-ul-Ulama-i-Pakistan, when
questioned at the Court of Inquiry which investigated
serious disturbances in the Punjab in 1953, who stated that
non-Muslim communities are neither *dhimmis* nor
mu'ahids (nor citizens). Muhammad Munir, who chaired
the Court of Inquiry and produced the report, condemns
this response as confused but Maulana Abdul Haamid
Badayuni was apparently given no opportunity to suggest
what category they did fall into.[65] Some Christians have
argued that Pakistani Christians fall into this third category,
for example, Dominic Moghal, director of the Christian
Study Centre in Rawalpindi,[66] and also the Catholic scholar
Geijbels who calls for *ijtihad* to determine the status of this
third type of minority in a contemporary Islamic state.[67]

The Shari'ah in Pakistan's legislation
It is in the Shari'ah that the status of *dhimmi* is codified.
The place of the Shari'ah in Pakistan's legislation is
therefore of the greatest importance in determining the
status of Christians.

---

65. *Report of the Court of Inquiry* pp.213-4
66. Moghal, Dominic "The status of non-Muslims in the
Islamic Republic of Pakistan: a confused identity" – a paper
given at a seminar on 'Religious Minorities in Pakistan: struggle
for identity' (July 1996) reproduced in a book of the same title
ed. Moghal, Dominic and Jivan, Jennifer (Rawalpindi: Christian
Study Centre, 1996) p.27
67. Geijbels, M. 'Pakistan, Islamisation and The Christian
Community. Part two: The Status and Calling of Christians'
Al-Mushir Vol. XXII No. 3 (Autumn 1980) p.105

Before independence

Throughout the history of the subcontinent, villages have had a significant degree of autonomy. Even under the sophisticated and highly centralised Mughal government (1526-1727) law enforcement rarely reached village level. The exceptions to this were cases involving a considerable breach of the peace or cases in which revenue due to the government had not been paid.[68] Thus the traditional village organization with all its Hindu institutions continued to function.[69]

Under British rule, a system known as Anglo-Muhammadan law developed, which was a fusion of British common law with Islamic law. Criminal justice was administered according to the British system, but personal law for Muslims continued to be governed by the Shari'ah (often as interpreted by British judges or by Indian judges with British training). Non-Muslims were unaffected by this law, apart from those who converted away from Islam, who, for example, lost their inheritance rights. It was this Anglo-Muhammadan law which became the original legislative system of the newly independent Pakistan.[70]

The origin of the campaign to enforce Shari'ah

The first constitution (1956) was carefully formulated to avoid references to the Shari'ah as the authoritative source of Islamic law. Rather, it referred to the "Holy Qur'an and the Sunna", intending to facilitate a new *ijtihad*, as envisaged by Muhammad Iqbal, which would be

---

68. Calkins, Philip B. "A note on lawyers in Muslim India" *Law and Society Review* Vol. III No. 2 (1968/9) pp.403-6
69. Mehdi, Rubya op. cit. pp.3-4
70. ibid. pp.4-9

formulated by parliament and the courts rather than by the *ulema*.[71] The various military and civilian governments which held power in the following two decades each made their own adjustments to the degree of attention paid by the law to Islam. The general trend, though rather superficial until 1977, was to give Islam an increasingly influential role and gradually to erode the rights of the non-Muslim minorities. (See chapter 2.)

The campaign to enforce Shari'ah began in 1977 with the Pakistan National Alliance and their anti-secular slogan, *nizam-e-Mustafa*, which was taken up by Zia's military government later the same year.[72] (See chapter 2.) Zia made the Islamization of the laws a primary objective.[73]

Shariat[74] benches and the Federal Shariat Court
In 1979 Zia created Shariat benches within the superior courts,[75] and soon followed this by an amendment to the

71. Lodhi op. cit. p.22; Ahmad, Salah-Ud-Din "Ijtihad" reprinted in *All Pak. Legal Decisions* Journal 1, p.1 (1980)

72. Amjad-Ali, Christine and Charles *The legislative history of the Shariah Act* (Rawalpindi: Christian Study Centre, 1992) p. 1

73. Khan, Justice Gul Muhammad "Islamization of the Laws in Pakistan" Presidential address at 5th Pakistan Jurists Conference, Karachi, reprinted in *All Pak. Legal Decisons* Vol. XXXVIII (1986) Journal 261; Korson, J. Henry 'Islamization and Social Policy in Pakistan' *Journal South Asian and Middle East Studies* Vol. 71 (1982) p.72

74. The Persian version of the Arabic "shariah", ending with 't' is often used in Pakistan.

75. President's Order 22 of 2 December 1978, Shariat Benches of Superior Courts Order, 1978, with effect from February 10, 1979 reprinted in *All Pakistan Legal Decisions* Vol. XXX (1978) Central Statutes 6

constitution to establish this reform.[76] According to Chapter 3-A, inserted into the 1973 constitution, Shariat benches were to be created within the High Courts when required to "decide the question whether or not any law or provision of the law is repugnant to the injunctions of Islam as laid down in the Holy Qur'an and the Sunnah of the Holy Prophet"[77] and this was to be done "notwithstanding anything contained in the Constitution".[78] Laws which were found not to conform with the injunctions of Islam were to be amended.[79] An explanatory note, however, excluded from the jurisdiction of Shariat benches virtually any kind of law which they might have been expected to examine. It ran: "In this Chapter, 'law' includes any custom or usage having the force of law but does not include the Constitution, Muslim personal law, any law relating to the procedure of any Court or Tribunal or, until the expiration of three years from the commencement of this Chapter, any fiscal law, or any law relating to the collection of taxes and fees or banking or insurance practice and procedure."[80] It is interesting to note the use of the word "Shariat" in the name of these benches. Although their task was defined as comparing the laws of Pakistan with the Qur'an and *Sunnah* (not with the Shari'ah), perhaps the very name indicates the beginning of a shift away from the concept of a new

---

76. President's Order 3 of 1979, section 2, with effect from February 7, 1979

77. Article 203-B of the 1973 Constitution of Pakistan, as inserted by Presidential Order 3 of 1979

78. Article 203-A of the 1973 Constitution of Pakistan, as inserted by Presidential Order 3 of 1979

79. Article 203-B (4)(a) of the 1973 Constitution of Pakistan, as inserted by Presidential Order 3 of 1979

80. Explanation appended to article 203-B

ijtihad and towards the use of the classical Shari'ah.

This effectively toothless constitutional provision was then ostensibly strengthened by General Zia in 1980 by the creation of a Federal Shariat Court.[81] This Court had the same role[82] accompanied by the same limitations as the Shariat benches had had. The Shariat Court had jurisdiction "notwithstanding anything in the Constitution" to 'examine and decide the question whether or not any law or provision of law is repugnant to the Injunctions of Islam, as laid down in the Holy Quran and Sunnah of the Holy Prophet'.[83] Further amendments to the Constitution with regard to the Federal Shariat Court were made in 1982, 1984 and 1985, which considerably strengthened its power. It gained the power to initiate examination of laws of its own volition[84] and the power to review any decisions or procedures of any other court enforcing *hadd* crimes, and to "enhance the sentence" if necessary.[85] Many laws, however, were still excluded from its jurisdiction.[86]

---

81. Constitution (Amendment) Presidential Order 1 of 1980, section 3

82. Article 203-D of the 1973 Constitution, as amended by Presidential Order 1 of 1980

83. Pakistan Constitution of 1973, article 203-D, amended 1982, in Mahmood, Safdar op. cit. p.938-41

84. Article 203-D section (1) of the Pakistan Constitution, amended by Constitution (Second Amendment) Presidential Order 5 of 1982

85. Pakistan Constitution of 1973, Article 203DD section (2)

86. Article 203-B (c) reads: "law" includes any custom or usage having the force of law but does not include the Constitution, Muslim personal law, any law relating to the procedure of any Court or Tribunal or, until the expiration of ten years from the commencement of this Chapter, any fiscal

By 1986 the Shariat Court had found portions of 55 federal laws (out of 512 examined) and 212 provincial laws (out of 999 examined) to be contrary to the Shari'ah.[87] These were mostly family and fiscal laws, but also included a whole range of constitutional, criminal and civil laws.

Hudood Ordinances and the Law of Evidence (Qanoon-e-Shahadat)

In 1979 a number of *Hudood* Ordinances were put into effect, enforcing *hadd* penalties[88] for the offences of drinking intoxicants (including drugs),[89] theft,[90] adultery,[91] and false accusation of adultery.[92] This was followed by legislation concerning the Islamic punishment of whipping,[93] the payment by Muslims of *zakat* (compulsory

---

law or any law relating to the levy and collection of taxes and fees or banking insurance practice and procedure;

87. Khan, Justice Gul Muhammad op. cit. pp.264-5

88. A *hadd* crime is an offence against the "boundaries" set by God, with a fixed punishment as stated in the Qur'an (or in the case of drinking alcohol, the *ahadith*) from which no deviation is allowed.

89. President's Order 4 of 1979, Prohibition (Enforcement of Hadd) Order, 1979 reprinted in *All Pakistan Legal Decisions,* Vol. XXXI (1979) Central Statutes 33-41 (1979)

90. Ordinance VI of 1979, Offences Against Property (Enforcement of Hudood) Ordinance, 1979 reprinted in *All Pakistan Legal Decisions* Vol. XXXI (1979) Central Statutes 44-51

91. Ordinance VII of 1979, Offence of Zina (Enforcement of Hudood) Ordinance, 1979 reprinted in *All Pakistan Legal Decisions* Vol. XXXI (1979) Central Statutes 51-56

92. Ordinance VIII of 1979, Offence of Qazf (Enforcement of Hadd) Ordinance, 1979 reprinted in *All Pakistan Legal Decisions* Vo. XXXI (1979) Central Statutes 56-60

93. Ordinance IX of 1979, Execution of the Punishment of

alms) and *ushr* (tithes),[94] and the enforcement of the Ramadan fast.[95]

The administration of justice under Islamic law depends heavily on the number of qualified witnesses who give evidence in court. In 1984 President Zia promulgated the *Qanoon-e-Shahadat* (Law of Evidence) which replaced a previous Law of Evidence dating from 1872. This had a grave effect on Christians and other non-Muslims because of the following proviso concerning who is competent to appear as a witness in a Court of Law:

> Provided further that the Court shall determine the competence of a witness in accordance with the qualifications prescribed by the injunctions of Islam as laid down in the Holy Quran and Sunnah for a witness, and, where such witness is not forthcoming, the court may take the evidence of a witness who may be available.[96]

This would give a judge trying a *hadd* case the freedom to define women as half-witnesses in comparison with men.[97] (It is relevant here to note that Article 17 specifies that business transactions require two male witnesses or one

Whipping Ordinance, 1979 reprinted in *All Pakistan Legal Decisions* Vol. XXXI (1979) Central Statutes 60-62

94. Ordinance XXIX of 1979, Zakat and Ushr (Organisation) Ordinance, 1979, reprinted in *All Pakistan Legal Decisions,* Vol. XXXI (1979) Central Statutes 277-285

95. Ordinance XXIII of 1981, Ehtram-E-Ramazan Ordinance, 1981, reprinted in *All Pakistan Legal Decisions* Vol. XXXIII (1981) Central Statutes 278

96. Law of Evidence Order, 1984, Chapter II, section 3, quoted in Dawood op. cit. p.113

97. based on Sura 2:282 "... and get two witness out of your own men, And if there are not two men, Then a man and two women..."

male and two female – four female witnesses are not allowed.) Likewise non-Muslims can be defined as half-witnesses in comparison with Muslims, making the evidence of a non-Muslim woman worth only a quarter of the evidence of a Muslim man. Furthermore, under the *Hudood* Ordinances there are certain cases in which women and non-Muslims are not admissible as witnesses at all[98] (see below). The effects of this on Christians brought to court under the *Hudood* Ordinances are clearly very negative. A report by the International Commission of Jurists in 1985 wrote of the inequalities resulting from the *Hudood* Ordinances:

> ... this is not being done on an entirely even handed basis since Muslims can give evidence against non-Muslims but not vice versa and, while the Presiding Officer in a trial of a non-Muslim for any of the offences other than 'Qazf'[99] must also be a non-Muslim, an appeal to the Federal Shariat Court will be heard by exclusively Muslim Judges. At least in some respects, therefore these ordinances may offend against the constitutional guarantees of freedom and equality before the law, but they are possibly immune from constitutional challenge because of the validation given to all the ordinances made by the President during Martial Law through the introduction of Article 270A(3) into the Constitution ...[100]

---

98. Dawood op. cit. p.111-123; Mehdi, Rubya op. cit. pp.147-150; Bouma, Cees "Pakistan's Islamization 1977-88: The Zia Era in Retrospect" in *Al-Mushir* Vol.31 No. 1 (Spring 1989) p.21

99. false accusation of adultery

100. *Pakistan After Martial Law* a report by the International Commission of Jurists, 1985 pp. 101-2, quoted in Shahani op. cit. p.4

Qisas and Diyat Ordinance

In 1990 the Shari'ah law of retaliation by causing similar hurt (*qisas*) and compensation (*diyat*) for murder and intentional bodily harm had been introduced by means of a presidential ordinance.[101] This law had been in preparation since Zia directed the Council of Islamic Ideology to start work on a draft in 1979, and had passed through numerous other committees and bodies.[102] The law caused resentment amongst Pakistani women because the *diyat* for female victims was only one half of the *diyat* of male victims, and because women were not admissible as witnesses in murder cases.[103] Christians were alarmed by the implication that, following the pattern of the Shari'ah, they would be considered to be worth only half the *diyat* of Muslims.[104] The Ordinance was not considered by Parliament and therefore lapsed after four months.[105]

In April 1997 an amended version was passed by Parliament, which had no discriminatory references to women or non-Muslims.[106]

---

101. Criminal Law (Second Amendment) Ordinance (No. VII of 1990) published *in Gazette of Pakistan Extraordinary* (5 September 1990) and reprinted in Mehdi, Rubya op. cit. pp. 298-323

102. Amin, Mohammad *Islamization of Laws in Pakistan* (Lahore: Sang-e-Meel Publications, 1989) pp.82-3

103. Mehdi, Rubya op. cit. pp.152-3

104. Shahani op. cit. pp.7-8

105. According to Article 89 (2) of the 1973 Constitution concerning the promulgation of ordinances by the president

106. Criminal Law (Amendment) Act (II of 1997) which substituted new sections 299 to 338 in the Pakistan Penal Code, available in an edition with commentary by Nizami, Muhammad Mazhar Hassan (Lahore: PLD Publishers, 1998) pp.277-321

The Eighth and Ninth Amendments

In 1985 General Zia introduced an Eighth Amendment to the constitution which served the dual purpose of ratifying various of his past actions and furthering the Islamization of the legislation. This amendment provided a constitutional basis for the separate electorates system (see chapter 4), and incorporated the Objectives Resolution as an integral part of the constitution,[107] rather than simply a preamble. Thus the clause stating that "Muslims shall be enabled to order their lives in the individual and collective spheres in accordance with the teachings and requirements of Islam as set out in the Holy Quran and the Sunnah" became legally obligatory (see chapter 2).[108]

The conservative religious groups considered the Eighth Amendment inadequate, since it did not extend the powers of the Federal Shariat Court to cover fiscal laws, Muslim personal laws and the judicial system; they voted for it only on condition that the government would introduce legislation to deal with this issue at a later date. When the government appeared to be delaying on this, two senators, Qazi Latif and Maulana Sami-ul-Haq, introduced a private Shariat Bill into the Senate on 13 July 1985. While this bill was at the committee stage, the government proposed a Ninth Amendment to the constitution which covered the areas that the conservative religious groups had considered lacking in the Eighth Amendment. The Ninth Amendment bill declared that "the injunctions of Islam as laid down in the Holy Quran and Sunnah shall be the supreme law and

---

107. Amjad Ali, Christine and Charles *The legislative history* p.2

108. Pakistan Constitution of 1973, article 2A (amended 1985) in Mahmood, Safdar p.842

source of guidance for legislation to be administered through laws enacted by the Parliament and provincial assemblies, and for policy making by the Government".[109] It allowed the Shariat Court to examine any law at all, excluding only the Constitution from its jurisdiction.[110] It also mandated that taxes, banking and insurance law be brought into "conformity with the injunctions of Islam".[111] The Ninth Amendment bill was passed unanimously by the Senate on 9 July 1986, but before it had finished its passage through parliament, Zia dissolved the National Assembly and dismissed the government (May 29, 1988). One of the stated grounds for the President's action was the failure of the government to Islamize the country. The Sami-Latif Shariat bill, having suffered major criticism by the select committee, had continued to be circulated for further comment and had also failed to become law.[112]

The Enforcement of Shari'ah Act (1991)
The newly developed power relationship between Parliament and the Federal Shariat Court – in which the law-making role of Parliament was subordinate to the law-checking role of the Federal Shariat Court – was reinforced by the Enforcement of Shari'ah Ordinance of 1988, promulgated by President Zia.[113] This stated that Shari'ah shall be the "supreme source of law in Pakistan and grund

---

109. Clause 2 of the Ninth (Constitutional) Amendment Bill
110. Clause 3 of the Ninth (Constitutional) Amendment Bill
111. Clause 4 of the Ninth (Constitutional) Amendment Bill
112. Amjad Ali, Christine and Charles *The legislative history* pp.2-3
113. Enforcement of Shari'ah (revised) Ordinance, 1988 reprinted in *All Pak. Legal Decisions* Vol. XLI (1989) Central Statutes 18

norm *(sic)* for policy making of the state" (clause 3).[114] The ordinance lapsed after Zia's death in August 1988[115] but its text formed the basis of the bill which was later passed as the Enforcement of Shari'ah Act (1991).[116]

After Zia's death, a Pakistan People's Party government (1988-90) was formed by Benazir Bhutto, having been voted into power. This government had no intention of furthering the lapsed Shari'ah legislation and sought, indeed, to repeal the Eighth Amendment. Nevertheless Qazi Latif and Maulana Sami-ul-Haq introduced another private bill, called The Enforcement of Shariah Bill, on 26 March 1989. Although based largely on General Zia's Shari'ah Ordinance this bill went a significant step further in speaking of the Shariah as the "supreme law in Pakistan" rather than the 'supreme source of law in Pakistan and grund norm *(sic)* for policy making of the state'. The bill was referred to a special committee, which made amendments and presented it to the Senate on 13 May 1990, which promptly passed it. However, the passage of the bill through Parliament was halted once again by the dissolution of the National Assembly and the dismissal of the government (6 August 1990).[117]

A new Islami Jamhoori Ittehad (IJI, Islamic Democratic

---

114. Amjad Ali, Christine and Charles *The legislative history* p.4

115. Pakistan Constitution of 1973, article 89, clause (1) (a) declares that a presidential ordinance will stand repealed four months after its promulgation

116. Enforcement of Shari'ah Act, 1991, reprinted in *All Pak. Legal Decisions* Vol. XLIII (1991) Central Statutes 373-378

117. Amjad Ali, Christine and Charles *The legislative history* pp.4-6

Alliance, formerly the Pakistan National Alliance) government was formed after elections in October 1990. While in opposition the IJI had spoken out in favour of the Enforcement of Shari'ah Bill, and Prime Minister Nawaz Sharif now formed a committee to examine the bill again.

Many minority groups, women's groups, human rights groups and Shi'a groups were strongly opposed to the bill.[118] They perceived a threat to the constitutional guarantee that all citizens are equal before the law and entitled to equal protection under the law. Another objection centred on the immense power to be given to the *ulema*, who could be appointed as judges, friends of court and lawyers, to interpret and determine what is, or is not, in accordance with Shari'ah; this would have effectively shifed the legislative power from parliament to non-elected individuals chosen by the president. A third objection concerned the vagueness of definition of the Shari'ah; a conservative rather than a progressive interpretation of the Qur'an and *Sunnah* was indicated but it was felt that the lack of precision would be likely to lead to conflicts between followers of different schools of Islam.[119]

---

118. Bouma, Cees "Ninth Amendment and Shariat Bill" *Al-Mushir* Vol. XXVIII No. 4 (Winter 1986) pp. 163-5; 'IJI determined to adopt Shariat Bill' *Frontier Post* (28 December 1990) p.1

119. "Observations, comments and reactions to the Shariat Bill submitted by the Christian group, meeting with the Shariat Bill Committee on 27th December 1990" signed by Bishop Alexander John Malik of Lahore Diocese of the Church of Pakistan and Rev. Dr Charles Amjad-Ali, director of the Christian Study Centre, Rawalpindi; letter to Prime Minister Nawaz Sharif on the subject of "Problems arising for Christians from the Shariat Bill" from Bishops Trinidade, Malik, Lobo,

The Enforcement of Shari'ah Bill was brought before the National Assembly on 11 April 1991, and again referred to a select committee. This bill was considerably more moderate than the initial bill presented by Sami and Latif, and was characterised principally by vagueness and "pious hopes"[120]. The substance was contained in just two of the 22 clauses. Clause 3 declared the Shari'ah to be the supreme law and Clause 4 instructed courts to interpret laws in the light of the Shari'ah. The bill was opposed not only by liberals but also by religious conservatives. The latter felt the bill was too weak owing to the use of the word "Shari'ah" which carried the implication of a variety of schools of law and a limited scope focusing mainly on inheritance and divorce. They wanted the "Qur'an and *Sunnah*" to be made the supreme law (as was later promulgated in the 1998 Shari'ah bill described below). Prime Minister Nawaz Sharif had promised to introduce another bill to amend the constitution to make the Qur'an and *Sunnah* the supreme law of the country, thus taking precedence over the constitution, but did not in fact ever table such a bill. The conservative religious parties held that such an amendment would be unnecessary if the preamble could refer (as it had done in the original Sami-Latif bill) to the Objectives Resolution, which since 1985 had been incorporated in the constitution. This change was duly made by the committee to the preamble of the draft

---

Pereira, Joseph and Azariah (4th December 1990)

120. Editorial in *The Muslim* (April 25, 1992) p.6. See also Khan, Shujaat Ali in *The News* (April 15, 1991) p.4 who argued that the bill was more like a declaration of intent than a draft law. Both cited in Amjad Ali, Christine and Charles *The legislative history* pp.10-11

bill. Opposition from the other end of the political/religious spectrum resulted in the government proposing amendments which were supposed to protect the constitutional rights of women and minorities and the existing democratic and political system. The value of these clauses was doubted by some observers, since the passing of the Shari'ah Act raised questions about the status of the constitution itself, which was now apparently secondary to the Shari'ah.[121]

The Enforcement of Shari'ah Bill was passed by the National Assembly on 16 May 1991 and by the Senate on 28 May 1991. Despite the amendments, its heart was still found in clauses 3 and 4 which made Shari'ah the supreme law in Pakistan and required laws to be interpreted in the light of the Shari'ah. The rest was mainly concerned with wide-ranging and ill-defined aims (such as 'eradicating social evils'), or with giving parliament powers and duties it already had. Two sub-sections (clauses 1(4) and 3(2)) were supposed to protect the minorities[122] but did not define

---

121. Amjad Ali, Christine and Charles *The legislative history* pp.15-16

122. See below for more detail. Clause 1(4) Nothing contained in this Act shall affect the personal laws, religious freedom, traditions, customs and way of life of the non-Muslims.

Clause 3(2) Notwithstanding anything contained in this Act, the Judgement of any court or any other law for the time being in force, the present political system, including the Majlis-e-Shoora (Parliament) and Provincial Assemblies and the existing system of Government, shall not be challenged in any court, including Supreme Court, the Federal Shariat Court or any authority or tribunal:

Provided that nothing contained herein shall affect the rights of the non-Muslims guaranteed by or under the Constitution.

what would happen in cases involving both Muslims and non-Muslims or non-Muslims and the state. The question remained as to whether a sub-constitutional enactment could decide what should be the "supreme law" of the country. The Objectives Resolution, which had been included in the preamble specifically to deal with this issue, does not in fact mention the word "Shari'ah" or its supremacy, but only states:

(para 5) Wherein the Muslims shall be enabled to order their lives in the individual and collective spheres in accordance with the teachings and requirements of Islam as set out in the Holy Quran and Sunnah;

Opponents of the Act also pointed out that the Islamization of laws had already been prescribed in Article 227 and Part IX of the Constitution, which stated that the process was to involve the recommendations of the Council of Islamic Ideology (CII); the Shari'ah Act itself was not based on the recommendations of the CII, and thus could perhaps be deemed unconstitutional. Charles Amjad Ali, former director of the Christian Study Centre, Rawalpindi, and his wife Christine summarized the constitutional status of the Shari'ah Act as:

... either the Act is meant to be understood and used in terms of the already existing constitutional provisions – in which case it is a superfluous piece of legislation, or it moves beyond the constitutional provisions – in which case it is unconstitutional.[123]

123. Amjad Ali, Christine and Charles *The legislative history* p.19

Another unresolved area was the nature of the Shari'ah which was now to be the supreme law of the country – no particular school of law was named. Furthermore, there was the question as to whether *every* part of the Shari'ah was to be made a legal requirement of the state, for example the injunction to pray five times a day or to wash the body in a certain way.[124]

Writing a year after the passing of the Act, Charles and Christine Amjad-Ali describe the effect of the Act, despite its vagueness:

> Where the Act has had an influence is in adding to a particular atmosphere of religious intolerance, anti-constitutionality, and a refusal to take into account the consequences of actions taken in the name of Islam.[125]

The following year a landmark ruling in the Supreme Court demonstrated the state's obligation to protect Islam, even when at variance with constitutional rights. In the case of Zaheer-ud-Din v. The State, which was concerned with the constitutional validity of some anti-Ahmadiyya legislation, Judge Abdul Qadeer Chaudhary held that the "Constitution has adopted the Injunctions of Islam as contained in the Qur'an and Sunnah of the Holy Prophet as the real and effective law. In that view of the matter, the Injunctions of Islam as contained in the Qur'an and Sunnah of the Holy Prophet are now the positive law." From this Chaudhary concluded that "every man-made law must now conform to the Injunctions of Islam as contained in the Qur'an and Sunnah of the Holy Prophet (p.b.u.h.) Therefore even the Fundamental Rights as given in the Constitution must not violate the norms of Islam ... Anything, even in any fundamental right, which violates the Injunctions of Islam thus must be repugnant."[126] As Lau points out, this was a new and much more restrictive interpretation of fundamental rights (including freedom of religion) which were listed in Part II, chapter I of the Constitution.[127] According to Chaudhary Islamic law was to be regarded as the positive law of the land, capable of restricting all fundamental rights, and binding on both the courts and the legislator. Lau comments that "consistently applied, such a principle would make the continued existence of statute law superfluous since judges could apply Islamic directly without any reference to other sources of law."[128]

The Fifteenth Amendment Bill[129]

On 28 August 1998 Prime Minister Nawaz Sharif introduced to the National Assembly a bill to amend the constitution so as to make the Qur'an and Sunnah "constitutionally and legally supreme".[130] This fifteenth

---

126. *All Pakistan Legal Decisions* Vol. XLV (1993) SCMR 1774-5

127. reproduced in Butt op. cit. pp.5-14

128. Lau, Martin "Islam and Fundamental Rights in Pakistan: the case of Zaheer-ud-Din v. The State and its impact on the fundamental right to freedom of religion" *Centre of Islamic and Middle Eastern Law Yearbook* Vol. 1 (1996)

129. Text of first version reproduced in *Dawn* (29 August 1998)

130. Sharif, Nawaz, speech to the National Assembly, 28 August 1998, quoted in *Dawn* (29 August 1998)

amendment bill was greeted by widespread condemnation, from the opposition Pakistan People's Party to the Islamic political parties such as the Jamaat-i-Islami and Jamiat-i-Ulema.[131] and even from some members of Nawaz Sharif's own Muslim League.[132] The bill was seen almost universally as a mechanism to increase the Prime Minister's power to an unacceptable level and by the minorities as also detrimental to their interests. Asma Jehangir, chair of the Human Rights Commission of Pakistan, asserted that if the bill were to be passed it would become impossible for the minorities to live in Pakistan.[133] Vociferous protests were made by many Christian organizations including the Pakistan Christian National Party,[134] the Pakistan Christian Action Forum,[135] the Christian Lawyers Association[136] and the Christian Liberation Front Pakistan.[137] Christian and other minority parliamentarians also spoke out against the bill and expressed their willingness to resign over the issue.[138]

---

131. *Newsline* (September 1998) pp. 16-18

132. For example, Abdul Hameed Jatoi MNA, interviewed by Faraz Hashmi in *The Herald* (September 1998) p.41

133. Interviewed by Asha'ar Rehman in *Newsline* (September 1998) p.26

134. "Christians Against 15th Amendment" *Dawn* (8 September 1998)

135. "Christians for withdrawal of 15th Amendment" *The News* (3 September 1998)

136. "Minorities to boycott Shariah Bill moot" *The News* (7 September 1998)

137. "CLF joins PPP in struggle against Shariah Bill" *The News* (2 September 1998)

138. "Christians reject Islamization bill" *Dawn* (3 September 1998); "Minority lawmakers to oppose bill" *Dawn* (5 September 1998); "Minority MNAs reject Bill" *The News* (18 September 1998)

The bill had only two changes to make to the constitution. Firstly, there was the introduction of a new article 2B. Section (1) of this stated that "The Holy Qur'an and *Sunna* of the Holy Prophet (peace be upon him) shall be the supreme law of Pakistan." This was explained as a logical step following the incorporation of the Objectives Resolution as a substantive part of the constitution. Furthermore, it will be remembered that the Enforcement of Shari'ah Act of 1991 had declared the Shari'ah to be the supreme law, but without any amendment to the constitution on this issue. Nawaz Sharif had promised at the time to make the required amendment, but had taken no action until this 1998 bill. The effectiveness of the constitution as a safeguard for the minorities[139] would be removed at a stroke by this article if passed.

Secondly, there were proposed amendments to Article 239 which set out new procedures for passing legislation with the purpose of removing any impediments in enforcing Shari'ah and implementing the injunctions of Islam. These new procedures reduced the majority required for constitutional changes and reduced the power of the upper house, giving the government – effectively the Prime Minister – vastly increased powers to amend the constitution and make laws. Hence the outcry from all

---

139. Joshua Fazl-ud-Din had recognised many years earlier that for non-Muslim minorities "their main source of strength lies in the fact that in the last resort they can always fall back on the Constitution as their mainstay". [Fazl-ud-Din, Joshua "Separate electorates: the Life-Blood of Pakistan" originally published in Punjabi Darbar (Lahore, date not given) and later reproduced in Grover, Verinder and Arora, Ranjana (eds.) *Pakistan Fifty Years of Independence* (New Delhi: Deep and Deep Publications, 1997) p. 182]

sides, for example, Sajjad Ali Shah, former Supreme Court Chief Justice,[140] even from Syed Munawar Hasan, the general secretary of the Jamaat-i-Islami.[141]

The minorities had further reason to protest, seeing more restrictions for themselves as the government would be required to "take steps to enforce the Shari'ah" (section (2) of article 2B) within which was included the traditional Islamic formula "to prescribe what is right and to forbid what is wrong". This was reinforced by sections (3) and (5) of Article 2B which asserted the government's power to override "any state functionary for non-compliance" and "anything contained in the Constitution, any law or judgement of any Court". Thus they feared they would have been left without any legal or constitutional protection.[142]

A revised version of the bill was presented to the National Assembly on 9 October 1998, and passed by 151 votes to 16. The revised bill omitted the proposed changes to

---

140. Interviewed by Idrees Bakhtiar in *The Herald* (September 1998) pp.38-40

141. He expressed support for the bill only on condition that Article 239 was removed. See "Special Report" *The News International* (12 September 1998)

142. Statements by, for example, Bishop Armando Trinidade (head of the Roman Catholic church in Pakistan) and Bishop Alexander Malik (head of the Church of Pakistan) at a press conference on 2 September 1998, reported in *Dawn* (3 September 1998), Dr R. Julius Sunday, a Christian member of the national assembly reported in *Dawn* (7 September 1998), a group of thirty minority organisations including Hindus, Sikhs and Christians, at a meeting convened by the Christian Liberation Front Pakistan reported in *Dawn* (7 September 1998), Joseph Francis, secretary general of the Pakistan Christian National Party, quoted in *The News International* (12 September 1998)

legislative procedure, thus obtaining broad support, but left unaltered the amendment to make the Shari'ah the supreme law and the government's obligation to take steps to enforce it, as well as to prescribe what is right and forbid what is wrong. The clause placing the government's power above constitution, law and courts remained.[143] Yet the revised bill was still condemned by the *amir* (equivalent to chairman) of the Jamaat-i-Islami, Qazi Hussain Ahmed, who said its purpose was to divert attention from the Prime Minister's failed policies on economics and law and order, and to "make the government supreme under the garb of the Qur'an and Sunnah". Interestingly Qazi Hussain Ahmed asserted that the existing constitutional provisions regarding the promotion of Islamic rule were sufficient.[144] The bill should have then passed to the Senate, where it would have been unlikely to obtain the two-thirds majority required.[145] On 14 December 1998 twenty-two religious parties announced that they had entered into an alliance called the United Shari'ah Front, with the aim of "besieging" all MNAs and senators who were opposed to the Shari'ah Bill until they changed their opinion.[146] In fact, the three months period during which the bill could have been considered by the Senate (ending 9 January 1999)

---

143. "National Assembly passes Shariat Bill" *The News* (10 October 1998); "Pakistan Deputies back Islamic law" *International Herald Tribune* (10-11 October 1998); "Betraying the Quaid" *The News* (12 October 1998)

144. "Jamaat chief warns of consequences of insulting national institutions" *The News* (12 October 1998)

145. "Pakistani Christians Fearful of Islamic Law" *Catholic World News Service* (3 November 1998)

146. "22 parties unite for Shari'ah" *The News* (15 December 1998)

passed without any Senate vote on it and, at the time of writing, it appears to have been unofficially set aside. However, on 30 January 1999 President Muhammad Tarar expressed his confidence that the bill would be passed by the Senate and that Pakistan's "real success" would come the day Shari'ah was imposed.[147]

Implementation of Shari'ah in certain areas
In 1994 an armed uprising in which scores of people were killed occurred in the Malakand Division of the North West Frontier Province (NWFP), led by the Tehrik-i-Nifaz-i-Shariat-i-Mohammadi (TNSM), demanding the imposition of Shari'ah law. *Nizam-i-Shari'ah* [Shari'ah system] regulations were introduced in Malakand as a response, including amputation for theft, stoning to death for adultery and flogging for consumption of alcohol. While these punishments were also possible in the rest of the country under the *Hudood* Ordinances, in Malakand they were now the only punishments legally permitted. Nevertheless they have never actually been enforced in Malakand, let alone anywhere else.

After Nawaz Sharif introduced the Fifteenth Constitutional Amendment Bill in August 1998, the TNSM became active again,[148] and on 16 January 1999 , the government of NWFP signed two statutes to promulgate Shari'ah in Malakand Division[149] and in the neighbouring

147. "Imposition of Shariah to be real success: Tarar" *The News International* (31 January 1999)
148. Hyman, Anthony "The Impact of the Taleban on Pakistan" *Dialogue* (published by the Public Affairs Committee for Shi'a Muslims, London) (May 1999) p.5
149. *Nifaz-i-Nizam-i-Shariat* [Promulgation of the System

Kohistan District of Hazara Division.[150] All judges in the area were required to go on a three-month refresher course in Islamic law, and were also able to call on *ulema* to assist them in reaching judgements. *Ulema* were to be allowed to act as lawyers. Non-Muslims in the areas were to have their cases tried under their own religious laws, but no statement was made regarding cases in which one party is a Muslim and the other a non-Muslim. The NWFP's chief minister, Sardar Mehtab Ahmad Khan, said that he saw these areas as a model for the rest of the province, and Maulana Sufi Muhammad, leader of the TNSM, said that in March 1999 they would re-start their "struggle for total enforcement of Shari'ah in the country"[151] but at the time of writing no further areas have been affected. Malakand – but not Kohistan – is part of the Provincially Administered Tribal Areas, lying along the Afghanistan border and inhabited by the Pakhtun, which have long been permitted a large degree of self-government. [152]

The Federally Administered Tribal Areas (FATA), also inhabited by the Pakhtun, have even greater freedom from central control than the Provincially Administered Tribal Areas. Society follows a rigid, highly traditional pattern. The supremacy of the Taliban for some years in nearby Afghanistan has motivated the religious groupings to take the law into their own hands and enforce Shari'ah. Various

---

of Shari'ah] Regulation, 1999

150. *Nizam-i-Adl* [System of (social) Justice] Ordinance, 1999.

151. "Country Focus" *Al-Mushir* Vol. 41 No. 1 (1999) pp.33-35

152. "Shariah enforced in Malakand, Kohistan" *The News* (17 January 1999)

groups, often described jointly as 'the Pakistan Taliban', are active in the FATA, one being the Tehrik-i-Tulaba in Orakzai Agency, whose declared goal is to fully Islamize first Orakzai, then all the FATA, and then the whole of Pakistan, by enforcing a system of Shari'ah, like that in use in the Taliban's Afghanistan. Already in Orakzai, music, television and games have been banned.[153] On 13 December 1998, a condemned murderer was publicly executed in Orakzai Agency on the orders of the 'Pakistan Taliban'. Khial Ghaffar was shot by his brother and uncle according to the Islamic principles of *qisas*, whereby the closest relative of the murderer must perform the execution. As announced by the Pakistan Taliban this was a significant step towards enforcing Shari'ah in the FATA.[154]

Official safeguards for religious minorities

Most discussions of minority rights focus primarily on the process of Islamization, but an alternative perspective can be considered, tracing the various ways in which legal and constitutional provision for the protection of minorities has been made. Some of these have already been discussed, but will be mentioned again below for the sake of completeness. The effectiveness or otherwise of these provisions is the subject of this study as a whole.

Jinnah and the Constituent Assembly (August 1947)
As described in chapter 2, Muhammad Ali Jinnah's famous speech as president of the Constituent Assembly, a day after the formation of the Constituent Assembly and three days

153. Hyman op. cit. p.5
154. "Murder executed Taleban style in Pakistan" *Straits Times* (15 December 1998)

before independence, emphatically asserted the fact that religion "has nothing to do with the business of the State" and that "there is no discrimination between one caste or creed or another".[155] As already noted, one of the first acts of the Constituent Assembly, accomplished even before independence, was to set up a committee called the Basic Rights Committee to advise it on the fundamental rights of citizens of Pakistan and on matters relating to the minorities.[156] Given Jinnah's lead, it was not surprising that this committee recommended the equality of Muslim and non-Muslim citizens. Its place was later taken by a Ministry of Minority Affairs, created in 1973.

United Nations Universal Declaration of Human Rights (December 1948)
The Universal Declaration of Human Rights, adopted by the United Nations Assembly on 10 December 1948, contains various provisions concerning freedom of religion and prohibiting discrimination on grounds of religion. The most relevant articles are:

> Article 2. Everyone is entitled to all the rights and freedoms set forth in the Declaration, without distinction of any kind, such as race, colour, sex, language, religion, political or other opinion, property, birth or other status....
> Article 18. Everyone has the right to freedom of thought, conscience and religion; this right includes the freedom

---

155. Jinnah's speech was made on 11 August 1947, and quoted in Munir *From Jinnah to Zia* p.30

156. Choudhury, Golam W. *Pakistan: transition from military to civilian rule* (Essex: Scorpion Publishing Ltd, 1988) p.120

to change his religion or belief, and freedom, either alone or in community with others and in public or private, to manifest his religion or belief in teaching, practice, worship and observance.

A year earlier, in December 1947, when the United Nations Assembly was discussing the draft Declaration, some Muslim delegates (mainly from Arab countries) expressed reservations with regard to Article 18, particularly the phrase guaranteeing the right to change one's faith. At the time of voting these delegates abstained. By contrast, the leader of the Pakistan delegation, Sir Muhammad Zafarullah Khan, was in favour of Article 18 and explained that his delegation approved it on the basis of the Qur'an's teaching in S.18:29.[157] He also argued that what the Qur'an condemned was not unbelief but hyprocrisy, and that Islam is a missionary religion and recognizes that other faiths also have the right to try to make converts.[158] It is relevant to note that Sir Muhammad Zafarullah Khan, as an Ahmadiyya, himself belonged to a religious minority which in later years was severely restricted and discriminated against (see chapter 5).

The Objectives Resolution (March 1949)
The Objectives Resolution, adopted by the Constituent Assembly in March 1949, listed a number of principles on which it was intended a future constitution should be based.

---

157. "Let him who will, Believe, and let him Who will, reject [the truth]"

158. "Islam en Godsdienstvrijheid" *Begrip* No. 45 (May/June 1979) pp.1-2, cited in Geijbels "Pakistan, Islamisation" pp.105-6

Amongst these were a guarantee of freedom of belief, faith and worship, provision for minorities "freely to profess and practise their religions and develop their cultures", and that "adequate provision shall be made to safeguard the legitimate interests of minorities and backward and depressed classes".[159]

As has been described in chapter 2, the Objectives Resolution was used as a preamble to all three constitutions, and was then given added authority by Zia in his 1985 amendments which made it part of the "substantive provisions" of the constitution (Article 2A). The minorities focused their aspirations on the clause stating that they should be able "freely to profess and practise their religion". This phrase was present in the 1956 constitution, but absent from the 1962 constitution, though within the 1962 constitution itself was the guarantee that every citizen had "the right to profess, practice (*sic*) and propagate any religion" (Article 6, principle 7(a)). The original wording re-appeared in the 1973 constitution's preamble but amongst the 1985 amendments was one which removed the word "freely" from this clause. This caused a furore amongst the minorities.[160]

---

159. Full text of Objectives Resolution is quoted in in Iqbal, Afzal op. cit. pp.42-3

160. Even in 1998 this was still a cause of complaint by the minorities, as reported by the Federal Minister for Religious and Minorities Affairs, Raja Zafarul Haq, when a delegation of minorities' leaders met Prime Minister Nawaz Sharif to discuss the proposed Fifteenth Constitutional Amendment Bill. The representatives of the Hindu community requested four amendments to the bill, including the re-insertion of the word "freely" in the Objectives Resolution. See "Nawaz meets minorities' representatives" *Dawn* (9 September 1998)

The Liaquat-Nehru Pact (April 1950)
In the context of deteriorating relations between Pakistan and India in the first quarter of 1950, communal disturbances, refugee movement between the two countries, and talk of outright war, an agreement was signed on 8 April between the Pakistani prime minister Liaquat Ali Khan and the Indian prime minister Jawaharlal Nehru. It opened with an undertaking by both governments that "each shall ensure to the minorities throughout its territory complete equality of citizenship, irrespective of religion, a full sense of security in respect of life, culture, property and personal honour, freedom of movement within each country and freedom of occupation, speech and worship, subject to law and morality".[161]

Nazir S. Bhatti, the president of the Pakistan Christian Congress, referred to the Liaquat-Nehru Pact in arguing for the rights of non-Muslims in Pakistan, particularly in calling for the establishment of a "Minority Commission" to present recommendations to protect the rights of minorities.[162] This commission has now been established, with committees at district level (see below).

Constitutions
The growing Islamization of the Constitutions has been traced in chapter 2. However, even the latest version retains a number of safeguards – explicit or implicit – for various

---

161. Ali, Chaudhri Muhammad *The emergence of Pakistan* (Lahore: Research Society of Pakistan, University of the Punjab, 1996) pp.273-4

162. Shazad, W. "Revival of Liaquat-Nehru Pact and establishment of Minority Commission in Pakistan demanded" reproduced in *Pakistan Christian Post* (7th August 2001)

rights of religious minorities, scattered throughout its text (in addition to the Objectives Resolution, discussed above). For example, the freedom of every citizen to profess, practise and propagate his faith (Article 20 (a)),[163] the right to establish, maintain and manage religious institutions (Article 20(b)),[164] the equality of all citizens before the law (Article 25(1)),[165] a safeguard against discrimination in the services on the basis of religion (Article 27(1)),[166] and a safeguard of "the legitimate rights and interests of minorities, including their due representation in the Federal and Provincial services" (Article 36).[167]

Legislation

Even the Shari'ah Act of 1991 and the Fifteenth Constitutional Amendment Bill of 1998 contain clauses apparently intended to safeguard the rights of minorities. The 1991 Act had two sub-sections referring to non-Muslims. One affirmed that nothing in the Act should affect their personal laws, religious freedom, traditions, customs or way of life,[168] the other that nothing in the Act should affect their constitutional rights.[169] However there was no indication of what would happen in cases involving both Muslims and non-Muslims or involving non-Muslims and the state.

---

163. Butt op. cit. p.11

164. ibid. loc. cit.

165. ibid. p.13. NB. Sections (2) and (3) of this article imply that the differences under consideration are sex and age rather than religion.

166. ibid. p.14

167. ibid. p.16

168. Clause 1(4) Nothing contained in this Act shall affect the personal laws, religious freedom, traditions, customs and way of life of the non-Muslims.

The Fifteenth Constitutional Amendment Bill of 1998 contained a clause which ran "Nothing in this Article shall affect the personal law, religious freedom, traditions or customs of non-Muslims and their status as citizens."[170]

It should be noted that Christians have their own laws for marriage, divorce, inheritance, charitable and religious trusts, religious and ecclesiastical property etc.[171] Various definitions of a Christian occur in these laws, making reference to racial background. The broadest is simply "Christian", used in respect of marriage law, which includes not only Pakistanis but "Christian British subjects domiciled in Pakistan, Anglo-Pakistanis, and British Pakistani subjects residing in acceding States". Marriage law also refers to "native Christians" who are "the Christian descendants of Natives of Indo-Pakistan sub-continent converted to Christianity, as well as such converts". For inheritance law the term "Pakistani Christian" is defined as "a native of Pakistan, who is, or in good faith claims to be, of unmixed descent and who professes any form of the Christian religion". It is noted by Joshua that professing Christianity

---

169. Clause 3(2) Notwithstanding anything contained in this Act, the Judgement of any court or any other law for the time being in force, the present political system, including the Majlis-e-Shoora (Parliament) and Provincial Assemblies and the existing system of Government, shall not be challenged in any court, including Supreme Court, the Federal Shariat Court or any authority or tribunal:

Provided that nothing contained herein shall affect the rights of the non-Muslims guaranteed by or under the Constitution.

170. Text quoted in *Dawn* (29 August 1998)

171. Manuals of Christian laws are available, the earliest by P.N. Joshua (1957) and a recent one by S.A. Khan (1995). See bibliography.

is a personal action, unrelated to any action of the Church.[172] The concept of conversion between Islam and Christianity and its legal implications for children, marriage and property are dealt with in detail.[173]

Institutional arrangments

A Minority Affairs Division has been established in the Federal Government to safeguard the minorities' rights, promote their welfare, protect them from discrimination, represent them on international bodies and conferences, and implement international agreements and commitments on minorities. Under the auspices of the Minority Affairs Division, a Federal Advisory Council for Minorities Affairs has been set up to advise the government. A National Commission for Minorities has been constituted by the government, chaired by the Minister for Minorities Affairs, to promote the minorities' welfare and uplift, to assist with the grievances of members of the minority communities, and to make recommendations to the Government to ensure the fuller participation of the minorities in national life. At a more local level, each District of the country has set up a District Minority Committee to try to resolve the problems of the minorities.[174]

---

172. Joshua, P.N. *A manual of laws for Christians* (Lahore: Punjab Religious Book Society, 1957) p.7

173. ibid. pp.8-12

174. Fourteenth Periodic Report of States parties due in 1996, Addendum Pakistan, submitted to the Committee on the Elimination of Racial Discrimination of the United Nations (International Convention on the Elimination of all Forms of Racial Discrimination) CERD/C/299/Add.6 (13 June 1996) pp.5-6

Attitudes to dhimmi (minorities), in particular Christians

Joshua Fazl-ud-Din wrote as early as 1949 that the Objectives Resolution had the potential to allow Christians to be treated as traditional *dhimmi* because it made a fundamental distinction between Muslims and non-Muslims: the former were to be enabled by the State to attain certain ends[175] but no equivalent provision was made for the latter.[176] Eleven years later he still believed that 'the problem of the minorities is the cornerstone of Pakistan as an Islamic state.'[177] He reviews the many commitments to the protection of the rights of the minorities made by Jinnah and the Muslim League before the formation of Pakistan[178] and applauds the economic help given to Christians and other non-Muslims by the government.[179] He identifies the source of the problems of the Christian community as two-fold: firstly, an inequitable distribution of land to Christians by the British before independence and, secondly, to a lack of "magnanimity" on the part of Muslims. This lack of maganimity he attributes to two causes – the two-nation theory[180] and the communalism fostered by British rulers before independence. "Under the influence of communalism the majority conducts itself with the

---

175. i.e. to "order their lives in the individual and collective spheres in accordance with the teachings and requirements of Islam as set out in the Holy Quran and the Sunna".

176. Fazl-ud-Din *Future of Christians* pp.114-5, 120

177. Fazl-ud-Din, Joshua *Pakistani Revolution and the Non-Muslims* (Lahore: The Punjabi Darbar Publishing House, 1960) p.32

178. ibid. pp.11-13

179. ibid. p.30

180. ibid. loc. cit

psychology of a minority which is always cautious and careful, even suspicious and disgruntled."[181] Forty years after independence and partition, Charles Amjad-Ali argued similarly that the Muslim attitude towards minorities in Pakistan was partly determined by "an anachronistic but historically real ... legacy of Islam and Muslims as being themselves a minority in undivided India". This he believes, in conjunction with the communal memory of the "humiliation of Islam" at the hands of the Christian West for the previous four centuries, created what he calls a "false sense of vulnerability" amongst Muslims so that they feel threatened by a Christian minority of only 2.5%.[182] Similarly the respected journalist Mubarik Ahmed describes as "preposterous" the argument that the non-Muslims of Pakistan, few in number, representing many different faiths and mainly very poor, could be seen as a threat to the Islamic character of Pakistan.[183]

While it is impossible to make definitive evaluations of theories about historical "folk memories" and their influence on contemporary attitudes and behaviour, a much clearer factor is the Shari'ah's teaching on *dhimmi* described above. Some Muslims have stated unambiguously that non-Muslims in Pakistan are *dhimmi* who are given protection by the Muslim majority.[184] Coming from the other end of

---

181. ibid. p.29

182. Amjad-Ali, Charles "Islamisation and Christian-Muslim Relations" p.78

183. Ahmad, Mubarik "Woes of the minorities" *The News International* (11 March 1997)

184. For example, Ismail Qureshi Advocate at the Supreme Court on 8 February 1994, reported in Ali, Rafaqat "Government takes ambivalent position" *The Muslim* (9 February 1994) p. 12

the Muslim spectrum, Akbar Hussein, writing in the influential *Herald* magazine, described what he saw as an irony in the use of the term "protected" with respect to non-Muslims who had no external enemy to threaten them.

> But more serious … is the humiliation non-Muslims suffer every day of their lives. And yet our leaders continuously reassure them that they will be protected. But protected from whom? The majority i.e. the Muslims? The implication of this assurance is that we are some kind of barbarians who pose a constant threat to the relatively few non-Muslims who still live in our midst.

> … when [Jinnah's] successors talk about "protecting" the minorities they make it seem as though some kind of endangered species is involved – and in a sense they are not far wrong, judging by the way we treat them. Given a free choice and the means to emigrate, how many non-Muslims would willingly stay in the Land of the Pure?[185]

Another extreme view is suggested by the columnist Riaz Ahmad writing in *Dawn*, who raises the question of whether there is any need now to maintain a distinction between the social identity of Muslims and non-Muslims, seeing that practice as appropriate only for certain historical contexts when "the cultural and social identity of the Muslims" had to be proved.[186]

Some aspects of the *dhimmi* traditions are or have been practised in Pakistan either officially or unofficially.

---

185. Hussein, Akbar "The Silenced Minority" *The Herald* (January 1992) pp.5-6.

186. Ahmad, Riaz "Non-Muslims in an Islamic State" *Dawn* (16 November 1979) p.7

Christians sometimes write of their perception that they are considered second-class citizens,[187] a phrase often used to summarize the restrictions placed on *dhimmi*.[188] A questionnaire answered by 60 Christians in Faisalabad (probably in 1980) revealed that almost 80% felt that Zia's *nizam-e-Mustafa* had heightened their feeelings of being second-class citizens. It is relevant to point out that most of those questioned had the relatively high status job of teachers in a secondary school.[189] Sometimes Christians assert their rejection of second-class status, as for example in the final statement of a seminar on the identity of non-Muslim minorities in Pakistan, held in Rawalpindi from 18 to 20 July 1996, which contained the pledge: "We do not accept ourselves as second class citizens of this country and we do not give anybody a right to impose these categories on us....We shall make concerted efforts to fight against those laws and legislations which have reduced our status of full citizens."[190]

A review of some of the specific ways in which the

---

187. David Paul, president of the Pakistan Christian Community Council writing passionately under the title 'The Untold and Unknown Christian Sufferings in Pakistan', speaks of Christians being "perhaps fourth or fifth class citizens" (unpublished paper, probably 1992)

188. It should be noted that none of the constitutions of Pakistan have defined the category of citizen, as pointed out by Charles Amjad Ali "Islamisation and Christian-Muslim Relations" p.72

189. Butler, R.A. "Islamic Resurgence in Pakistan and the Church" – a lecture given to the pastoral workers of the Catholic Archdiocese of Karachi in September 1980, and reproduced in *Al-Mushir* Vol. XXIII No. 2 (Summer 1981) p.49

190. reproduced in *Al-Mushir* Vol. 38 No. 3 (1996) p. 105

traditional restrictions on *dhimmi* are experienced by non-Muslims in Pakistan is given below.

The right of dhimmi to hold high office
Traditionally, *dhimmi* were prohibited from high political office in an Islamic state so that they were not in a position to make major political decisions, nor sit in judgement over Muslims or take the initiative in matters concerning Islam.[191] Some of the most conservative *ulema* in Pakistan have asserted their belief that *dhimmi* should be far more restricted than that. The Munir Report records Maulana Abul Hasanat Sayyad Muhammad Ahmad Qadri's statement that *dhimmis* in an Islamic state of Pakistan should "have no voice in the making of laws, no right to administer the law and no right to hold public offices".[192] Maulana Ahmad Ali held that "they will have no say in the making of law and no right to administer the law. Government may, however, permit them to hold any public office."[193] Maulana Abdul Haamid Badayuni, president of the Jami'at-ul-Ulama-i-Pakistan, asserted that "non-Muslims cannot be taken in the army or the judiciary or be appointed as Ministers or to other posts involving the reposing of confidence."[194] The same view was expressed by Maulana Shabbir Ahmed Osmani in the Pakistan Constituent Assembly in the course of the debate on the Islamic state.[195] Mawdudi held that non-Muslims could hold any position except "key-posts" such as those connected

191. Cahen op. cit. p.229
192. *Report of the Court of Inquiry* p. 213
193. ibid. loc. cit.
194. ibid. pp.213-4
195. Choudhury, Golam W. *Islam and Modern Muslim World* p.55

with the formulation of state policy or the control of "important departments". Examples he gave of the kind of posts which a *dhimmi* could hold were Accountant-General, Chief Engineer or Post-Master General.[196] He held that *dhimmi* could not perform military service in an Islamic state.[197]

In Pakistan, as mentioned above, the constitution forbids non-Muslims from holding the posts of President or Prime Minister. They are not forbidden to hold posts in the military, judiciary, civil service or police, and have reserved seats in the National Assembly (see chapter 4). There is, however, a perception amongst Christians that they are in practice excluded from senior posts in the government, civil service, medical professions, judiciary, armed forces and academia. Mohan Lal Shahani, a Christian lawyer, was appointed Advocate General in Sind in 1996 and then in 1997 made a judge in the Sind High Court. However, his appointment was not renewed in 1998, apparently because of complaints that he was a "committed Christian".[198] This kind of discrimination with respect to senior posts has been vocalized by, for example, Joseph Francis, Secretary General of the Pakistan Christian National Party, and Saleem Sylvester, General Secretary of the Christian Organisation for Human Rights,[199] David Paul, President of the Pakistan Christian Community Council,[200] and the

---

196. Maududi *Rights of Non Muslims* p.30
197. ibid. pp.22-3
198. "Interview with Mohan Lal Shahani" in *Rutherford International* Vol. 2 Issue 8 (August 1998) p.2
199. Sadiq op. cit. p.3; Balchin, Cassandra "Some are less equal than others" *Frontier Post* (27 December 1991)
200. Paul, David (President of the Pakistan Christian Community Council) "Recruitment policy and minorities" *The Frontier Post* (24 January 1992); Paul, David "Do minorities

participants at a 1996 seminar on "Religious Minorities in Pakistan: Struggle for Identity".[201] However, in the past there were greater numbers of Christians in positions of high office, for example, Chief Justice Alvin Robert Cornelius[202] who was largely responsible for the drafting of the 1973 constitution and Air Vice Marshal Eric G. Hall, who was Deputy Chief of the Air Staff of the Pakistan Air Force.[203] Some Christians assert that the state appears "embarrassed when it finds itself having to acknowledge the national value of a particular person from the minority community whose status makes that recognition unavoidable". For example, Christians felt aggrieved that no one from the federal or provincial government attended the funeral of Chief Justice Cornelius and that official condolences and obituaries omitted to mention his religion,[204] and his draft constitution had to be re-worked because President Z.I. Bhutto felt that the constitution of a Muslim state should not be written by a *dhimmi*.[205]

It is difficult to find accurate recent figures, but according

---

enjoy equal rights" *The Frontier Post* (2 March 1992)

201. Final Statement of the seminar published in Moghal, Dominic and Jivan, Jennifer (eds.) *Religious Minorities in Pakistan: Struggle for Identity* (Rawalpindi: Christian Study Centre, 1996) p.96

202. Ahmad, Mirza Mahmood "A.R. Cornelius a giant among mortals" *The News International* (28 December 1991)

203. Ansari, Athar Hasan "Minorities Contribution to Pakistan" *The Muslim* (9 July 1998)

204. Amjad-Ali, Christine "Opening the curtains: minorities and women in Pakistan" *Al-Mushir* Vol. 33 No. 4 (Autumn 1991) pp.131-2

205. Samdani, Zafar "Cornelius, a man always at peace with himself" *Dawn* (22 December 1991)

to government figures for January 1983, there were no non-Muslims in the two highest grades of federal government civil servants. The overall percentage of Christian employees was 1.15%, a little lower than the census estimate two years earlier of the percentage of Christians in the country's population (1.6% – a low figure according to many Christians). Of the Christian employees, 69.8% were in the lowest three grades and 0.1% in thee highest three grades. The comparable figures for Muslims were 28.7% and 0.5%, indicating that, if similar levels of education amongst Christians and Muslims are assumed, it would appear that Christians are indeed discriminated against with regard to the higher posts.[206]

Similar statistics are available for 1986 for employees of autonomous and semi-autonomous corporations / bodies under the administrative control of the federal government. These indicate that Christian employees number 1.9%, possibly slightly higher than their number in the population as a whole. But, of these, 87.5 % are in the lowest three grades and only 0.2% in the highest three grades. The equivalent figures for Muslim employees are 66.8% and 0.7%. Here the difference between Muslims and Christians is less marked, though it still exists.[207]

In examining figures such as these, it is essential to know whether Christians are as well qualified and well educated as Muslims when seeking to establish whether there is

206. Figures from the Government of Pakistan's Public Administration Research Centre, reproduced in Kennedy, Charles *Islamization of Laws and Economy: Case Studies on Pakistan* (Islamabad: Institute of Policy Studies, 1996) p.178

207. Figures from the Government of Pakistan's Public Administration Research Centre, reproduced in Kennedy op.cit. p.179

discrimination in the allocation of more senior posts. Mano Rumalshah, Church of Pakistan Bishop of Peshawar, has quoted the latter set of figures for Christians as evidence of the lowly social position of Christians[208] without specifying whether this is due to discrimination or to lack of qualifications. On the other hand Sardar Feroze Khan, a former moderator of the United Presbyterian Church in Pakistan, sees the problem as one of poverty leading to lack of educational opportunities and hence a lack of better jobs.[209] The influential journalist Cassandra Balchin similarly considers the problem to be complicated by "the discrimination process which begins from birth where Christians are less likely to have access to health and education facilities than members of the majority community [i.e. Muslims] of the same socio-economic background. Less educated and in poorer health, they are automatically poor employment material".[210] Nevertheless, religion can be a conscious factor as in the case of Vivian John, an engineer who found many difficulties put in the way of his promotion and was told that if he were to embrace Islam all the problems would speedily solved.[211] It would appear that religious discrimination *per se* is the primary cause, but a lower level of education is the cause in some cases.

---

208. Rumalshah, Mano *A New Paradigm: the Future of the Christian Community in Pakistan* (unpublished paper produced by Diocese of Peshawar, Lent 1996) p.2

209. Khan, Sardar Feroze *An overview of Pakistan and socio-economic-political and religious issues facing the Christian community* (unpublished paper, probably 1991)

210. Balchin op. cit.

211. ibid.

Law of evidence

According to the Shari'ah, specific and complex rules govern the system of witnesses and the weight to be attached to their evidence at any trial. The number and sex of witnesses required to gain a verdict varies according to the severity of the crime. Thus, under Hanafi law, the school of law which predominates on the Indian subcontinent, adultery requires four male witnesses, whereas for other *hudood* crimes and *qisas*, two male witnesses are sufficient. In other cases, two male witnesses or one male and two female witnesses will be acceptable.[212] An exception is matters about which men should not be required to make an inspection, such as virginity and childbirth. For these the evidence of a single woman is permitted.[213] These witnesses must be adult Muslims, not disqualified by virtue of insanity, servitude or any other of a number of possible factors.[214] Non-Muslims, in Hanafi law, may give evidence for and against each other, though in the other schools of law the evidence of a non-Muslim is never permitted.[215]

As described above, Zia promulgated a new law of evidence (*qanoon-e-shadat*) in October 1984, which replaced the existing law, dating from 1872, which he – and many others – had condemned as un-Islamic.[216] Despite a strongly Islamic draft produced by the Council of Islamic Ideology, the final version of the new law hardly

212. Mughal, Dr Justice Munir Ahmad writing in the foreword to Anwarullah *The Islamic Law of Evidence* (Lahore: Research Cell, Dyal Singh Trust Library, 1992) pp.4-5; *The Hedaya* Vol. II Book XXI pp.666-7

213. Mughal, Dr Justice Munir Ahmad op. cit. p.5; *The Hedaya* Vol. II Book XXI p.668

214. Anwarullah *op. cit.* pp.671-2

differed from the 1872 law, except in replacing the statement "No particular number of witnesses shall in any case be required for the proof of any fact" with a requirement for two men, or one man and two women, to attest documents "pertaining to financial or future obligations" (Article 17). The same section also stipulated that "the competence of a person to testify and the number of witnesses required in any case shall be determined in accordance with the injunctions of Islam as laid down in the Holy *Quran* and *Sunna*".[217] While Kennedy claimed that the new law made virtually no difference,[218] many women were indignant,[219] and Benazir Bhutto called for its repeal.[220]

For non-Muslims the significant aspect of the law was the freedom given to courts to decide whether any individual was a competent witness according to the Qur'an and *Sunnah*, specified not only in Article 17 but also in Article 3. The possibility of different courts coming to different conclusions on this question was envisaged by various lawyers,[221] but non-Muslims feared that they would

215. ibid. pp.690-1

216. Kennedy op. cit. p.39; Tanzil-ur-Rahman, Tanzil-ur-"Some Aspects of the Islamic Law of Evidence" *All Pakistan Legal Decisions* Vol. XXXV (1983) 199-207

217. Article 17 of the *Qanoon-e-Shahadat* Order (1984) is quoted in full in Mehdi, Rubya op. cit. p.149

218. Kennedy op. cit. pp.41,76

219. for example, Mehdi, Rubya op. cit. p.148; Patel, Rashida *Islamization of laws in Pakistan?* (Karachi: Faiza Publishers, 1986) p. 81

220. Kennedy op. cit. p.76

221. Mehdi, Rubya op. cit. p.148; Patel op cit. p.80; Changez, Justice (retd.) A.R. "The Qanune-Shahadat, 1984" *Pakistan Times* (8 November 1984)

be deemed inadmissible as witnesses in cases involving Muslims, in accordance with Hanafi law described above.

Worse still for non-Muslims, some of the *hudood* ordinances prohibited non-Muslim witnesses in cases involving a Muslim defendant. For example "at least two Muslim adult male witnesses" are required when a Muslim is accused of theft,[222] and "at least four Muslim adult male witnesses" when a Muslim is accused of adultery.[223] This clear discrimination against non-Muslims, following closely the requirements of the Shari'ah concerning *dhimmi*, is a matter about which Christians have voiced protests,[224] just as women have protested the discrimination they suffer from the same legislation.

Restrictions and attacks on places of worship
Early Muslim jurists were almost unanimous in interpreting in a very restricted sense the undertaking made on behalf of Muslims to uphold the places of worship of non-Muslims. This undertaking was generally considered to apply only to buildings which were already in existence at the time of advent of the Islamic power, with the result that new buildings were forbidden (at least in and near Muslim centres of population).[225] This aspect of *dhimmi* status is a major problem in certain other Muslim countries today, notably Egypt and lately in Indonesia, but it is less

---

222. Offences against property (Enforcement of *Hudood*) Ordinance (VI of 1979) section 7 (b) reproduced in *All Pakistan Legal Decisions* Vol. XXXI (1979) 44-51

223. Offence of zina (enforcement of *hudood*) Ordinance (VII of 1979) section 8 (b) reproduced in *All Pakistan Legal Decisions* Vol. XXXI (1979) 51-56

224. for example, Bouma "Pakistani's Islamization" p.21

225. Cahen op. cit., p.228

prominent in Pakistan. Nevertheless difficulties do occur in erecting new churches,[226] and also in the closely linked problem of establishing new Christian cemeteries. The Bishop of Lahore, Alexander John Malik, appealed in 1991 for land to be allotted for new churches and cemeteries.[227] Seven years later, the Bishop of Peshawar reported that it was becoming increasingly difficult to get permission to build new churches.[228] In some parts of the country, such as the North West Frontier Province, overt church buildings are not allowed at all. Churches can only be erected if they are described as "community centres".[229]

Another kind of problem relating to church property is exemplified by a small plot of land in the centre of Rawalpindi on which a priest's house stood. The land had been leased to the church by the British army in 1908 under a perpetual lease yet was sold improperly in 1989, and the house demolished by the purchaser. Probably it had been enclosed by Muslims, who later went on to sell it. In this

---

226. Sadiq op. cit. p.3

227. Malik, Alexander John (Bishop of Lahore) Welcoming speech at the 31st session of the Church of Pakistan Lahore Diocesan Council (24 October 1991)

228. Rumalshah, Munawar "Being a Christian in Pakistan" the testimony of Bisho Munawar (Mano) Rumalshah of the Diocese of Peshawar, Pakistan before the Senate Foreign Relations Committee on 17 June 1998, reproduced in Sheridan, Sharon *Hear the cry! Standing in solidarity with the suffering Church* Report of a consultation organised by the Episcopal Council for Global Mission, New York, April 1998 (New York: Anglican and Global Relations, 1998) p.46

229. Rumalshah "Hear the cry" p.42; Sneddon, Sandy, a missionary with the Church of Scotland Board of World Mission who is Secretary of the Development Board of Peshawar Diocese, interview with the author (9 August 1999)

case the authorities have now responded to Christian protests by taking steps to facilitate the reversion of the land to the church, including the posting of army guards to protect the site.[230]

Separate from official restrictions, but related to the issue of Islamic attitudes to places of worship is the phenomenon of communal violence. Christian buildings are liable to be attacked[231] and this has increased in recent years. The Church of Pakistan's Diocese of Lahore had many difficulties with erecting a building in Islamabad. Land was allocated and work began on a new building in 1986, but soon met opposition because of its proximity to mosques. In January 1989 construction re-started, but within weeks was forcibly halted after angry Muslim students attacked the site. Further attempts to continue the construction were opposed by the police who feared more violence. A protest march resulted in Prime Minister Benazir Bhutto using her influence to have an alternative site offered.[232] In all, the building work had to be begun three times before the church was finally built.[233] More recently, existing Christian buildings such as churches and schools have been attacked in riots, for example, those in Shanti Nagar and Khanewal in February 1997 (see chapter 5). On 28 January 1998 a United Presbyterian pastor, Rev. Noor Alam, was stabbed to death, apparently by Muslims who believed him

---

230. "Church claims its land sold illegally" *Dawn* (4 September 1998); "Property being restored to church" *Dawn* (18 September 1998)

231. Sadiq (op. cit.) p.3

232. "Foundation only in Islamabad" *Berita NECF* (April/May 1990)

233. Rumalshah "Being a Christian in Pakistan" p.46

determined to erect a church building in Sheikhupura, near Lahore. The partly finished building had been demolished by a Muslim mob on 5 December 1997, and threats issued against the pastor should he plan to re-build it.[234] On 23 December 1997 a Catholic church in Faisalabad was attacked by Muslims, who pulled down the crucifix and Bible and removed the microphone system.[235]

It is important to note that the issues are not only practical but also psychological. The lack of church buildings and cemeteries is inconvenient at the very least for the Christian community, and their destruction is expensive. But also there is a powerful symbolism in the visible presence of a Christian community through its buildings. Lack of a visible presence – especially its violent removal – generates feelings of insecurity and diffidence for the community.

Low social status
Many of the restrictions imposed on *dhimmi* at different periods of Islamic history served to reinforce visibly their inferior position in society. Such rules included sometimes the part or side of the road on which they could walk, the height of their buildings and doorways and the kind of animal they were permitted to ride.

234. "Pakistani pastor murdered in church land dispute" *Compass Direct Flash News* (Santa Ana: Compass Direct, 4 February 1998, an electronic mail service)
235. ibid.
236. *The Friday Times* (29 May – 4 June 1998)
237. For example, Khan, Sardar Feroze op. cit. pp.7-8; Rumalshah *A New Paradigm* p.2
238. for example, Nazir-Ali *Pakistani Christians* p.2

While no such rules exist in Pakistan, there is a widespread understanding that Christians are rightly poor and hold a lowly position in society. A newspaper cartoon[236] depicts a Christian by showing him wearing patched clothes and carrying a broom, thus signifying his poverty and his dirty and despised job as a sweeper. Christians themselves complain of their resourcelessness and powerlessness.[237] Large numbers are indeed "sweepers" cleaning the streets and sewers, a job not only unpleasant and dangerous, but held in great contempt by Muslims (though there are small numbers of Muslim sweepers). The majority of bonded labourers (effectively slaves) are Christians (see chapter 4).

The situation is not uniform, and some Christians are keen to point out that members of the Christian community are in respected positions within the professions,[238] while the percentage of Christians who are actually sweepers has decreased in the last twenty years from 70% to 40%.[239] Nevertheless there is undoubtedly a perception amongst Christians that they are generally considered inferior by Muslims, in keeping with the *dhimmi*'s status as a second class citizen. A powerful comment made by a Muslim lawyer in 1992 ran: "Christians must realize that they have become the 'niggers' of this country, even though the cottonfield chores may have been replaced by that of sweeping the city streets."[240]

Some Christians attempt to raise their social status by changing their family name to that of a higher and more

---

239. Moghal, Dominic *Changing Realities and Churches' Response* (Rawalpindi: Christian Study Centre, 1997)

240. Malick, Mohammad "Minorities large and small" *Horizons* (The *Frontier Post* magazine) (7 January 1992) pp.8-9

prestigious caste (The family name and the place of origin – which must conform with each other in order to convince – are very important in determining social status in Pakistan, more so than, for example, accent.) The desire to be dissociated from low castes can sometimes lead to a decrease or absence of the *biradari* system, whereby members of a group of inter-related extended families (the *biradari*, somewhat akin to a clan) take responsibility for each other's well being. Christians who are unwilling to admit to their low caste origins may refuse to take on this responsibility for members of their *biradari*. [241]

Marriage regulations
The Shari'ah permits a Muslim man to marry a *dhimmi* woman but forbids a *dhimmi* man to marry a Muslim woman.[242] One consequence of this is that if the female partner of a *dhimmi* marriage converts to Islam, her husband must either convert also or allow the marriage to be dissolved. This ruling has been affirmed several times in Pakistani courts, for example, the case of Mukhtaran Bibi in the Lahore High Court in 1992[243] and the case of Safia Bibi, also in the Lahore High Court, in 1996.[244] In both cases the marriage was dissolved because the wife had embraced Islam. The existence of this law is the basis of the Muslim practice of abducting Christian women, forcibly converting them to Islam and then marrying them (see chapter 4).

241. Ismail, Zafar, interview with the author (December 1996)

242. Cahen op. cit. p.228

243. Judgement sheet in the Lahore High Court at Lahore, Judicial Department on appeal no. 4835-B/ of 1991.

244. "Convert Muslim woman's marriage with non-believer

Jizya

The primary mark of *dhimmi*, the payment of *jizya*, has never been enforced in Pakistan, though the possibility was raised by Fazl-ud-Din in 1949 with respect to possible future repercussions of the Objectives Resolution.[245] Some Christians expected it as a result of Zia's Islamization process,[246] but still it did not come. The introduction of *jizya* was, however, cited by one commentator as an example of the kind of changes which could be introduced on the word of a single high court judge as part of the federal government's obligation "to prescribe what is right and to forbid what is wrong" according to the proposed fifteenth amendment to the constitution.[247] The same fear was expressed by the Pakistan Christian Action Forum at a meeting to protest about the draft fifteenth amendment on 2 September 1998.[248] It is certainly likely to be considered an obvious omission to be rectified in the eyes of religious conservatives wishing to re-create a traditional Islamic state in Pakistan. The lawyer Naheed Jehan Lodhi argues that *jizya* would bring harmony between Muslims and Christians and goes so far as to suggest that therefore "the possibility exists that the ruling class of Pakistan attempted to abrogate the *jizya* tax to selectively victimise the Christian minority of Pakistan".[249]

---

stands dissolved" *Pakistan Times* (10 February 1996)

245. Fazl-ud-Din *Future of Christians* p.120

246. Butler op. cit. p.48

247. Raja, Salman Akram "A blow to the federal structure of the state" *The News International* (12 September 1998)

248. "Christians for withdrawal of 15th amendment" *The News* (3 September 1998)

249. Lodhi, Naheed Jehan *Pakistan: Religious Minorities and Adultery (Muslim laws)* (Lahore, date unknown) p.5

Conclusion

A process of Islamization of the laws and constitution of Pakistan has taken place, which has served to negate the ideals of equality between Muslims and non-Muslims with which Jinnah founded the nation. This began as early as 1949 with the Objectives Resolution and proceeded more or less without interruption though at varying rates. Exceptions to the direction of change were Ayub Khan's liberal constitution of 1962, which was reversed within two years, and the 1997 amendment to the *Qisas* and *Diyat* Ordinance.

The gradual Islamization has inevitably eroded the status of non-Muslims to some extent, despite the safeguards ostensibly built into each new constitution or relevant piece of legislation. For if the Shari'ah deems non-Muslims to be *dhimmi*, different from and inferior to Muslims (albeit protected), then each step towards greater enforcement of the Shari'ah brings as an automatic 'by-product' a lessening in status of non-Muslims. This may not always involve practical changes in the law, but will at the very least take place simply by reinforcing in the mind of Pakistani Muslims the place of the Shari'ah in their faith, including its teaching on the rights and status of *dhimmi* in comparison with the rights and status of Muslims. An indication that this has been occurring in Pakistan can be seen in the increasing number of incidents of anti-Christian violence against both buildings and individuals in recent years; while this violence has been illegal, its growth has accompanied the growth of legal Islamization. The premeditated murder of nine Christians, including children and babies, in Nowshera, near Peshawar, on 18 November 1998 was linked by both the Bishop of Peshawar[250] and leader of the opposition Benazir Bhutto[251] to a change in Muslim attitudes due to the Fifteenth Constitutional Amendment Bill going through Parliament at the time.[252] Other possible factors contributing to the growing anti-Christian violence include a perceived increase in "Islamophobia" in the "Christian" West and reaction against Pakistani Christians' demands for the abolition of the blasphemy law.

It can be argued that a Muslim-majority state, even if democratic in form, can never result in permanent equality for non-Muslims. Sooner or later steps will be taken to alter the status of non-Muslims to be more in line with the Shari'ah's teaching. Democracy will not hinder this process unless a majority of citizens embrace democratic principles to such an extent as to give them pre-eminence over Islam. Rather, democracy will provide an easy mechanism for the Muslim majority constitutionally to enforce their will with regard to non-Muslims. Wilfred Cantwell Smith reasons that :

> ... the rights accorded to any minority or other non-powerful group in any state depend on the ideal of those in power... A state may be democratic in form but unless it is democratic also in ideal, unless the majority of its citizens are actively loyal to the transcendent principles

250. Bishop Mano Rumalshah, interview with the author (25 November 1998)

251. "Murderers claim dead Christians were using black magic" *The Guardian* (20 November 1998)

252. The fact that these murders were later discovered to be non-sectarian does not invalidate the significance of the comments by the Bishop and Mrs Bhutto which are still indicative of the general "climate of opinion".

of democracy, recognizing the ideal validity of every man's status as a man, then the arithmetic minority has, through the democratic form, no right at all... Many outsiders and several Pakistani Christians and Hindus ... have stated or supposed that these minorities would be better off if Pakistan was simply a "Democratic" instead of an Islamic state. This is irresponsibly glib. For if Muslims do in fact treat non-Muslims unjustly then a democratic framework (without the Greco-Roman and religious tradition of democracy to vitalize it) would merely give them as a majority the constitutional authority for doing so without let or hindrance.[253]

It is therefore not surprising to find that the articles and clauses in constitutions and laws considered above which ostensibly safeguard the rights of non-Muslim citizens, are not invariably effective. All can be relativized if the Shari'ah is given precedence. A phrase like "all citizens" begs the question as to whether non-Muslims are full citizens of an Islamic state. Similarly, the phrase "legitimate rights of a minority" raises the question as to what are the "legitimate rights" of non-Muslims according to the Shari'ah – not necessarily the same as the "legitimate rights" of Muslims. Provisos to safeguards with wordings such as "subject to law, public order and morality" have been used in other Muslim countries, for example Egypt, to suppress religious freedom. A common argument by the authorities in those countries is that conversion from Islam to Christianity is going to cause such outrage in the community that the convert must be placed in detention in order to preserve

---

253. Cantwell Smith, Wilfred *Pakistan as an Islamic state* (Lahore: Shaikh Muhammad Asraf, 1951) pp.41-3

public order. It is for this reason that non-Muslims and human rights bodies have been so concerned about the Fifteenth Constitutional Amendment Bill to make the Shari'ah supreme in constitution as well as in law.

Other – non-Islamic – reasons for discrimination against Christians in Pakistan will be considered in the next chapter.

FOUR

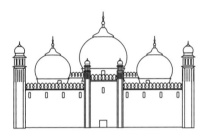

De facto discrimination against Christians

Introduction

The previous chapter examined the extent to which the traditional restrictions on *dhimmi* are practised (or not) against Christians in Pakistan, whether officially according to laws and constitution, or unofficially by virtue of individual and community actions. But there are other forms of discrimination that Pakistani Christians encounter which are not included within Islamic teaching on *dhimmi*. These include the two issues of greatest concern to Christians, namely, the "blasphemy law" which is unique to Pakistan (see chapter 5) and the system of separate electorates (see below).

The most significant single reason for discrimination not sanctioned by the Shari'ah appears to be the resilience of the Hindu caste system. This has remained entrenched in the community consciousness of Pakistanis in Punjab and Sind (the two provinces where most of the Christians live), despite the conversion of almost all from Hinduism to Islam many generations ago.[1] As seen in chapter 1, the vast majority of Pakistani Christians, wherever they may now be living, are Punjabis,[2] and it is amongst Punjabis that the caste system remains particularly strong.[3] The great majority of Punjabi Christians are descendants of converted Chuhras, who had occupied the lowest place in the caste system, being in fact scheduled castes. Formerly known as outcastes, the scheduled castes were without any caste at all and therefore without any status at all. The stigma of impurity they carried had three distinct origins – the nature of the work they did, the fact that they ate carrion (strongly prohibited in both Islam and Hinduism) and their very dark skins.[4] This social stigma has by and large remained with the Christian descendants of the Chuhras. This is not only from other Punjabis, but also from non-Punjabi Muslims in Pakistan. According to Vemmelund, it is their low social status as sweepers which is the primary reason for the isolation of Punjabi Christians in the North West Frontier Province from the Pathan Muslims who constitute the majority in the province.[5] It is important to note that the

1. Streefland op. cit. p.16
2. Moghal states that 98% of Pakistani Christians are ethnically Punjabis, though many do not live in the Punjab. See Moghal, Dominic *Human Person in Punjabi Society: a tension between religion and culture* (Rawalpindi: Christian Study Centre, 1997) p.10
3. Moghal discusses the caste system in Punjabi culture in *Human Person in Punjabi Society* pp.43-9
4. Streefland op. cit. pp.3-4

social stigma of the Chuhra-descent Christians appears to have spread to their co-religionists of higher caste status, for many Christians report examples of discrimination on this basis irrespective of their actual caste background.[6]

Discrimination which apparently originates from the remnants of the caste system is rationalized by the Muslims who practise it as a religious duty against non-Muslims. In other words, a religious pretext is used to justify a social phenomenon which existed centuries ago when Punjabis were all Hindus, rather than (mainly) Muslims and Christians. The link is the concept of purity and impurity within Pakistani Islam. One of the causes of impurity, which would prevent a Muslim from praying because of his defilement, is touching certain objects such as excrement. Those, such as many of the Chuhras, whose work involves doing this, therefore, make themselves "impure".[7]

A second important reason for what might be termed "non-*dhimmi* discrimination" appears to lie in the political consciousness. The condemnation of Christians by village mullahs in Friday prayers[8] increases with events such as the Gulf War of 1990-1 (perceived by many Muslims as a Western-Islamic conflict). Similarly the occupation of the

---

5. Vemmelund op. cit. p.118

6. For example, the experience of Christian journalist Noshin Jacob and her sister and Christian friends, described in her article "Stranger at home" *The News* (24 July 1997). See also Streefland op. cit. pp.21-22

7. Streefland op. cit. pp. 2-3; Dumont, Louis *Homo Hierarchicus: the caste system and its implications* translated from the French by Mark Sainsbury, Louis Dumont and Basia Gulati (London, 1970) p.47

8. Ahsan, Ijaz "A religious civil war" *The Nation* (2 March 1997)

Ka'ba by a mixed group of Sudanese and others in November 1979 (considered by many Pakistanis to be an Anglo-American conspiracy) resulted in unusual anti-Christian violence such as an attack on a Christian hostel.[9] This phenomemon might be compared with the hardening attitude of Muhammad (and his successors the Caliphs) towards Christians as the military conflict with the Byzantine Empire developed (see chapter 3).

A distinct but similar third factor could be termed the side-effects of the Islamization process. It can be postulated that, as the laws and constitution become increasingly Islamic and therefore increasingly anti-Christian, public attitudes evolve in response to become less tolerant of minorities. Attitudes may be expressed in actions, and thus more discriminatory behaviour towards Christians and other non-Muslims occurs. (This can also apply to *dhimmi*-type discrimination, as discussed in chapter 3.)

A fourth important factor is the *jajmani* system.[10] This term refers to the land-ownership and economics of rural areas, which is based on the power of small numbers of *zamindars* who own most of the land.[11] Often translated "landlord", *zamindars* are immensely powerful local figures, wielding huge influence in local society and politics in rural

---

9. Ismail, Zafar, who was living in the hostel which was attacked, interview with the author (18 February 1999)

10. Campbell op. cit. p.19

11. Khan, Mahmood Hasan *Underdevelopment and Agrarian Structure in Pakistan* (Lahore: Vanguard Publications Ltd, 1994) pp. 134-138. Moghal states that in Punjab 70% of the cultivated land is owned by 15% of the people, who are *zamindars*. See Moghal *Human Person in Punjabi Society* p.9

areas,[12] in a system somewhat akin to Europe's medieval feudal system. As the local patron, the *zamindar* can confidently rely on being elected to the National Assembly should he choose to stand, which almost all of them do. His word carries great weight. Not only the local agricultural labourers but also the local mullah and local police are effectively under his control. There is little possibility of getting a job in the civil service without a *safarish* (recommendation) from the local Member of the National Assembly (MNA), i.e. the local *zamindar*. Until partition, the majority of Christians lived in rural areas and, being mostly landless, were thus at the mercy of the local *zamindar* economically and socially.[13]

While the *jajmani* system is not intrinsically biased against non-Muslims, in combination with the separate electorates system it adds greatly to the difficulties of Christians and other minorities in rural contexts. There is no incentive for a *zamindar* to assist non-Muslims. Thus, some Christians feel that *zamindars* could have prevented the development of the practice of misusing the blasphemy law against Christians (see chapter 5), if they had chosen to speak out against such injustice in the early days after the introduction of the legislation. As will be seen below, the immigration of Muslims from India at partition forced many rural Christians into the cities. While this enabled them to escape the *jajmani* system, it left them with little option but to do sweeping jobs, a lowlier position in society than agricultural work.

Having considered possible general reasons for "non-

---

12. Even Jinnah did not dare to antagonize the *zamindars* – see Khan, Mahmood Hasan op. cit. p. 139

13. Comfort op. cit. p.6

dhimmi discrimination", some of the more common ways in which this occurs will now be surveyed. Documentation on this kind of discrimination is rather rare, but records of various individual cases have been collected by the National Commission for Justice and Peace (NCJP). This body was established by the Catholic Bishops' Conference of Pakistan in 1984, as the process of Islamization gathered speed.

Separate electorates[14]

The concept of separate electorates for religious minorities originated amongst Muslims in India before partition, and was practised under British rule from 1909 until partition in 1947. After the formation of Pakistan, some Islamic parties continued to press for separate electorates for the purpose of preserving the Islamic character of the state.[15] The 1956 constitution permitted the National and Provincial Assemblies to decide whether elections would be held with a joint electorate or separate electorates (Article 145).[16] The four provinces of West Pakistan

---

14. Since completing this book, there has been an important change in the situation regarding separate electorates in Pakistan. On 16th January 2002 the Government of Pakistan announced that the system of separate electorates would be abolished. However, at the time of going to press (March 2002), there is still much dispute from both Christian and Muslim parties as to the best way forward.

15. See for example Maudoodi, Syed Abul A'la "Psychological Basis of Separate Electorates" originally published in *The Punjabi Darbar* (Lahore, date not given) and later reproduced in Grover, Verinder and Arora, Ranjana (eds.) *Pakistan Fifty Years of Independence* (New Delhi: Deep and Deep Publications, 1997)

16. Reproduced in Government of Pakistan Ministry of Law

decided in favour of separate electorates, but East Pakistan (now Bangladesh) decided to have a joint electorate. However, no elections were ever held under the 1956 Constitution. In the 1962 constitution, certain seats were to be reserved for women (Article 162)[17] but there were no distinctions made on religious grounds. The 1973 constitution specified direct elections by a joint electorate with no special treatment on the basis of sex or religion. There were, however, in the National Assembly ten extra seats reserved for women and six extra seats reserved for religious minorities, which were to be filled by indirect election i.e. election by the directly elected members of the Assembly (Article 51).[18] Interestingly, there was a time limit on the special representation of women of ten years or two general elections, but no time limit for the special representation of religious minorities. At least some Christians interpreted this as an indication that women were expected soon to become integrated into society to such a degree that they would cease to need special representation, whereas apparently non-Muslims were not expected to do so.[19]

The system of separate electorates, so much resented by Christians and other minorities, was introduced by Zia in 1978[20] and ratified by means of the Eighth Constitutional Amendment in 1985 (see chapter 3). In this system, the

---

The Constitution of the Islamic Republic of Pakistan p. 43
    17. Reproduced in Mahmood, Safdar op. cit. p. 560
    18. Reproduced in Butt op. cit. pp.25-7
    19. Amjad-Ali, Christine "Opening the Curtains" p.135
    20. Election Commission (Amendment) Order, 1978, issued by President Zia on 24 September 1978 (text reproduced in *Pakistan Times* 27 September 1978)

minorities were not permitted to vote with their Muslim neighbours for someone to represent their local constituency, but had to vote from a list of candidates of their own religion, each of whom represented the whole country. Ten seats are reserved for the minorities: four for Christians, four for Hindus, one for Ahmadiyyas and one for the Sikh, Buddhist and Parsi communities and any other non-Muslims (Article 51(2A)).[21] In the Provincial Assemblies, seats are similarly reserved for the minorities, the figures varying in the different provinces in proportion to the populations of the various non-Muslim communities in each province (Article 106 (3)).[22] There are no seats reserved for minorities in the Senate.[23]

Before the introduction of this system, some Christians had been actively seeking it. Joshua Fazl-ud-Din considered that non-Muslim minorities could only enjoy religious freedom and their constitutional rights if their elected representatives could "reflect their deepest thoughts and feelings in their entirety and utmost sublimity".

---

21. The history of the introduction of separate electorates is reviewed in various places, for example, Amjad-Ali, Christine "Opening the curtains" pp. 134-6

22. Reproduced in Butt op. cit. p. 65

23. The lack of minority senators is very rarely discussed, but one example is a letter from F. Ali of Karachi published in *The Muslim* (25 March 1996). This letter expresses warm appreciation on behalf of the minorities to Benazir Bhutto's government for their proposal of a dual voting system for minorities, but raises the fact of the complete absence of minority representation in the Senate, since the current constitution came into effect. The writer ends by asking the Prime Minister, in the light of forthcoming Senate elections, not to "miss this opportunity to set right a wrong being done for the last 23 years.".

(Likewise, he felt that Muslims should not be represented by non-Muslims.)[24] Others called for separate electorates on the basis that it would at least guarantee them some co-religionists in the National Assembly whereas in the joint electorate system there were unlikely to be any Christians elected.[25] However, once the system had been introduced and put into practice (which occurred for the first time in February 1985, when Pakistan's third general election was held) the disadvantages soon became manifest. At this election there were 26 Christian candidates, each of whom had to canvass the whole country for votes. They were assisted in this by government permission to spend twice as much on campaigning as Muslim candidates could and by some free airtime on radio and TV. Newspapers, especially *The Pakistan Times*, reported the activities of minority candidates. Nevertheless it was an immense undertaking. Non-Muslim voters also had practical difficulties, as the Christian candidates could not provide polling station workers to assist them and the Muslim staff were too busy with Muslims to give any help to non-Muslims.[26]

But these practical difficulties were overshadowed by the long-term repercussions of the fact that the non-Muslim

---

24. Fazl-ud-Din "Separate Electorates" p. 176

25. For example, the Christian Democratic Party, as referred to in "Separate electorate demands criticised" in *The Pakistan Times* (18 April 1977). See also Christians welcoming the new system when introduced in "Minorities wanted separate electorates" *The Pakistan Times* (2 January 1979); "Masihi leader hails separate electorates" The Pakistan Times (3 January 1979); "Separate electorate welcomed" *The Pakistan Times* (22 February 1979)

26. Kraan, J.D. "News from the country" *Al-Mushir* Vol. XXVII No. 1 (Spring 1985) pp.60-63

vote was of no value to Muslim MNAs representing a local constituency. So the non-Muslim opinion could be safely disregarded by the local *zamindars* and other Muslims with political power. Thus there was no incentive for these influential Muslims to treat their Christian workers well.

The powerlessness and loss of political weight which resulted from the separate electorates system has been described recently by one Christian leader as turning Christians into "political *dhimmi*"[27] and earlier by others as "political death".[28] The system was condemned by Benazir Bhutto on the grounds that it had "isolated minorities from the mainstream of the national politics".[29] In the words of Asma Jehangir of the Human Rights Commission of Pakistan, speaking of the brick-kiln workers, who are mainly Christian:

> Their owners beat them severely. They would not treat Muslims like this, their only concern is votes. The Christians complain that no MNA or member of the local bodies is concerned about them. Even the police do not listen to them... These Christian brothers think they would have been better off making their Muslim brother their representative, at least he would have paid attention to their needs.[30]

---

27. Ismail, Zafar, international director of the Open Theological College, Lahore, interview with the author (16 September 1998)

28. Joseph Francis (General Secretary of the Pakistan Christian National Party) and Saleem Sylvester (General Secretary of the Christian Organisation for Human Rights), quoted in Sadiq op. cit. p.3

29. *The Frontier Post* (2 September 1993)

30. Jehangir, Asma "Minorities and Women in Pakistan" pp.129-30

Another example is given by the National Commission for Justice and Peace (NCJP) which reported the case of Benyamin Masih, a Christian school-teacher who received no salary for the entire four years (1993-1997) of his service in various government primary schools. The reason given was that his school exam marks were not high enough, though Benyamin Masih claimed to know 30 Muslims in his district with the same marks who were in the same kind of job. He held the separate electorates system responsible for the discrimination he suffered.[31]

A further shortcoming of the separate electorates system is that successful candidates for the minorities are virtually certain to come from areas that have large minority populations. This is a natural result of the propensity of people to vote for a candidate known to them or known to come from the same area, and a system in which the four candidates with the highest number of votes are elected. The candidates with the highest number of votes will always be those who come from the areas of densest Christian population. In the National Assembly elections in 1985,[32] 1988 and 1990 all the Christian MNAs came from the densely Christian areas of the Punjab. When Christians in other parts of the country faced problems which needed the help of a MNA, they had to travel large distances to meet their MNA or even their MPA (Member of the Provincial Assembly).[33] Furthermore, the few votes of

---

31. *Human Rights Monitor 97: a report on the religious minorities in Pakistan* (Lahore: National Commission for Justice and Peace, Catholic Bishops' Conference of Pakistan, 1998) p.12

32. Kraan "News from the country" p.62

33. Mendes, Bonnie "The Separate Electorate: Election 90" *Focus* Vol. 12 No. 4 (1990)

Christians in areas of sparse Christian population are of
little value to Christian candidates who may concentrate
all their attention on the populous Christian community of
central Punjab with little detrimental effect on their chances
of being elected. Thus a Christian in the North West Frontier
Province, for example, finds that his vote is of negligible
value to the national Christian candidate and none at all to
the local Muslim candidate, so neither is likely to be
interested in his affairs or well-being.[34]

Many church leaders have protested against the separate
electorates system. These include Roman Catholic leaders
Bishop Paul Bonaventure, Bishop Armando Trinidade
(Vice-Chairman of the Roman Catholic Bishops'
Conference of Pakistan) and Fr James Chanan (Major
Superior of the Dominicans in Pakistan), and Protestants
Bishop John Alexander Malik (Church of Pakistan Bishop
of Lahore), Col. Farman Masih (of the Salvation Army and
Chairman of the National Council of Churches of
Pakistan), Chaudhry Naeem Shakir (Chairman of the
Justice and Peace Committee), leaders of the YWCA, and
many others.[35]

In 1988, the Human Rights Commission of Pakistan
launched a signature campaign against separate
electorates.[36] In 1993, as the next election approached, a
spate of protests was voiced by Christian leaders.[37] The

---

34. Mehdi, Tabir "Polls Apart" *Newsline* (January 1997)
p.104

35. Amjad-Ali, Christine "News from the country" *Al-Mushir* Vol. 35 No. 3 (Winter 1993) p.98

36. *The Christian Voice* (23 October 1988)

37. See for example "Church leaders demand joint electoral
system" *The Muslim* (23 September 1993)

Justice and Peace Commission of the Major Religious Superiors of the Roman Catholic Church called for a boycott of elections by minorities as long as they were held under the separate electorates system.[38] Although this call generated substantial publicity in the national media, when the elections were held in October that year the figures indicated that it had made little difference to the number of minority voters. Very likely this was at least in part due to the Protestant attitude, which, led by the National Council of Churches of Pakistan, was to participate in the elections but "under protest".[39]

The reason the Protestant leaders did not want to urge their followers to boycott the elections is that they were fielding a Christian candidate in the Provincial Assembly elections as a test case. While the constitution clearly prohibited non-Muslims from standing as candidates in the National Assembly (Article 51(1)), there was no specific constitutional prohibition on non-Muslims standing for election to a Provincial Assembly (Article 106 (1)). The Awami Jamoori Party nominated as its candidate for the Punjab Assembly (constituency PP-126 in Lahore) a Christian, Chaudhry Naeem Shakir, a lawyer and human rights activist, who was chairman of the Justice and Peace Committee. After some delays by the Returning Officer and the Lahore High Court, an appeal to the Supreme Court resulted in a provisional ruling allowing Chaudhry Naeem Shakir to file his nomination papers.[40] The

38. Justice and Peace Commission (of Major Superiors of Pakistan) News Letter Vol. 1 No. 1 (September 1993)
39. Amjad-Ali, Christine "News from the country" p.99
40. Babar, Najma "Minorities want joint electorate" Dawn (30 September 1993)

Supreme Court also ordered the Election Commission to prepare joint voting lists in that constituency "since, prima facie, both Muslim and non-Muslim voters of PP-126 are eligible to vote in the elections in this constituency and are to be allowed to do so". On October 4, just days before the elections, the Supreme Court reversed its decision[41] and the elections went ahead in the normal way with only Muslim candidates and only Muslim voters.[42]

If Chaudhry Naeem Shakir had been permitted to stand in the Punjab Provincial Assembly elections in 1993, and if non-Muslims had been permitted to vote, the non-Muslims would have had two votes – one in the main election and one for the specially reserved non-Muslim seats. Such a system of "dual votes" for non-Muslims was proposed by Benazir Bhutto's government in February 1996 to be applied throughout the country.[43] (A very similar system, in which minorities could contest the general seats and also vote in separate electorates, had been proposed seventeen years earlier by P.S. Ramdasia, secretary-general of the Pakistan Minority Alliance.[44]) Welcomed by the minorities[45] and defended by Qazi Jamil, the Attorney General,[46] the proposal was vehemently opposed by some

41. Abbasi, Ansar "SC withdraws order granting minorities right to joint electorate" *The News* (5 October 1993)

42. Amjad-Ali, Christine "News from the country" pp.101-2

43. Ismail, Muhammad "Major electoral reforms approved" *The Frontier Post* (27 February 1996)

44. "Minority alliance's appeal to Zia" *The Pakistan Times* (12 October 1979)

45. "Minorities welcome dual voting right" *The Frontier Post* (2 March 1996)

46. Jan, Matiullah "Dual voting right: a constitutional discovery?" *The Frontier Post* (29 February 1996)

of the Islamic religious groups,[47] such as the Tanzeem-i-Islami[48] and the Milli Yak' Jahti Council[49] and came to nothing. However, calls for a joint electorate continue to be voiced by Christians and human rights bodies, with support being added in 1997 by the Election Commission.[50]

Women

Another area in which the Christian community feels extremely vulnerable and powerless is the abuse of its women by Muslim men. Abduction, rape, forced conversion to Islam and marriage to the kidnapper are the kinds of abuse most often practised, and it is extremely rare that the perpetrators of the crimes are brought to justice. This is particularly common in rural areas where the women of poor families are needed to contribute to the economic support of the family, and thus must be out and about in the village and fields. (Whole families work together as agricultural labourers and brick kiln workers). Moreover, the more remote the area, the more difficult it will probably be to communicate with city-based human rights organizations – a necessity given the near impossibility of poor Christians getting just treatment from their local police.[51]   However, Alexander John Malik, Church of

---

47. Moghal "The right of dual vote" passim

48. "Protest against dual vote right" *Dawn* (12 March 1996)

49. "MYC to oppose dual voting rights" *Dawn* (31 March 1996)

50. "Election Commission for joint electorate" *The Nation* (5 September 1997)

51. For example, when a Christian woman and her two daughters from Gujranwala were kidnapped and raped by an influential local Muslim, the local police did not lodge a case

Pakistan Bishop of Lahore, asserted in 1991 that the
abduction and forced conversion to Islam of Christian
women was beginning to happen in cities as well as
villages.[52]   Hindu women also are vulnerable,[53] but
Christians are more so because, as described by Mohani
Ghosh of the Young Women's Christian Association, some
Muslims believe them to have lax morals so they "can be
seduced very easily".[54] This belief arises mainly because
of Western films depicting immorality which is taken as the
behaviour of Christians, all Westerners being considered
Christians. A second reason why Christian women are
more vulnerable than Hindu women stems from the
distribution of their respective communities. Most Hindus
live in a large, solidly Hindu area, and therefore tend not
to meet Muslims in their daily lives. Christians, however,
are much more scattered, and often live amongst
Muslims.[55] The NCJP wrote in its 1997 report on human
rights in Pakistan:

> The incidents are rampant where minority women are
> deprived of their rights. They are even more vulnerable
> than ordinary citizens and Muslim women in the
> contemporary male dominated society in Pakistan.

---

against him until forced to do so by the High Court because
of a writ petition filed by the Centre for Legal Aid, Assistance
and Settlement (CLAAS), as described in CLAAS's *Update*
(1 January – 30 June 1996) p.5
52. Malik, Alexander John "Welcoming speech"
53. Hussain, Sheher Bano in *Newsline* (August 1997) p.79
54. Quoted in Sadiq op. cit. p.3
55. See Addleton op. cit. pp.32-39

While coping with the underdevelopment and marginalization which [the] majority of the non-Muslims are also facing, the minority women carry an additional burden of being legally and socially disadvantaged. Personal laws and social norms of their own communities are obsolete and meant to sustain male supremacy. To make economical *(sic)* contribution to their families, they have to be socially active but there is a price for such daring.

The non-Muslim women living in remote rural areas are most prone to mischief.[56]

It is hard to estimate the real scale of this problem. The kidnapping of seven girls from seven different places in upper Sind in a single month (January 1994) resulted in an organized protest by the non-Muslim community leaders,[57] which suggests that this was probably an abnormally high rate of abduction. The knowledge that the police are unlikely to act, combined with the high risk of finding themselves accused of *zina* (adultery, a crime which is punished by lashing), keeps many Christians from reporting rapes and abductions. The case of Angelina Peter, a sixteen-year-old Christian girl from Tharparkar who was raped by a Hindu in June 1997, is noteworthy. In this case, Angelina's family managed (with the help of protests from the Christian community) to persuade the police to register a case against her rapist, who was a well known criminal in the area. Whether the fact that he was a Hindu rather than

---

56. *Human Rights Monitor 97* p.18
57. " 'Minorities' rights in serious danger' " *The Frontier Post* (16 February 1994)

a Muslim had anything to do with this success is unclear, but many other people then submitted complaints of rape and sexual harassment. This is interpreted by NCJP as an indication that Angelina's success encouraged others, who had previously thought themselves unlikely to succeed.[58]

The NCJP report details various cases in which women and girls were abducted or rape was attempted, most of whom were not able to obtain justice. One problem is the legal system itself, particularly the *Hudood* Ordinances (see chapter 3) whereby the evidence of a Christian woman carries only a quarter of the weight of the evidence of a Muslim man. Furthermore, while a human rights organization may fight a court case for such women, the victims and their families continue to have to earn their livelihood in the village where the attackers are probably also living, released or bailed by the police, and free to intimidate or harass the family.

Another major cause of miscarriages of justice is the claim of "conversion and marriage", which is often used to disguise the facts of crime and coercion.[59] Behind this lies the ruling in Islamic law (and also in Pakistani law –see below) that conversion of a Christian woman to Islam automatically dissolves her marriage with her Christian husband, since a Christian man is not allowed to be married to a Muslim woman. It should be emphasized that the conversion is necessary only in order to dissolve the existing

---

58. *Human Rights Monitor 97* pp.21-22; Fleming, Fr James "One victim's ordeal" *The Herald* (September 1997)

59. Sylvester, Saleem, General Secretary of the Christian Organisation for Human Rights, and Ghosh, Mohani, leader of the Young Women's Christian Association, as reported in Sadiq op. cit. p.3

marriage and free the woman to marry again. There is nothing in the Shari'ah to prevent a Muslim man from marrying a single or divorced Christian woman, who is permitted in theory (though often not in practice) to continue in her original faith.

While women may agree publicly with their new husbands that they have converted to Islam and re-married of their own free will, it is easy to suppose that many do so out of fear of the consequences should they disagree. A statement by Rajan Victor, a Christian man, alleges that his wife Mary was abducted. When he found her, under the wing of Wajid, an influential Muslim who had abducted her temporarily once before, he says "there were many people and she appeared to be terrorised. She appears to have been tutored and said that she had converted to Islam on 17th May 1993 at Amrot Sharif and on 18th May 1993 she married with Wajid son of Rustam Kandhro."[60] The NCJP cites the case of two sisters from Sheikhupura, Veronica and Sonica Bashir, who were abducted by police officers on their way home from college in 1996. Six months later the girls stated to the High Court that they had converted to Islam , married the policemen and therefore did not want to return to their parents. However in January 1997 both sisters returned to their parents. Veronica, who was pregnant, went back to her husband again briefly but soon divorced him. Sonica did not return to her husband. In the words of the NCJP, " the outcome of this case amply explains what must have been the reality".[61] Nasreen

---

60. Statement by Victor, Rajan addressed to the Station Officer, Lakhidar Police Station, District Shikarpur (22 May 1993)

61. *Update on cases from July to December 1997* Centre

Daniel, a fourteen year old Christian girl was claimed to have been kidnapped by a Muslim, but the alleged kidnapper told the police who arrested him that she had converted to Islam and married him. The police refused to register a case against him. According to NCJP the police were very hostile to Nasreen and her father, who claimed that his daughter had been held in custody by the police and even raped by them. Shahida Mughal, a fourteen-year old Christian girl from Faisalabad, dropped out of school in 1990 because the principal of the school, a Muslim, demanded custody of her, on the basis that she had converted to Islam and entered into a marriage contract with him. Shahida denies this and believes that, in the process of filling out admission forms for her matriculation examinations, the principal tricked her into signing a blank sheet of paper which he later used to forge appropriate documents. The case was decided in the principal's favour in April 1996.[62]

Those who attempt to make protests or lodge complaints against rape and abduction often find themselves ignored.[63] Worse, they may be targeted in retaliation. A common way to do this is to have the woman accused of *zina* (adultery). When the case concerning Sonica and Veronica Bashir was registered, it was not under Sections

for Legal Aid Assistance and Settlement (Lahore) p. 14; *Human Rights Monitor 97* pp.18-20; "Special Report of CLAAS" *Human Rights Today* (May-June 1996)

62. *Human Rights Monitor 97* p.20

63. For example the cases of the abduction of seven unmarried girls from seven different towns in Sind in January 1994, reported in ""'Minorities' rights in serious danger '" *The Frontier Post* (16 February 1994)

64. Nizami op. cit. pp.340-1

364 and 365 of the Penal Code[64] which are concerned with kidnapping. It was registered instead under section 10 of Ordinance VII (1979) of the *Hudood* Ordinances, that is, *zina*.[65] This choice which was challenged in the High Court by the Centre for Legal Aid, Assistance and Settlement on the grounds that "the police created a vagueness in charges to protect the accused".[66]

Another way in which those who complain of abduction or rape may be targeted is through unrelated accusations against the woman's relatives. In 1997 Ghulam Masih, a Christian from the village of Sharqpur, District Shekhupura in the Punjab, found his seven-year-old daughter being raped by four Muslim men in a cow shed. Many other villagers who saw the men running away from the cow shed gave their names to the police. The hospital confirmed that the child had been raped. The rapists were arrested but then released on the grounds of insufficient evidence. But Ghulam Masih continued to press for justice, and nineteen months later received £200 in compensation from the Human Rights Ministry. A few days after receiving this, in October 1998, he was arrested by the Sharqpur police, accused of the murder of an elderly woman. The only witnesses of the alleged murder were his daughter's rapists, whereas other villagers stated that Ghulam had been working in the fields at the time of the murder. Speaking to journalists from the *Sunday Times*, the police inspector, Mushtaq Ahmed, explained that his prisoner was a Christian whereas his accusers were good Muslims and he had no reason to disbelieve them. "My first duty is to Islam.

---

65. This section is headed *zina or zina-bil-jabr liable to tazir* and can be found in "Shariat Criminal Laws"in Nizami op. cit. p.10 of the section on Shariat Criminal Laws

66. "Special Report of CLAAS" *op. cit.*

The courts will take a similar view, and Ghulam Masih will be hanged. You'll see."[67] This prediction could well prove to be correct, as in the case of Gul Pervaiz Masih who was convicted on the evidence of a single Muslim witness whose beard convinced the judge that, as a good Muslim, he must be speaking the truth (see chapter 5).

An interesting twist is given to the tactic of accusing the accusers by the fact that a Christian wife who converts to Islam is automatically divorced from her Christian husband. This rule, from the Shari'ah, applies also in Pakistan and was upheld by the Lahore High Court in March 1992[68] (thus reversing the decision of a lower court in Faisalabad which had ruled in November 1991 that the woman's conversion was not genuine and therefore her abductor had probably committed an offence).[69] It allows Muslim abductors and rapists of Christian women to evade conviction by forcing their victim to convert to Islam (i.e. to recite the *shahada* – Muslim creed – in front of two witnesses, who can sign a mullah's certificate confirming her conversion). If this is accomplished, the woman's former marriage is

---

67. Scott-Clark, Cathy and Levy, Adrian "Beyond Belief" *The Sunday Times Magazine* (24 January 1999) pp.29-30

68. Judgement sheet in the Lahore High Court at Lahore, Judicial Department on appeal no. 4385-B/ of 1991. A similar decision was reached in the Federal Shariat Court on 14th April 1988, a precedent which was referred to in the hearing in the Lahore High Court.

69. The additional sessions judge in Faisalabad wrote in his judgement dated 12 November 1991: "Moreover, in my view, this is not the proper *(sic)* to abduct a woman and then claim that she has embraced Islam and contracted marriage especially in this case where Mst. Mukhtaran Bibi is the mother of seven children. The petitioner is using Islam as a tool to specify *(sic)* his sexual desire and he cannot be allowed to do so."

annulled, and her abductor can freely and legally marry her (conditional, strictly speaking, on her consent).

The bizarre legal consequences which can follow from this are illustrated by the case of Yunis Masih, which began in the early 1990s. He and his wife Piari had been married since 1976 and had five children. One day Piari did not come home from the rice factory in Lahore, where she and her husband both worked. After several days of searching for her, Yunis Masih filed a complaint at the police station. Some time later he received a letter from the first wife of Gulam Rasool, the Muslim owner of the rice factory, saying that Piari had been forcibly converted to Islam, forcibly married to Gulam Rasool and that she wanted to return to Yunis Masih. Yunis then found his wife and brought her home (31 July 1992). Gulam Rasool filed a complaint against Yunis Masih under section 16/7/79 of the *Hudood* Ordinances which is entitled "Enticing or taking away or detaining with criminal intent a woman".[70] Yunis was duly arrested and imprisoned. Piari was returned to Gulam Rasool, whose eldest son murdered her on 8 July 1994, while Yunis was still in prison. Gulam Rasool registered a murder case against his son, but later withdrew it. The son was released on bail.[71] Yunis was released on bail in 1998

---

70. "Enticing or taking away or detaining with criminal intent a woman – Whoever takes or entices away any woman with intent that she may have illicit intercourse with any person, or conceals or detains with that intent any woman, shall be punished with imprisonment of either description for a term which may extend to seven years and with whipping not exceeding thirty stripes, and shall also be liable to fine." – Nizami op. cit. pp. 11-12 of section on Shariat Criminal Laws

71. Centre for Legal Aid Assistance and Settlement *Update* (1 January – 30 June 1996) p.3

but has to live in hiding.[72] What is striking about this case is that, because of Piari's conversion to Islam, the law is all on the side of her Muslim abductor, despite the fact that the evidence strongly suggests that she converted against her will.

To set these events in context, it must be made clear that Christian women do sometimes choose to convert to Islam, generally in order to escape an unhappy marriage.[73] (While Christian men can divorce their wives on the grounds of adultery alone, it is much harder for Christian women to divorce their husbands, as they have to provide more reasons.[74]) Yet it appears that the existence of this law, which removes most of the risk for a Muslim man who abducts and/or rapes a non-Muslim woman, must surely be a factor in the prevalence of this form of abuse.[75]

It could be argued that rape occurs in every country

---

72. Joseph Francis, co-ordinator of the Centre for Legal Aid Assistance and Settlement (Lahore) in interview with Zafar Ismail (January 1999)

73. Bokhari, Sadia "More sinned against..." *The Nation* (Sunday Review) (25 May 1997) p. 4

74. Section 10 of the Divorce Act (1869) reproduced in Khan. S.A. op. cit. p.97, see also p.76. A woman must show more than her husband's adultery in order to have valid grounds for dissolution of the marriage. Such grounds can include (1) her husband has left his Christian faith and married another woman (2) incestuous adultery (3) bigamy with adultery (4) rape, sodomy or bestiality (5) cruelty and adultery (6) adultery coupled with desertion of his wife for two years or more

75. This opinion was expressed by the Rt Rev. Dr John A. Malik [actually Alexander J. Malik], Church of Pakistan Bishop of Lahore, as reported in "Bishop criticizes discrimination against Christians" *Dawn* (21 November 1997) p. 6

and even in Pakistan it is not always the rape of a Christian woman by a Muslim man. This is, of course, true, but it is noteworthy that the rape of a Muslim girl by a Christian man is reported in the press[76] whereas the reverse is rarely publicized. Christine Amjad-Ali has asserted that rape is used in Pakistan as a means of punishment or even political intimidation.

> In Pakistan, as in the rest of the world, rape is a constant feature of the reality of women. While the fact of rape is universal, however, the particular social shape it takes varies from situation to situation. In Pakistan, as well as being an act of violence perpetrated by an individual man against an individual woman, rape is also a means of "punishment" or "teaching a lesson" carried out by one family or class group against another family or class group. Thus the police, as agents of the status quo, routinely use rape against lower class women as an instrument of intimidation. In Sindh particularly the intelligence agencies have used rape as a means of political intimidation.[77]

The phenomenon Amjad-Ali is describing does not have a religious element, but clearly demonstrates an attitude from which it is but a small step to seeing rape as a weapon against a despised minority.

---

76. For example "Christian man molests Muslim girl" *The News* (20 August 1997)

77. Amjad-Ali, Christine "Opening the curtains" pp.132-3

Land and property issues

As indicated above, one of the areas in which Christians feel particularly vulnerable through lack of local political representation is in relation to *zamindars*. Forced eviction of Christians is a commonplace occurrence, with legal restitution a rarity.[78] The 1997 report of the NCJP lists five cases under the heading "Eviction, demolition and land grabbing" some of them involving the homes of dozens of individual Christians. Noteworthy features of these cases include the use of firearms by the Muslims seizing the land, the Christians' feelings of insecurity and helplessness even if they form the majority in a particular village, and false criminal accusations made by the landlords against the Christians.[79] In Sahiwal in September 1998, the homes of 600 Christians – and their church – were razed by bulldozers. A few weeks later the Christians returned and began to re-build from the rubble. In October a Muslim mob marched on the community and destroyed the buildings again. Posters were put up stating "The Christians are into suspicious activities against Islam."[80] Christian cemeteries and graveyards are often encroached on, seized or damaged with apparent impunity.[81]

Another way in which Christians face discrimination in relation to their property is the provision of amenities such as street lights, gas and sewerage. The *Frontier Post* reports examples in which Christian districts had completely inadequate amenities whereas nearby Muslim districts were well provided for.[82]

---

78. Malik, Alexander John " Welcoming speech"
79. *Human Rights Monitor 97* pp. 26-30
80. Scott-Clark and Levy op. cit. pp.35-6
81. *Human Rights Monitor 97* p.30; Sadiq op. cit. p.3
82. Sadiq op. cit. p.3

Employment

While chapter 3 examined the obstacles faced by some Christians in gaining promotion, in line with traditional Islamic teaching about the role of *dhimmi*, there is a separate but related issue which has no basis in the Shari'ah. This is the high proportion of Christians found in the worst jobs. Higher castes often deem it appropriate for the Christians, as Chuhras, to perform the dirty and menial jobs (which, following the underlying pattern of Hindu thinking still held by many Punjabi Muslims, may cause religious defilement as well as being physically dirty). In 1997 it was reported that a Christian in prison (for possessing illegal videos) was forced by the Muslim prisoners to clean the latrine – a not unusual situation. When he refused, they beat him up and made him lick the excrement from the bottom of the latrine.[83] Advertisements for vacancies as sweepers occasionally state "only for Christians". In the early 1990s the mayor of the Lahore Municipal Corporation ordered that only Christians were to be recruited as Corporation sweepers. Although this was presented as positive discrimination designed to assist the economic uplift of the Christian minority, the fact that Christians were discriminated against in other sectors of the Corporation tended to negate this explanation.[84] As well as Christians, low-caste Hindus also are employed as "sanitary workers" – a euphemism for "sweepers", a term embracing not only street-sweeping but other dirty jobs such as cleaning houses and sewers.

---

83. Shirvanee, Imran "Crisis of identity" *The News International* (27 December 1997)
84. Balchin op. cit.

There are also some Muslim sanitary workers, but in much smaller numbers. The NCJP reports an example of a company whose work included keeping clean the city of Lahore which had 8,000 Christian employees and 500 Muslim employees. (Strangely, when Christmas came and all the Christians went on holiday, all the Muslims were found to have left their jobs.) Though Muslims may be employed as sanitary workers, they normally delegate their actual work to non-Muslims thus avoiding the social disgrace associated with the job, but continuing to draw their wages. Typically, the Muslim divides his wages between himself, the Christian who performs his work for him and the supervisor who knows about the arrangement. In August 1997 Christian sanitary workers in Lahore threatened to go on strike, demanding that the Muslim sanitary workers be asked to perform the work they were employed for.[85]

The working conditions of sanitary workers are often very poor, failing even to meet legal requirements. For example, workers often do not receive compensation for accidents or injuries, nor a pension when they retire, even though they are in government service. Several deaths are reported each year, but little official concern is expressed. Those who have attempted to go on strike find themselves dismissed or new workers are brought in to do their jobs. Wages may be left unpaid for long periods of time, and female workers beaten and mistreated.[86]

The population movements and consequent demographic changes which resulted from partition

---

85. *Human Rights Monitor 97* p.42
86. ibid. pp.43-5; Balchin op. cit.

created an increase in the number of Christians in sweeper jobs. Many of them had previously worked as agricultural labourers for Hindu and Sikh landowners, who migrated to India. Their land was given to the Muslim *muhajirun,* who migrated simultaneously to Pakistan from India. Considered to have given up everything for Allah, these newly arrived Muslims had great prestige in Pakistan and were given the land left by the Hindus and Sikhs. Because there were so many *muhajirun* they tended to get rather small parcels of land, which they could work themselves without hiring other labourers. If they did want labourers, they often preferred Muslims.[87] Large numbers of Christians were left without any means of earning their livelihood from the land and moved to the towns and cities to look for work, where many of them became sweepers.[88] This was a step down the social hierarchy for former agricultural labourers for whom sweeping had been only a small part of their work before. Even worse, much of the "sweeping" in the cities was "wet" work i.e. sewers etc. which was more despised even than "dry" work such as street-sweeping and cleaning houses.[89] Nevertheless it was work, and the only kind of job for which the Christian applicants would not find themselves in competition with the respected *muhajirun.* In fact, there were extra numbers of sweeper jobs available because of the growth of urban populations and the migration of some former town-based

---

87. Comfort op. cit. pp.6,14
88. Streefland op. cit. pp.10-11; Jardine, Kenneth W.S. "Church and State in Pakistan" *The East and West Review* Vol. XV No. 4 (October 1949) p. 115
89. Streefland op. cit. pp.12-13

sweepers to India.[90] If cleaning private houses it could even be a relatively well-paid job.[91]

Not all Christians are sanitary workers, but many find difficulties in getting promotion to a level appropriate to their qualifications and experience, or in getting a job at all. Reports in 1991 indicated that the Habib Bank had a policy of not employing Christians and that the Punjab government stopped recruiting Christian nurses for one of its hospitals in 1989.[92] Najma Sadeque, a respected feminist journalist, writes:

> One of the saddest reflections of the bias and the state of mind that poorer Christians constantly live with is when they seek jobs and ask tentatively whether the prospective employer has any objection to a Christian working on Muslim premises. As 'people of the Book', that question should not have to arise, yet if often does. The grounds sometimes given is *(sic)* that they were originally converts from Hinduism and not even genuine Christians. Now that begs the question: what were the sub-continent's Muslim ancestors before Islam came to South Asia.[93]

This highlights an interesting phenomenon. Apparently there is a feeling among some Muslims that genuine *dhimmis* would be eligible for employment but Christians are considered only pseudo-*dhimmis*. Presumably the reluctance to concede full *dhimmi* status to Christians is

---

90. ibid. pp.14-15

91. ibid. p.24

92. Balchin op. cit.

93. Sadeque, Najma   "Leaving some issues to God" *The News* (26 May 1998)

because only a few generations have passed since the conversion of the Hindu ancestors of most of today's Christians. A distinction appears to be drawn, consciously or unconsciously, with Muslims who have many centuries of Muslim ancestors between them and their Hindu forebears. Whether this is normally a sincere religious conviction or a pious excuse to keep Christians out of the workplace is hard to determine.

The question of being refused appropriate promotion is hard to analyse since each individual case would need to be examined on its merits to determine if there is religious discrimination or whether the employee is less well qualified than he or she believes. Illuminating statistics are difficult to obtain, but it is relevant to state that the literacy rate amongst Christians has traditionally been high relative to the population as a whole. The 1911 census showed that Christians in the Punjab (meaning both the Punjab of modern Pakistan and the part which remained in India after partition) had a higher percentage of literacy than Muslims and Sikhs, though lower than Hindus. However, the percentage of literate people who were also literate in English was about four times higher for Christians than for the other faith-communities.[94] In 1978 it was reported that the literacy rate in Christian villages ranged from 30% to 60%, whereas the national average was 20%.[95] Apart from the question of education and ability, an important factor is undoubtedly that Christians tend to lack influence

---

94. Webster op. cit. pp.228-230

95. *The Role of Minorities in National Development* – papers from a seminar held 27-29 April 1978 under the auspices of the Institute of Political and Social Studies of F.C. College, Lahore p.42

and influential friends, which is significant in a society where jobs are often allocated on the basis of favours owed or friendships sought.[96] Whatever the true figures and reasons, it is a very commonly expressed cause of frustration for Christians who see a disproportionately large number of their co-religionists being passed over for promotion.[97]

Bonded Labour

Illegal but widespread, the practice known as "bonded labour" is effectively slavery. Families of labourers, including men, women and children, work long hours in atrocious conditions[98] (usually in brick kilns or agricultural work) for no money, on the basis that they are paying back a family debt owed to their *zamindar*. Commonly the debt originated several generations earlier, and the labourers have no paperwork to indicate their progress in paying it off. They are bought and sold by their *zamindars*. Some are chained to prevent them running away. Those who do run away may be rounded up by men with dogs and rifles.[99] According to the NCJP some are kept in the private jails of their *zamindars*, though this was denied by Justice (Retd.) Salahuddin Mirza, the Sind provincial ombudsman.[100]

---

96. Streefland op. cit. p.20

97. For example the story of Christofer Anderson, a video engineer, as reported in Shirvanee op. cit.

98. The conditions of women and children in particular are described in detail by Asma Jehangir in a report to the Supreme Court in the famous Darshan Masih case in which she represented Darshan Masih. "Submission of report the Hon'ble Supreme Court in the matter of bounded *(sic)* labour A.R. (L)/88-S.C.J. in *All Pakistan Legal Decisions* Vol. XLII (1990) SC583-588

99. Scott-Clark and Levy op. cit. p.36

100. *Human Rights Monitor 97* p.46

Being an illegal practice which the *zamindars* involved usually take care to disguise, estimates of the numbers of bonded labourers are hard to find. The NCJP, which seeks to release bonded labourers, claimed at the end of 1997 that there were "thousands" of people living in bondage.[101] It has found that most of the bonded labourers it has recovered or reported were Christians.[102] This may be compared with a statement by the Human Rights Commission of Pakistan's Special Task Force in Sind concerning 4,000 agricultural workers from Sind whom they had enabled to gain their freedom since 1995, of whom a large majority were Hindus.[103] If both these statements are true, it indicates that the numbers of Christian bonded labourers in the country as a whole must be many times greater than 4,000. A long-term investigation of bonded labour by Human Rights Watch/Asia, begun in late 1993, asserts that this practice involves "millions" of workers.[104] With regard to brick-kiln workers, Asma Jehangir of the Human Rights Commission of Pakistan estimates that 80% of brick-kiln workers are Christians.[105] Human Rights Watch/Asia comments that Christians form "a high proportion" of bonded brick-kiln workers in the Punjab relative to their numbers in the total population.[106]

---

101. ibid. loc. cit.

102. "Bonded labour in agricultural sector: dead souls are stalking in Punjab" *The Mirror* Vol. 1 issue 3 (October/December 1997)

103. reported in *Human Rights Monitor 97* p.46

104. *Contemporary Forms of Slavery in Pakistan* (New York: Human Rights Watch/Asia, 1995) p.1

105. Jehangir, Asma "Minorities and women in Pakistan" p.129

106. *Contemporary Forms of Slavery in Pakistan* p.31

Bonded labour in the agricultural sector is known in both Sind and the Punjab. The NCJP comments that it is not a problem specific to the religious minorities, but the predominance of Christians involved is because "their social vulnerability as a minority group must have contributed to their plight."[107]   Similarly, Khalil Ramdey, Advocate-General of the Punjab, commented in 1988 about brick-kiln workers: "Most of the workers in this industry are Christians and even on this score being the minority they perhaps do not feel confident enough to challenge the maltreatment being meted out to them by the Brick-Kiln Owners who belong to the majority class with all the resources, political involvements at their disposal."[108] Human Rights Watch/Asia "found it difficult to document particular abuses against non-Muslim bonded labourers as non-Muslims" but quoted the comment of a Christian lawyer in Lahore, who wished for safety reasons to remain anonymous, that "Christian bonded labourers suffer double exploitation as religious minorities and as bonded labourers". They also reported that eight Christians and three Hindus interviewed said they were forced to work harder and punished more brutally than Muslim bonded labourers.[109]

Bonded labour is prohibited in the constitution.[110]   A

---

107. "Bonded labour in agricultural sector: dead souls are stalking in Punjab" *The Mirror* Vol. 1 issue 3 (October/December 1997)

108. Ramdey, Khalil report submitted to a meeting held under the direction of the Supreme Court of Pakistan (31st August 1988) *All Pakistan Legal Decisions* Vol. XLII (1990) SC555

109. *Contemporary Forms of Slavery in Pakistan* pp.15,31

110. "Slavery, forced labour etc." are prohibited by Article

number of individuals have obtained their freedom by legal proceedings, either under Section 100 of the Pakistan Penal Code[111] or by filing Habeas Corpus petitions.[112] A landmark case was that of Darshan Masih and twenty other Christians in 1988-9, in which the court ordered that the workers repay current debts to the brick-kiln owners and return to work, while the brick-kiln owners were to cancel past debts of the workers and refrain from coercive methods to retain the workers against their will. Further provisions attempted to stop any future debts getting too large or women and children being made to work against their will.[113] The court was concerned to avoid having to try similar cases in the future and set up a committee to make recommendations regarding long-term measures to prevent bonded labour practices in brick-kilns.[114] In 1992 the Bonded Labour System (Abolition) Act was passed, which required all bonded debts to be cancelled and prescribed a prison sentence and fine for those who compelled anyone to render bonded labour.[115] A set of rules related to the implementation of this Act was published by the

---

11 of the Constitution, Butt op. cit. p.9

111. Concerned with the right of private defence of the body

112. See *All Pakistan Legal Decisions* Vol. XLII (1990) SC528,532

113. *All Pakistan Legal Decisions* Vol. XLII (1990) SC540-544

114. The case and the deliberations of the committee are reported in *All Pakistan Legal Decisions* Vol. XLII (1990) SC513-595.

115. Bonded Labour System (Abolition) Act, 1992, reproduced in Shafi, M. and Shari, P. *Labour Code of Pakistan* 13th edition (Karachi: Bureau of Labour Publications, 1999) pp.32A-32F

government in 1995.[116]   Nevertheless, it remains very difficult for bonded labourers to gain their freedom. Society as a whole, and the police in particular, do not see much to object to in the practice, and therefore do little to assist.[117] The wealth and influence of the *zamindars* helps them evade the consequences of the law, whereas the lack of education and lack of confidence of the labourers themselves have the opposite effect.[118]

Schools and education

In chronologies of their grievances, Pakistani Christians often list in first place the so-called "nationalization" of the Urdu-medium Christian schools and colleges, which began in October 1972. (English-medium schools were unaffected.) These institutions – originally founded by missionaries – are generally recognized as one of the Christian community's greatest contributions to Pakistan, because of their high quality.[119]   Their loss was bitterly resented.[120] Between 1972 and 1974 all the Urdu-medium

116. Bonded Labour System (Abolition)Rules (20 July 1995) reproduced in Shafi, M. and Shari, P. *Labour Code of Pakistan* 13th edition (Karachi: Bureau of Labour Publications, 1999) pp. 32G-32L

117. Several cases in which the police ill-treat runaway Christian bonded labourers or refuse to help them or return them to their *zamindars* are described in *Contemporary Forms of Slavery in Pakistan* pp.29,39,41

118. "Bonded labour in agricultural sector: dead souls are stalking in Punjab" *The Mirror* Vol. 1 issue 3 (October/ December 1997)

119. Hussain, Sheher Bano writing in *Newsline* (August 1997) pp.81-2

120. See for example Malik, Alexander John, Bishop of Lahore *Serving Community* (Lahore: Tanzeem-i-Nau, no date

Christian schools and colleges in the Punjab and Sind were nationalized, along with private Muslim schools. This was a decision made at provincial level and did not affect the few Christian schools in Baluchistan and North West Frontier Province.[121] No compensation was given since the churches remained the nominal owners i.e. they held the title deeds, although management passed to the provincial governments. At the time of nationalization it was promised that the character of the Christian schools would be maintained, but in 1979 a policy of Islamizing education was introduced. Christians voiced concern at the gradual loss of the Christian character of the schools.[122] This included a growing emphasis on the teaching of Islam (*Islamiyat*) and the ideology of Pakistan in all schools, whatever their origin. *Islamiyat* was made a compulsory subject in board examinations for Muslims, and non-Muslim students were not allowed to offer their own religion as a subject, or even study it at school.[123] Instead non-Muslims were allowed to study "ethics". However, no practical arrangements were made for this, and anyway most non-Muslims chose to study *Islamiyat* because it was a necessary qualification for all tertiary education.[124] Christians also complained that some textbooks gave

but before April 1982) pp.16-19

121. *Human Rights Monitor 97* p.58

122. Butler op. cit. p.50

123. *The Christian Voice* Vol. XXXIX No. 31 (31 July 1988)

124. Tebbe, J.A. "Separate Curriculum in Religious Education for Christians" in "News from the Country: the Christian community" *Al-Mushir* Vol. XXVII No. 2 (Summer 1985) p. 120; Kraan, J.D. "Education in Pakistan: developments in 1984-1985" *Al-Mushir* Vol. XXVII No.1 (Spring 1985) pp.9-10

inaccurate information or information biased against Christians.[125]   It became difficult for Christians to gain admission to (Muslim) state schools – applications were often refused on the grounds that there were "no places" or that Christians should go to Christian schools. (All Christian schools were fee-paying so not accessible to many poorer Christians.) Of those Christians who did gain places in the Muslim state schools, many performed poorly, played truant or dropped out altogether. When this happened it was generally attributed by the Christians to the discrimination and hostility which Christian students suffered at school, sometimes even being deliberately failed in their examinations.[126]   Those from sweeper families were easily recognizable by their "sweeper culture" manifested in language, outward appearance and hygiene habits. Specifically the "sweeper culture" includes coarse language, the wearing of old and dirty clothes, and the habit of using the public road as a latrine, all of which contribute to the Christians being despised.[127]

At tertiary level also, Christians found it hard to get places to study, and there was a perception that places were not granted on merit. The Bishop of Lahore expressed the opinion of many Christians when he complained that it was hard for Christians, as an impoverished community, to study at college, for good marks were only obtained by bribes

125. Butler op. cit. p.51
126. Ismail, Zafar *Pakistan: the Islamic state and the Christian community* unpublished paper presented at a consultation held at Glen Eyrie, Colorado Springs, 8-12 November 1992
127. Comfort op. cit. p.119
128. Malik, Alexander John "Welcoming speech"

and most Christians did not have the financial resources for bribery![128] Many Christians believed that the main purpose of the nationalization of the schools and colleges, which so dramatically changed the character of Christian schools while scarcely affecting Muslim schools, was to weaken the Christian influence in Pakistan.[129]

Continued Christian protests eventually resulted in a promise to denationalize the educational institutions including the Christian ones, but it was many years before this was put into practice for the Christian schools and colleges.[130] The process began in 1990 in the Sind. In 1996 the Punjab announced its decision to offer nationalized schools back to their previous owners/managements conditional on meeting certain financial conditions.[131] The following year, some schools were indeed returned to the control of their original owners, in return for a deposit of six months salary for the teachers, but by 1999 there were still many which had not yet been returned.[132]

Assumed disloyalty to the state

The rationale behind many of the restrictions on *dhimmi* is their assumed disloyalty to the Islamic state. Sardar Feroze Khan writes that "It is generally suspected by orthodox [Muslim] religious elements that as Christians we are tied to the culture, civilization and politics of the West

---

129. "Pakistan" (author not given) in Barrett op. cit. p. 544
130. "Bishop criticizes discrimination against Christians" *Dawn* (21 November 1997)
131. "Nationalized schools to go to previous owners" *The Nation* (27 July 1996)
132. "10 Christian schools to be denationalized" The Muslim (27 November 1997); "Bishop criticizes discrimination against Christians" *Dawn* (21 November 1997)

and that our supposed links and western orientation can sabotage the very foundational ideology – Islam – of the state."[133]   Naseem George, a Christian politician, summarizes the situation by saying that Pakistani Christians are considered to be foreigners "belonging to the West".[134] Thus, for example, the loyalty of non-Muslim Pakistanis was considered suspect during the war with India in 1965, and non-Muslim war veterans received minimal recognition.[135]   Khurshid Ahmad attributes Christian opposition to Shari'ah to the influence of past colonialists.[136] The kind of Muslim attitude which, at least in Christian perception, is so widespread is that of Naheed Jehan Lodhi who writes:

> Muslims in an ideological Muslim state cannot permit
> the substance of sovereignty to slip from their hands.
> There is an impression of militancy associated with a non-

---

133. Khan, Sardar Feroze op. cit. p.8. See also Charles Amjad-Ali's use of the term "fifth column" in "Islamization and Christian-Muslim Relations" p.78

134. George, Naseem "The role of religious minorities in Pakistan's politics and the future direction" – a paper given at a seminar on "Religious Minorities in Pakistan: struggle for identity" (July 1996) reproduced in a book of the same title ed. Moghal, Dominic and Jivan, Jennifer (Rawalpindi: Christian Study Centre, 1996) p.89

135. Jacob, Peter "The Question of Identity for Religious Minorities" – a paper given at a seminar on "Religious Minorities in Pakistan: struggle for identity" (July 1996) reproduced in a book of the same title ed. Moghal, Dominic and Jivan, Jennifer (Rawalpindi: Christian Study Centre, 1996) p.54

136. Siddiqui, Ataullah *Christian-Muslim dialogue in the twentieth century* (Basingstoke: Macmillan Press Ltd, 1997) p.134

Muslim dominated government in any state where Muslims are in majority. It is not advisable to allow for the formation of hostile government at war with the mainstream majority's welfare.[137]

Similarly, Qazi Hussein Ahmad of the Jamaat-i-Islami caused outrage amongst Christians when he stated on 9 December 1990 that Christians cannot be the friends of Muslims.[138]

While some Christians do feel and demonstrate a greater loyalty to the Western "Christian" world,[139] Sardar Feroze Khan and many other Christians in Pakistan are at pains to assert their loyalty to their motherland, Pakistan. Justice Cornelius even described himself as a "constitutional Muslim".[140] At the time of the 1990-1 Gulf War, the National Council of Churches of Pakistan held a press conference in which they stated that Christians in Pakistan were loyal citizens of Pakistan and their loyalty should not be doubted.[141] Many other affirmations of their desire to work for the good of the country as a whole, not just for Christians or non-Muslims, are given in various forums.[142]

---

137. Lodhi, Naheed Jehan op. cit. pp.4-5
138. Statement of protest issued by M. Joseph Francis of the Pakistan Christian National Party (undated, but shortly after 9 Dec 1990)
139. George op. cit. p.89
140. cited in Butler op. cit. p.52
141. Saroia, Yousaf G. (executive secretary of the National Council of Churches of Pakistan) and Bakhsh, Bishop J.S. (vice-president of the National Council of Churches of Pakistan) at a press conference reported in the *Daily Imroz* (Urdu) (3 February 1991)
142. For example Final Statement of the national seminar on "Religious Minorities in Pakistan: Struggle for Identity"

Media

Many Christians in Pakistan feel that they and their faith are routinely misrepresented in the electronic and print media.[143]   Christians and other non-Muslims are often portrayed unsympathetically in screen and radio dramas or on posters. Alternatively, their existence is ignored altogether. Christians call for a greater emphasis and recognition to be given to the positive contribution they have made to the country.[144]   Non-Muslim religious festivals do not pass unrecognized by the Muslim majority. For example, there are normally short Christmas programmes on television and messages from the President and Prime Minister. Newspapers often take the opportunity to describe Christmas traditions, the charity work of a Christian organization or sometimes the discrimination which Christians face.[145]   However, a seminar on the religious minorities in 1996 called for more positive coverage of all non-Muslim festivals in order to "develop better understanding among the people of Pakistan".[146]

Until early 1999, it was normal for the word *isai* (followers of Jesus, *Isa*) to be used in the media to refer to Christians. This is a derogatory term which carries negative connotations as it has come to mean "sweeper". Christians themselves therefore did not use this word, but referred to

pp. 96-7; Malik, Alexander John *Serving Community* passim

143. Khair Ullah, F.S. "The future of Christians in Pakistan" *Al-Mushir* Vol. XV No. 1 (1973) p.6

144. Final Statement of the national seminar on Religious Minorities in Pakistan: struggle for identity p. 104; Butler op. cit. p.50

145. Amjad-Ali, Christine "Opening the curtains" pp.137-8

146. Final Statement of the national seminar on Religious Minorities in Pakistan: struggle for identity pp.104-5

themselves as *masihi* (followers of Christ/Messiah, *masih*) A one-man letter-writing campaign was mounted in December 1998 by Altaf Naseem, a Christian who appealed to the president, prime minister and others in the government to stop the practice of using the derogatory term *isai* in the media.[147] A directive was duly issued by the government to television stations and newspapers, which soon began to refer to Christians as *masihi*.[148]

Food and utensils

One of the forms of discrimination most clearly linked to Chuhra origins is that related to food and the refusal of some Muslims to eat and drink with Christians or share utensils with them. This is a consequence of the belief that the impurity of the Chuhras will be passed on by physical contact with them.[149] A young Christian journalist found that a female Muslim typist would not eat with her for this reason.[150] An elderly Christian man who staffed the press lounge at the National Assembly was banned by the National Assembly canteen staff from touching any canteen utensils or even carrying a tray.[151] A Christian student of science at the Islamia College in Karachi was forbidden by his fellow students to drink from the tap.[152] Five Christian

147. For example, e-mail from Altaf Naseem to Mushahid Hussain, the Federal Minister of Information ()12 January 1999) who replied by e-mail saying "I have given necessary instructions in this regard" (14 January 1999)

148. Zafar Ismail noticed the change in terminology in the media in March 1999.

149. Streefland op. cit. pp. 2-3,19

150. Jacob, Noshin op. cit.

151. Baabar, Mariana "Apartheid at NA canteen" *The News* (6 November 1997)

schoolgirls from St Mary's School. Gujrat, who were taking a Home Economics practical examination on 25 February 1997, found that the Muslim examiner would not test or mark the food they had cooked. She ordered the Christians' food to be put in the dustbin, but tested the food of their eight Muslim classmates in the normal way.[153]

This kind of behaviour is actually forbidden[154] though by no means uncommon in rural areas. In the cities it is quite rare, as demonstrated by the outrage of Muslim journalists when the Christian staff member in the National Assembly press lounge explained why he was not able to bring them any tea from the canteen.[155] Indeed, many restaurants are run by Christians and staffed by Christian chefs. Nevertheless, when this form of discrimination does occur, it is personally very hurtful to those who experience it. A Christian man who earns his living by cleaning six Muslim homes, while his wife cleans for various other families, commented wistfully, "We have to have our own utensils in order to eat or drink at any house in case they offer something. We are also human beings with emotions and passions." When his wife gave birth to a longed-for

152. See the case history of Daniel Scot in chapter 5. The refusal to share a tap with Christians is noted by Streefland op. cit. p.19.

153. "Christian students humiliated" *Dawn* (1 March 1997); Centre for Legal Aid, Assistance and Settlement *Update on Cases from January till June 1997* pp.9-10

154. Article 20 of the 1956 constitution runs "Untouchability is abolished, and its practice in any form is forbidden and shall be declared by law to be an offence." Government of Pakistan Ministry of Law *The Constitution of the Islamic Republic of Pakistan* p.6

155. Baabar op. cit.

son at last, the man brought a cake as a gift to one of his employers to celebrate the birth. The employer himself ate the cake willingly but his wife and children were reluctant to share it.[156]

Identity cards and passports

The identity cards issue concerns a move proposed in 1992 which was abandoned in response to the protests of the non-Muslim minorities. However, the memory of this "narrow escape" still lingers and continues to be referred to by both Muslims and non-Muslims as an example of a successful minorities' protest.[157]

Under Prime Minister Nawaz Sharif, a government proposal was made to indicate on identity cards the religion of the bearer. The demand originated with the Islamic parties,[158] who suggested cards of a different colour for non-Muslims,[159] and was modified by the government to the insertion of a "religion column" on the card. This procedure was agreed on 13 October 1992 but Christians responded with press conferences, posters, letters, street meetings, rallies, processions, sit-ins, strikes, hunger strikes etc. The minority MNAs passed a motion opposing it[160] and – less predictably – the Provincial Assembly of Sind

---

156. Shirazi, Saj "Meet your sweeper" *The News* (22 June 1997)

157. For example Abbas, Azhar "Standing apart" *The Herald* (February 1997) p.69

158. Ahmad, Eqbal "Sectarianising national identity" *Dawn* (18 October 1992)

159. "'Fundamentalists creating problems'" *Frontier Post* (27 February 1992)

160. "Religion column: MNAs move motion in NA" *Dawn* (8 November 1992)

passed a unanimous resolution opposing it.[161]   The Sind
Provincial Assembly at this time was dominated by the
socialist-leaning Pakistan People's Party and the liberal,
educated Muttahidda Quami Movement, both of which
voted on principle against this proposal. By December it
appeared the government was trying to find a way to
reverse the decision, and on 25 December an official of
the Ministry for Interior Affairs announced that ID cards
would continue to be issued as before.[162]

Religious identification on passports was introduced in
1977 and has not been a cause of distress to Christians,
because they are not in use in daily life. The chief
complainants against this are the Ahmadiyyas who consider
themselves Muslims but whose faith prevents them signing
the declaration of belief which Muslims must sign in order
to be described on the passport as a Muslim.[163]

Conclusion

Discrimination against Christians in Pakistan is a complex
phenomenon, in which Islamic tradition, Pakistani law, a
prevailing culture of corruption, and a deep-rooted caste
system originating from Hinduism are all contributory
factors. The poverty of the Christians has a double effect
making them not only despised but also powerless in a
society where bribery of the police and judiciary is
commonplace. The scarcity of Christians in positions of

161. "Sindh PA rejects religion column" *Dawn* (3 November
1992)

162. Mendes, Bonnie "Looking back at the ID card issue"
Focus supplement Vol. 13 (1993);

163. "Religion column in passport to stay" *The Frontier
Post* (14 January 1997) p.4

authority is also detrimental for the community as a whole, since having influential friends and contacts is another important way to attain a goal in Pakistani society. According to Balchin's analysis, "For the marginalised communities, the 'scratch my back and I'll scratch yours' syndrome is a disaster; alienated from the mainstream, Christians automatically have less to 'offer'".[164] Despite an excellent secular legal system, they can rarely gain redress for the wrongs done to them. This can be either because of the use of Shari'ah-derived legislation such as the *Hudood* Ordinances, or because of the bias of those members of the judiciary, that bias originating either from honest conviction or from fear of reprisals from Islamists.

All the kinds of discrimination described in this chapter are in addition to those prescribed by the Shari'ah for *dhimmi*. Village Christians in Pakistan do not even have the theoretical rights and protection due to *dhimmi*. Furthermore, a recent report has concluded: "Today, Christians in Pakistan are worse off than the untouchables of India: socially stigmatised for being poor as well as for their faith."[165] History and geography have combined to make Pakistan's Christian community – or at least the impoverished majority of the Christian community – not only more discriminated against than non-Muslims in an Islamic context but also more discriminated against than scheduled castes in a Hindu context.

Writing in 1996, Dominic Moghal of the Christian Study Centre in Rawalpindi declared his desire to see Pakistan become a true Islamic state because he believed the position

---

164. Balchin op. cit.
165. Scott-Clark and Levy op. cit. p.36

of Christians would improve. He asserted that the implementation of the "Islamic values of tolerance, equality, brotherhood and social justice" would give Christians a better position than the feudalism, class and caste systems of the present.[166] It should be noted that Moghal's understanding of the status of non-Muslims in an Islamic state seems to be derived largely from a work by Hamidullah[167] which asserts the unusual position that non-Muslims had equal status with Muslims during Muhammad's lifetime and hence also in an ideal Islamic state. Nevertheless, this is indicative of the multiple burden borne by the majority Christians in Pakistan – their faith, their poverty, and their caste origins. Moghal's stance is unusual, despite the assertion of Khurshid Ahmad, a deputy leader of the Jama'at-i-Islami and founder of the Islamic Foundation in Leicester, that the Christians and some of the leaders of the Hindu scheduled castes in the First Constituent Assembly demanded the establishment of an Islamic State, believing that their rights would be better safeguarded in such a state.[168]

As a response to the needs of the minorities, the government allocates certain sums of money for the economic development of the minority communities.[169]

---

166. Moghal "The right of dual vote" p.76 [of English version]

167. Hamidullah, M. *Status of non-Muslims in Islam* Publication no. 40 (Islamabad, Da'wah Academy, International Islamic University, 1989)

168. Ahmad, Khurshid's editorial footnote in Maududi *The Islamic Law and Constitution* p.70

169. A list of the various funds and schemes for financial assistance of the minorities is given in the United Nations Fourteenth Periodic Report of States pp.7-8

In 1997-8 this amounted to Rs65 million (about one million pounds sterling) which included revolving loan funds for scholarships, financial gifts at Christmas, the Hindu festival of Divali, and Parsi religious festivals, for needy Christians, Hindus and Parsis respectively, and a scheme of National Cultural Awards with prizes in various kinds of arts for which only the minorities were eligible. However, the sums involved are so small that few seem to benefit beyond the friends and family of the minority MNAs.[170]

Looking to the future, a significant new factor is the growing anti-Western sentiment amongst Pakistani Muslims, a response to the perceived Muslim-Western conflict in various parts of the world, for example, Iraq. This attitude can manifest itself in anti-Christian action, following the age-old equating of the Western world with the Christian world. This suggests that anti-Christian prejudice in society, police and judiciary is likely to increase rather than decrease, and therefore the problems of poor Christians will tend to grow.

As suggested in the introduction to this chapter, a likely additional cause of non-*dhimmi* discrimination against Christians is that it is in a sense a "by-product" of the discrimination which is legitimized by the Shari'ah. In other words, if the Shari'ah teaches Muslims to discriminate in

---

170. "No systematic discrimination against minorities in Pakistan" *The News* (31 July 1997); see also the alleged misappropriation of Rs2,500,000 intended for the welfare of Christians by a Christian MNA reported in "Complaint against Salhotra lodged" *The Frontier Post* (27 February 1992). Other reports of government funds for minority development are given in "Rs18.44m earmarked for minorities development" *The News* (21 October 1997) and "Govt committed to minorities welfare: Zafar" *The Muslim* (22 September 1998)

certain ways against Christians, it is not surprising to find that individual Muslims may also discriminate against Christians in other ways, not listed in the Shari'ah. The Shari'ah creates a mindset of anti-Christian discrimination which individuals may put into practice with greater or lesser attention to the limits set out in the Shari'ah. If this is indeed a factor tending to produce *de facto* discrimination, it is likely that the increasing Islamization of Pakistan's laws and society will bring increasing *de facto* discrimination against Christians in its wake.

FIVE

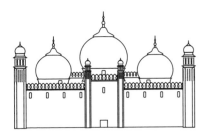

The development of national legislation and attitudes to blasphemy and apostasy, and their outworkings in practice

Blasphemy

Introduction

Blasphemy has become one of the most pertinent current issues for the Christian community in Pakistan. Indeed, it affects other minorities and even the Muslim majority. From independence in 1947 until the 1980s, only six cases of blasphemy were registered. The maximum two-year sentence was rarely awarded. Between 1986[1] and 1995, however, at least sixteen blasphemy cases were brought against Christians, at least nine against Muslims and at least

---

1. The year in which the key part of the "blasphemy law", Section 295-C of the Pakistan Penal Code was added to the legislation.

100 against Ahmadiyyas.[2] By June 1997 three Christians, one Sunni Muslim and two Shi'a Muslims had been sentenced to death under Section 295-C (defiling the name of Muhammad), though all were acquitted on appeal.[3]

The blasphemy legislation has become a weapon in the context of personal disputes, biased as it is in favour of the accuser – for the accuser has nothing to lose, the accused everything, even his life. This includes not only disputes between Muslims and non-Muslims but also between Muslims themselves. A famous case of the latter is that of Dr Akhtar Hameed Khan, an active reformist Muslim, who had accusations of blasphemy made against him by militant Muslims who were "utilising the blasphemy law to delegitimise him and enforce their own notion of orthodoxy".[4]

Unofficial changes made by the Government in 1995 to procedures for filing blasphemy charges (see below) have been followed by a significant drop in the number of blasphemy charges.[5] Nevertheless, the law is still a

---

2. Figures for Christians from Haider, Ejaz "A live given to a worthy cause" *The Friday Times* (15-21 May 1998) which lists fifteen with name, date and place for each case. In addition there is the case of Daniel Scot (see below). Figures for Muslims and Ahmadiyyas from U.S. Department of State *Country Reports on Human Rights Practices for 1995* (Washington: U.S. Government Printing Office, April 1996) p.1344 which mentions only nine Christians.

3. Amnesty International *Pakistan: Time to Take Human Rights Seriously* Index ASA 33/12/97 (1 June 1997) p.23

4.. Forte, David F. "Apostasy and Blasphemy in Pakistan" *Connecticut Journal of International Law* (Fall, 1994) p. 57

5. Statement by Human Rights Commission of Pakistan, reported in U.S. Department of State *Country Reports on Human Rights Practices for 1996* (February 1997) p.1474

fearsome instrument to which Christians are particularly vulnerable. Though the number of Christians directly affected is small in absolute terms, the blasphemy law is felt to be a sword of Damocles[6] and has developed a huge symbolic signficance which contributes substantially to the atmosphere of intimidation of Christians. The detrimental effect of the law on community relations is most dramatically illustrated by the incident at Shanti Nagar in February 1997 in which tens of thousands of rioting Muslims destroyed hundreds of Christian homes and other Christian property, following an accusation of blasphemy.

Furthermore, the blasphemy law has engendered a "wave of private violence".[7] Equating blasphemy with apostasy (see below) and influenced by "the tradition of direct violent action and self-help, which goes back to the earliest times of Islam", some Muslims feel that they are entitled to enforce the death penalty themselves.[8] While no one has yet been executed by the state for blasphemy, four Christians[9] charged with blasphemy have been murdered with little police investigation of the murders (see below). In addition one Muslim was murdered because he was mistaken for a Christian who had been accused of blasphemy.[10] Death threats against Christians are not

---

6. This metaphor was used by Dr Ruffan Julius, a Christian Member of the National Assembly, quoted in *Dawn* (September 7, 1998) p.8

7. Forte op. cit. pp.54-56

8. An-Na'im, Abdullahi Ahmed *Toward an Islamic Reformation: Civil Liberties, Human Rights and International Law* (Syracuse: Syracuse University Press, 1990) p.184,

9. Full list given below in section on "Misuse of the blasphemy law.

10. Emmanuel Luther, a Christian, was accused of

uncommon, and an entire Christian community may be forced to move away from the place where they have lived for generations.[11] This phenomenon of unofficial punishment according to the blasphemy law is very important, particularly in that the judiciary and police often appear to be intimidated themselves by the strength of religious feeling against alleged blasphemers, and therefore do not move to control or punish the violence.[12] Writing after the first two murders of Christians accused of blasphemy, Chaudhry Naeem Shakir, a Christian High

---

blasphemy with respect to the Urdu translation of a book he had published in English in 1989 on the life of Muhammad. He went into hiding and escaped to the United States in January 1991. A Muslim called Abdul Rehman Lothar from Gujranwala was murdered because extremists confused his name with Luther's. See Dildar, Peter Jacob and Mughal, Alexander Aftab *Section 295-C Pakistan Penal Code: A Study of the History, Effects and Cases under Blasphemy Laws in Pakistan* (Faisalabad: National Commission for Justice and Peace, 1995) pp.43-44 In addition Dr Sajjad Farooq, a Muslim, was murderd by an angry Muslim crowd on 21 April 1994 after he had been accused of blasphemy. See Khan, Aamer Ahmed "The blasphemy law: the bigot's charter?" *The Herald* (May 1994) pp.46b-50

11. For example, the 32 Christian families in the village of Ratta Dhotran where Salamat Masih, Rehmat Masih and Manzoor Masih, all arrested for blasphemy on 11 May 1993, had lived. In addition, 18 Christian families had to leave the village of Arifwala (Chak 353/E.B) following the arrest of Ayub Masih for blasphemy under Section 295-C on 14 October 1996. *The Herald* (May 1994) pp.52-54; "Update on cases from 1st July – 31st December 1996" Centre for Legal Aid, Assistance and Settlement, Lahore

12. U.S. Department of State *Country Reports on Human Rights Practices for 1998*, Vol. II (Washington: U.S. Government Printing Office, 1999) p.1951

Court advocate, spoke of the "general scare and insecurity" amongst non-Muslims.[13] After the murder of the fourth, George Clement, a Roman Catholic Member of the National Assembly, commented on how insecure this made the minorities feel.[14] After the protest suicide of Bishop John Joseph of Faisalabad in May 1998, his fellow-bishop, Joseph Coutts, Bishop of Hyderabad wrote of "the fear and tension in which minority communities are living because of the misuse of this law by extremist and unscrupulous elements".[15] It must be emphasised that this violence is a new phenomenon which has followed the introduction of Section 295-C. In the words of Bishop Michael Nazir-Ali, there was no pre-existing "law of the jungle" which might have been considered to need dealing with by the introduction of this Section of the Penal Code.[16]

Basis in Shari'ah

The Shari'ah does not emphasise blasphemy nearly as forcefully as it does apostasy; it is a *ta'zir* offence,[17] rather than a *hadd* offence. The definition of blasphemy is rather more broad than simply insulting God, for a denial of any of the essential principles of Islam is defined as blasphemy.[18] This opens the way for condemning as a

---

13. Shakir, Chaudhry Naeem "Fundamentalism, enforcement of Shariah and the law on blasphemy in Pakistan" *Al-Mushir* Vol. 34 No. 4 (1992) p.114

14. "Blasphemy law being misused, say MNAs" *Dawn* (22 April 1994)

15. Coutts, Joseph letter published in *Dawn* (28 May 1998)

16. Rt Rev. Dr Michael Nazir-Ali, interview with author (11 May 1998)

17. i.e. the punishment is discretionary

18. Hughes, T.P. *Dictionary of Islam* (Lahore: Premier Book House, 1885)

blasphemer anyone with a different interpretation of Islam.
Forte comments that "none of the great intellectual leaders
of Pakistan's pre-history, from Muhammad Iqbal even to
Muhammad Ali Jinnah, would have been immune to
attack".[19]

In South Asian forms of Islam the figure of Muhammad
is invested with a special sanctity, as veneration of the
Prophet developed in association with Sufism.[20]   Hence
alleged insults to Muhammad are treated in the same way as
insults to God, or as even worse.[21]   Thus Mohammad Asrar
Madani, a much respected conservative Pakistani scholar
(now director of the Islamic Research Institute, Toronto),
whose opinion is followed by Pakistan's Shari'ah Court, gives
a definition of blasphemy which is centred on Muhammad:

> Reviling or insulting the Prophet (peace be upon him)
> in writing or speech; speaking profanely or
> contemptuously about him or his family; attacking the
> Prophet's dignity and honour in an abusive manner;
> vilifying him or making an ugly face when his name is

---

19. Forte op. cit p.67

20. Schimmel, Annemarie *And Muhammad is his messenger:
the veneration of the Prophet in Islamic piety* (Lahore:
Vanguard, 1987) passim, especially pp.239-256 on how love of
the Prophet coloured the work of Muhammad Iqbal; Lewis, P.
"The Shrine Cult in Historical Perspective" in *Al-Mushir*, Vol.
XXVI No. 2 (Summer 1984) pp.54-9; Geibels, M. "The Prophet
Muhammad's Birthday Festival" in *Al-Mushir* Vol. XXVIII No.
4 (Winter 1986) pp. 133-145

21. Halliday, Fred "'Islam is in danger': Authority, Rushdie
and the Struggle for the Migrant Soul" in Hippler, Jochen and
Lueg, Andrea (eds.) *The Next Threat: Western Perceptions of
Islam* transl. Laila Friese (London: Pluto Press, 1995) footnote
10

mentioned; showing enmity or hatred towards him, his family, his companions and the Muslims; accusing or slandering the Prophet and his family, including spreading evil reports about him or his family; defaming the Prophet; refusing the Prophet's jurisdiction or judgement in any matter; rejecting the Sunnah al-Nabawiyya; showing disrespect, contempt for or rejection of the rights of Allah and His Prophet or rebelling against Allah and His Prophet.[22]

Traditionally Islam (apart from the Hanafi school)[23] taught that a Muslim found guilty of blasphemy was to be sentenced to death.[24] This is the opinion of Ibn Taymiyya (1263-1328), the reformist Hanbali scholar and jurist, who dealt extensively with the issue of insulting Muhammad in his work *Kitab al sarim al maslul ala shatim al rasul*.[25] According to Ibn Taymiyya, anyone who defames the Prophet **must** be executed, whether the offender is a Muslim or not. Such opinions have survived into the modern age, as exemplified by Madani who asserts that an insult to Muhammad is considered to be an insult, injury and threat to the entire Muslim *umma*.[26] In addition, he

22. Madani, Mohammad Asrar *Verdict of Islamic Law on Blasphemy and Apostasy* (Idra-E-Islamiat, Lahore, Pakistan, 1994) pp.19-20

23. Lewis, Bernard "Behind the Rushdie Affair" *Am. Scholar* (1991) 185,188

24. Hughes op. cit. ; Madani op. cit. passim

25. Hyderabad, 1905. See also Thomas Michel in *Ibn Taymiyya, A Muslim Theologian's Response to Christianity* pp. 69-71. Both cited in Ruthven, M. *A Satanic Affair* (London, Hogarth, 1991) p.51

26. Madani op. cit. p.12

states that "respect for [the Prophet] and his family ... is part of the Divine scheme for the preservation of His deen. The Messenger's integrity, honour and dignity are essential for the propagation of the message."[27]

According to Madani, basing his reasoning on the hadith collection of Al-Saif al-Sarim, while Muhammad lived he had the option of forgiving blasphemers, but now apologies and repentance from blasphemers cannot be accepted – the offender must be killed.[28] Ibn Taymiyya also insists that repentance will not save the offender from execution.[29] (This contrasts with the apostasy law which, according to some schools, allows a three-day period for possible repentance so as to avoid execution.)

With regard to blasphemy committed by non-Muslims, there is variation according to different schools of law. The Maliki school teaches that a *dhimmi* who criticises Muhammad is only guilty of blasphemy if his criticism goes beyond merely stating what is a necessary part of a non-Muslim's belief. This school also teaches that a non-Muslim blasphemer who **is** guilty according to the above definition may still escape execution by converting to Islam.[30] This option was practised in Sukkur in 1995 when a fourteen-year-old Christian girl, Carol Daphne, was obliged to convert to Islam after having submitted an allegedly blasphemous answer in a school test. Carol and her relatives had received many death threats and processions led by extremist Muslims had called for the

---

27. ibid. p. 40
28. ibid. pp.109,126
29. Ruthven op. cit. p.51
30. "Al-Risala" (Maliki manual) 37.19 Crimes Against Islam in *Lawbase* (London: The Islamic Computing Centre, 1993?)

death penalty for the girl and her headmistress. Ironically, some *ulema* in Sukkur insisted that the child was still responsible for her blasphemy even after her conversion to Islam.[31] Salman Rushdie also tried the same in December 1990 but found that re-converting to Islam – without condemning his allegedly blasphemous *The Satanic Verses* – did not result in the lifting of the Ayatollah Khomeini's death sentence.[32]

Madani quotes a *fatwa* of Ibn Taymiyya which specifically contradicts the teaching that execution can be avoided by converting to Islam: "In the case of a non-Muslim who embraces Islam after committing the crime, his conversion cannot save him from the punishment."[33]

The case with Shafi'i law, which is one of the two schools applied in the Indian sub-continent, is very different. Here the same offence is to be punished by death, whether committed by a Muslim or a non-Muslim, i.e. there is no exemption for non-Muslims who are merely stating the beliefs that make them non-Muslims. The argument is that a *dhimmi* who blasphemes the Prophet has broken his contract of subjection and is thus no longer protected but liable to the same penalty as an apostate.[34]

---

31. Sardar, Asawal "Test of faith" *Newsline* (September 1995) p.59

32. Kharroufah, Prof. Dr Ala'ul Deen *The Judgement of Islam on the Crimes of Salman Rushdie "Death Sentence Still in Force"* (Kuala Lumpur, Percetakan Sentosa (KL) Sdn. Bhd., 1991) passim but especially pp.9-11; Rushdie, Salman "Why I have embraced Islam" in his *Imaginary Homelands* (London: Granta Books, 1992)

33. Madani op. cit. p.124

34. *The Hedaya* Vol. II p.221 There is one difference between a *dhimmi* and an apostate which is that if the *dhimmi* flees to

However, the school of law which is predominant in the Indian subcontinent is the Hanafi. The main Hanafi text relating to blasphemy committed by non-Muslims in the *Hedaya*[35] runs as follows:

If a Zimmee *(sic)* refuse to pay capitation-tax, or murder a Mussulman *(sic)*, or blaspheme the prophet, or commit whoredom with a Musslima, yet his contract of subjection is not dissolved; because the thing in virtue of which the destruction of Zimmees is suspended is the submitting to capitation-tax, not the actual payment thereof; and the submission to it still continues. Shafei has said that the contract of subjection is dissolved by a Zimmee's blaspheming the prophet; because if he were a believer, by such blasphemy his faith would be broken*; and hence, in the same manner, his protection is thereby broken, since the contract of subjection is merely a substitute for belief. The argument of our doctors is that the blasphemy in question is merely an act of infidelity proceeding from an infidel; and as his infidelity was no obstruction to the contract of subjection at the time of making it, this supervenient act of infidelity does not cancel it.

* That is, he would become a virtual apostate, and forfeit the protection and privileges of a believer. The consequence attending a breach of the contract of subjection is mentioned a little further on.

---

infidel territory and that territory is later conquered by Muslims who also capture the *dhimmi*, the *dhimmi* will be enslaved rather than killed as an apostate in the same situation would be.

35. *The Hedaya*: Vol. II p. 221

To summarize, according to Hanafi law, a Christian or Jew who blasphemes against the Prophet Muhammad is only acting as a non-Muslim naturally would act, and therefore should not be penalized. This is an even more lenient stance than the Maliki law, and runs contrary to the strict blasphemy legislation contained in the Pakistan Penal Code – an illustration of the fact that the traditionally dominant Hanafi law is not always followed.

Development of the legislation
Blasphemy is dealt with under Section 295 of the Pakistan Penal Code. The original law, based on the British Indian Law's Indian Penal Code of 1860 and amended by the insertion of Section 295-A in 1927,[36] simply stated that defiling any place of worship or deliberately insulting the religious beliefs of any group was to be punished with up to two years' imprisonment:

> 295. Injuring or defiling place of worship, with intent to insult the religion of any class : Whoever destroys, damages or defiles any place of worship, or any object held sacred by any class of persons with the intention of thereby insulting the religion of any class of persons or with the knowledge that any class of person is likely to consider such destruction, damage or defilement as an insult to their religion, shall be punished with imprisonment of either description for a term which may extend to two years, or with fine, or with both.

> 295-A. Deliberate and malicious acts intended to outrage

36. Criminal Law (Amendment) Act, XXV of 1927

religious feelings of any class by insulting its religion or religious beliefs : Whoever, with deliberate and malicious intention of outraging the religious feelings of any class of the citizens of Pakistan, by words, either spoken or written, or by visible representations insults the religion or religious beliefs of that class, shall be punished with imprisonment of either description for a term which may extend to two years, or with fine, or with both.[37]

This was far more liberal than the English blasphemy law which protects only a single Christian denomination – the Church of England – and has no requirement for criminal intent.

In 1982, under Zia, an amendment was added which made wilfully defiling or damaging a copy of the Qur'an an offence, punishable with mandatory life imprisonment (Section 295-B).

295-B. Defiling, etc., of Holy Qur'an : Whoever wilfully defiles, damages or desecrates a copy of the Holy Qur'an or of an extract therefrom or uses it in any derogatory manner or for any unlawful purpose shall be punishable with imprisonment for life.[38]

In 1986, an amendment added the crime of insulting the Prophet Muhammad (*Gustakh-e-Rasool*) in the form of Section 295-C:

295-C. Use of derogatory remarks, etc., in respect of the Holy Prophet : Whoever by words, either spoken or

---

37. Nizami op. cit. pp.269-271
38. ibid. pp.271-2

written, or by visible representation, or by any imputation, innuendo, or insinuation, directly or indirectly, defiles the sacred name of the Holy Prophet (peace be upon him) shall be punished with death or imprisonment for life, and shall also be liable to fine.[39]

Section 295-C is significantly harsher than the rest of Section 295 in that it omits any requirement for the offence to be committed deliberately or with criminal intent. This harsher attitude is more closely in line with English blasphemy law.

In 1991, a ruling made by the Federal Shari'at Court in October 1990[40] came into effect. This disallowed the more lenient option, on the basis that it was "repugnant to the injunctions of Islam", and the death penalty became mandatory.[41] This was supposedly in accordance with the constitutional obligation to amend any law to the extent that it has been found un-Islamic by the Federal Shari'at Court.[42]

Benazir Bhutto, then in opposition, criticised the Shari'at Court for increasing the severity of punishment for blasphemy. In response to this Maulana Abadu Sitar Niazi, the Federal Minister for Religious Affairs issued a *fatwa* in 1992 which declared her to be a "*kafir* who is liable for the

---

39. ibid. p.272

40. Points 67 and 69 of a judgement given by Gul Muhammad Khan in a case against Muhammad Ismail Qureshi (Shariat Petition No. 6/L of 1987) Federal Shariat Court, 30 October 1990 *All Pakistan Legal Decisions* Vol. XLIII (1991) FSC35

41. Khwaja, Imrana "Guilty even if proven innocent" *The Friday Times* (27 Feb – 4 Mar 1992) p.5

42. *Impact International* (13 Sept-10 Oct 1991) p.3

death penalty".[43] By denying what was considered to be an essential truth of Islam, Ms Bhutto was deemed to have committed blasphemy and thus made herself a *kafir*, effectively an apostate. (See below.) The following year, as prime minister, a case was registered against her in the Lahore High Court under Section 295-C by Zia Ul Islam, leader of the Pakistan Movement Workers, for criticizing the blasphemy law and separate electorates system.[44]

In 1993 a bill targeting Shi'as was introduced which provided for severe penalties for those guilty of defiling the names of Muhammad's family and Companions.[45] The bill was rejected by the National Assembly in July 1994.[46]

The Federal Shari'at Court had also recommended in 1991 that a clause be added to Section 295-C to include other prophets so that defiling the name of any prophet would carry a mandatory death sentence.[47] In June 1994 Judge Mian Nazir Akhtar expressed his hope that "the provision be made more comprehensive to as to make blasphemy qua other Prophets including the Holy Christ,

---

43. "Nearer, my God, to theocracy" *The Economist* (Sept 5-11, 1992) p.38; Dildar and Mughal op. cit. p.64

44. "Persecuted" *Newsline* (Nov/Dec 1993) p.26; Human Rights Commission of Pakistan, *State of Human Rights in Pakistan 1993* (1994?) p.27; Dildar and Mughal p.64. The First Information Report of the case registered against Benazir is not available to the public.

45. U.S. Department of State *Country Reports on Human Rights Practices for 1993* (February 1994) p.1377

46. "Pakistani Parliament Rejects Religion Bill" (UPI, 24 July 1994) cited in Forte op. cit. p.41

47. Point 68 of a judgement given by Gul Muhammad Khan in a case against Muhammad Ismail Qureshi (Shariat Petition No. 6/L of 1987) Federal Shariat Court, 30th October 1991 *All Pakistan Legal Decisions* Vol. XLIII (1991) FSC35

punishable with the same sentence of death".[48] The problem here is that if a Christian were to declare his or her belief that Jesus is the Son of God this would be blasphemy to a Muslim.[49] However, no such case has so far been brought.

On 16 February 1994, the Pakistan Law Commission decided to send Section 295-C to the Council of Islamic Ideology for further examination.[50] Amendments to the legislation were proposed by Benazir Bhutto's government in 1994 with the aim of somewhat redressing the balance between accuser and accused. Her cabinet approved an amendment whereby a case could not be registered until a court had enquired into it and found that there was a case to answer. If the court found the complaint to be false, the complainant would be liable to a prison sentence.[51] Her cabinet also twice examined the possibility of changing the mandatory death sentence into a prison sentence. It considered making blasphemy a non-cognizable offence in which the State had no responsiblity. It also considered the possibility of requiring proof that the blasphemy was uttered deliberately and with malicious intent.[52] When, however, on 6 May 1994 the Federal Law minister

---

48. Riaz Ahmed v. State, Criminal Miscellaneous No. 140/B of 1994, 9 June 1994 *All Pakistan Legal Decisions* Vol. XLVI (1994) Lahore 502. See also Lahore 494 for the arguments of the lawyer representing the Christian parties in this case.

49. "Pakistan: Prophet and Loss" *The Economist* (7 May 1994) p.78

50. "Draft of blasphemy law would be sent to CII" *The Frontier Post* (February 17, 1994)

51. "Amending the blasphemy law" *Dawn* (May 9, 1994)

52. Irfan, Ahmad "47 years! Time to roll back Islam" in *Impact International* (August 1994) pp.8-9; "Pakistan: Prophet

announced two amendments designed to discourage false accusations and prevent the exploitation of suspects by the police, radical Islamic groups immediately offered $40,000 for his death.[53] The government then abandoned their efforts to introduce the amendments. In February 1995 Prime Minister Benazir Bhutto stated that she still intended to amend the law, but she did not achieve this before being ousted from power.[54]

However, according to the Human Rights Commission of Pakistan (HRCP), unofficial changes made by the Government in 1995 to procedures for filing blasphemy charges have been followed by a significant drop in the number of blasphemy charges. Under the new procedures, magistrates are required to investigate allegations of blasphemy to see if they are credible before filing formal charges. The HRCP reports that in 1996 one charge was brought against a Christian, three against Ahmadiyyas and none against Muslims.[55] In May 1999 the Federal Minister for Religious Affairs, Raja Zafar-ul-Haq, announced that the initial invesitgation of an accusation of blasphemy must be made by a six-member enquiry committee comprising two noted religious leaders each from the Muslim and Christian communities, the deputy commissioner and the

---

and Loss" *The Economist* (7 May 1994) p.38 ; "Pakistan May Amend Blasphemy Law" Agence France Presse (8 May 1994); Sarwar, Beena "Pakistan: Blasphemy Law to Stay, Minor Modifications" Inter Press Service (19 July 1994)

53. "Extremists Put Contract on Law Minister" *The Independent* (11 July 1994) p.11

54. *The News International* (February 14, 1995); *International Herald Tribune* (February 15, 1995)

55. Reported in U.S. Department of State *Country Reports on Human Rights Practices for 1996* (February 1997) p.1474

Senior Superintendent of Police of the district concerned. This committee would visit the place where the case of blasphemy had been reported to verify the facts before a First Investigation Report would be registered.[56]

Also relevant is Section 298 of the Penal Code.

298. Uttering words, etc., with deliberate intent to wound religious feelings : Whoever, with the deliberate intention of wounding the religious feelings of any person, utters any word or makes any sound in the hearing of that person or makes any gesture in the sight of that person or places any object in the sight of that person, shall be punished with imprisonment of either description for a term which may extend to one year, or with fine, or with both.[57]

An amendment was added in 1980.

298-A. Use of derogatory remarks, etc., in respect of holy personages : Whoever by words, either spoken or written, or by visible representation, or by any imputation, innuendo, or insinuation, directly or indirectly, defiles the sacred name of any wife (*Ummul Mumineen*), or members of the family (A*hle-bait*), of the Holy Prophet (peace be upon him), or any of the righteous Caliphs (*Khulafa-e-Rashideen*) or companions (*Sahaaba*) of the Holy Prophet (peace be upon him) shall be punished with imprisonment of either description for a term which may extend to three years, or with fine, or with both.[58]

Further amendments were added in 1984 (298-B and

---

56. Research staff of the Christian Study Centre "Country Focus" *Al-Mushir* Vol. 41 No. 2 (1999) p.84

57. Nizami op. cit. p.274

58. ibid. pp.275-6

298-C) concerning the activities of Ahmadiyyas, specifically forbidding them from using certain Islamic epithets, descriptions and titles, from calling themselves Muslims, and from preaching or propagating their faith (see below). These amendments do not affect Christians.

At the time of writing it seems unlikely that any further amendments to these laws will be passed, owing to the atmosphere of intimidation. Death threats were issued in 1998 by the "Pakistan Taliban" against Christians and Ahmadiyyas who might protest against Section 295-C. They also threatened the "groups which were supporting the Christians' cause" and the government, should it attempt to change Section 295-C.[59] An illuminating remark was also made by the Speaker of the Pakistan National Assembly, Elahi Bux Sumro, who indicated that change in the law is unlikely. He attempted to lay blame for the current situation on both President Zia and the American government, asserting that during the 1980s the American government had sought Zia's help to oust the Russians from Afghanistan. In return the Americans refrained from challenging the passing of Section 295-C and other Islamic measures, which have now become so firmly entrenched that they cannot be changed. Whether or not this is factual and accurately interpreted, it is noteworthy that he, as a representative of the upper echelons of the government, sought to dissociate himself from Section 295-C and to place the responsibility elsewhere.[60]

What is certain is that during the 1980s the United States,

59. "Deobandis for forming "Taliban-e-Pakistan" *The News* (29 August 1998)

60. Elahi Bux Sumro, Pakistan High Commission, London,

through the CIA, did provide financial support to Pakistan's radical Islamists (as well as funds and weapons totalling over $3 billion to similar groups across the border in Afghanistan) as part of their efforts to force the Soviets out of Afghanistan.[61] This undoubtedly did much to strengthen the Islamist groups in Pakistan and increased their influence in the country. It could be said that American money funded the Islamization of Pakistan. Similarly, according to Ahmed Rashid, CIA money and weapons may have been what enabled the Taliban to gain control in Afghanistan.[62]

Illustrations

(a) **Daniel Scot** – *the first case to be registered under Section 295-C* [63]

Daniel Scot was born into a Christian family in 1951 and brought up in a Christian village in Punjab Province. In 1968, he was sent to the Islamia College Garu Mandir in Karachi. Out of 8,000 students in the science section

---

interview with author (13 May 1998)

61. Weaver, Mary Anne, untitled article reproduced in *Pakistan Christian Post* (7th September 2001) passim; Manyon, Julian "Blood and Fundamentalism" *The Spectator* (22nd September 2001)

62. Rashid, Ahmad *Taliban: Islam, Oil and the New Great Game in Central Asia* (London and New York: I.B. Tauris & Co. Ltd, 2000) pp.19,46

63. The following account is taken from Daniel Scot's own written testimony (July 1996). His case is also mentioned in Gul, Muhammad Shan "Courting the Law" *Friday Times* (29 May – 4 June 1998) p.23 and described, though with some inaccuracies particularly on dates, in Chaudhry, Gulzar Wafa "A prophetic kiss: self-sacrifice for liberation" *The Minorities' View* (September – October 1998) pp.3,5

there were only two Christians, Daniel and one other. The other Christian student deliberately did not reveal his faith, but Daniel was open about his. As a result, he was banned by his fellow students from drinking from the tap, in accordance with the belief that Muslims cannot share cooking or eating utensils with Christians (see chapter 4).

Later the same year, he entered into debate with an Ahmadiyya student in his class. The Ahmadiyya student criticised Jesus Christ, and Daniel responded by criticising the founder of the Ahmadiyya sect, Mirza Ghulam Ahmed, concluding that Mirza was insane and not a prophet. As a result the Ahmadiyya student gathered about 25 others in order to kill Daniel. The group dragged him from the room in order to push him off the edge of the balcony, but his life was saved when a professor intervened.

Always active in trying to spread the Christian faith, Daniel was accused in 1969 by Muslim students of being an American spy propagating a Western religion. In 1974 during the third year of his B.Sc. degree Daniel had a talk with Professor Kahar Ali Khan. In the context of a discussion of relativistic mass, the professor condemned Christians for not believing in Muhammad's journey to heaven. Daniel pointed out to him that many Muslims also do not believe that this journey took place physically but rather spiritually. The professor was angry, but did not refute what Daniel had said. That year, Daniel received the minimum marks to pass in all his subjects, which he believes was the result of having angered Professor Khan. The next year this professor left and Daniel received a first class M.Sc. degree.

In 1976, Daniel began teaching at a nationalized mission college in Lahore. He was transferred in 1985 to the

Government Degree College in Okara, which was a centre of the Jamaat-i-Islami. In 1986 Section 295-C of the Penal Code was introduced, and Daniel noticed a change in attitude and behaviour of his Muslim colleagues at the College. Later in the year, one of the senior physics professors asked Daniel what he thought of the Qur'an. He replied that the differences between the Bible and the Qur'an indicated that they could not have the same source. The following day, Daniel was summoned before the College Council and told that he must give up preaching Christianity and become a Muslim. If he refused a case of blasphemy would be filed against him, under the new legislation. Daniel replied that if he were to reject his Saviour Jesus Christ, who else would save him? One of the professors declared that Muhammad would save him. Daniel then quoted from the Bible, the Qur'an and the Hadith to support the sinlessness of Christ and the fact that Muhammad was not sure of his own salvation, let alone anyone else's.

As a result, Professor Changase Mohammad and Professor Omar Ali filed against Daniel a case of insulting Muhammad. The professors incited the students against him and 5,000 students turned out, many of them armed with guns and daggers, trying to find him to kill him.

A case was registered against Daniel under the newly passed Section 295-C, the First Information Report being registered on 24/26 September 1986. On 27 October 1986, 120 Christian leaders, including foreign missionaries as well as Daniel, met President Zia ul-Haq. Daniel was told that the case against him could not be dismissed, but that nothing serious would happen to him immediately. He and his wife and children spent several months in hiding in various places and eventually managed to get visas to leave for Australia.

Daniel's case was the first charge made against a Christian of defiling the name of Muhammad. It was uncharacteristic of subsequent cases against Christians in two ways:

Firstly, it appears that the conversation for which Daniel was accused of blasphemy was deliberately contrived by his opponents. Thus he did indeed criticize Muhammad, whereas in many other blasphemy cases the accused and their witnesses have vehemently denied that any derogatory remarks were made.

In most cases of blasphemy registered against Christians, it appears that the complainant has had some sort of earlier grudge against the accused and is using the blasphemy law as an easy weapon of retaliation. In Daniel's case this is also true in that his openness about his Christian faith, and his constant evangelizing had created many enemies. It is, however, unusual that the cause of the quarrel should be simply and directly religious.

(b) Gul Pervaiz Masih – *the first Christian to be convicted under the Blasphemy Law*[64]

Gul Pervaiz Masih, a Christian, lived in a village to the east of Sargodha. In 1991 he was asked by the other

---

64. Zaidi, Mazhar "Doomed by Faith" in *Newsline* (May 1994) pp.132-3; *The 'Blasphemy' Episodes: An HRCP inquiry* (Human Rights Commission of Pakistan, no date given); Judgment in the Court of Khan Talib Hussain Baloch, Additional Sessions Judge, Sargodha, Sessions Case No. 6 of 1992, Sessions Trial No. 6 of 1992, The State vs. Gul Masih s/o Dolat Masih caste Christian r/o Chak No. 46 N.B. City Sargodha

villagers to have the communal water tap repaired, and he was given 35 rupees to get the job done. The tap was repaired, but soon failed again, and on 10 December 1991 Gul's neighbour, Sajjad Hussain, allegedly a member of the Sipah-e-Sahaba (SSP), a militant Sunni group which is violently anti-Shi'a, questioned Gul about the faulty repair job, implying that Gul had pocketed the money. A heated argument followed, moving on to politics and religion, drawing other villagers to listen, including Gul's brother Bashir. Bashir persuaded Gul and Sajjad Hussain to make peace.

However, Rasheed Tunda, an employee of a local landowner called Mohammad Aslam Kachela, went to the local police station and filed a First Information Report (FIR) dated 13 December 1991 against the two Masih brothers on behalf of Sajjad Hussain. According to Gul Masih, Rasheed Tunda had had a grudge against him, because Gul admonished him for harassing the village women.

The brothers were arrested by the police on 14 December 1991. In the FIR, Sajjad Hussain accused Gul of making derogatory statements about the Prophet Muhammad and his wife Aisha. He also alleged that Gul had condemned some local maulanas, saying that they often indulged in adultery.

According to Bashir Masih, his brother had not made any defamatory remarks, but Aslam Kachela had manufactured the incident as part of his campaign to get elected in the local bodies election. There was a dispute between him and Aziz Masih, a brother of Gul and Bashir, who was also prominent in local politics and who had formerly been his ally.

The police declared Bashir innocent and released him on 13 January 1992. They also said there was no substance in the case against Gul, but they were not empowered to release him. No lawyer could be found to represent the Masihs, until their case was taken up by the Human Rights Commission of Pakistan. Posters put up in the town by mullahs called for the death of both brothers. They also appointed death squads of young college students to carry this out. After the release of Bashir Masih there were demonstrations in the streets calling for him to be re-arrested and both brothers to be killed.

At the trial two prosecution witnesses denied that Gul had made any derogatory statements against the Prophet Muhammad or his wife. Only Sajjad Hussain spoke against him. Nevertheless the Sessions Judge stated in his judgement of 2 November 1992:

> Sajjad Hussain is a young man of 21 years age, student of the 4th year with a beard and out look *(sic)* of being a true Muslim and I have no reason to disbelieve him... In my view the prosecution has succeeded to prove the guilt of the accused beyond any reasonable doubt. I see no mitigating circumstances in favour of the accused nor any such is pointed out to me, therefore, accused is convicted u/o. 295-C PPC and sentenced to death and fine of rupees five thousands.[65]

---

65. Judgement in the court of Khan Talib Hussain Baloch pp. 10-11

Gul Masih lodged an appeal against the death sentence on 5 November 1992.[66] He was acquitted by the Lahore High Court on 27 November 1994, and released from prison.[67] He is now living in Europe.

Gul Masih was the first Christian to be convicted under Section 295-C. His case is a clear illustration of a feature which typifies the majority of blasphemy cases against Christians, namely, that the accusation is made by someone who already has a reason to dislike the accused and to want to harm him. The blasphemy law is thus being used as a safe way to retaliate. In Gul Masih's case, there appear to have been two factors – Gul's ongoing disagreement with Rasheed Tunda about the treatment of women (they had even come to blows about this) and the local political situation described above. In Tahir Iqbal's case (see below), both accused and accuser offered coaching to children, but Tahir Iqbal had recently started to offer his lessons free of charge thus undercutting his accuser Peerzada Ali Ahmed Sabir. In the case of thirteen-year-old Salamat Masih, accused in regard to an incident on 9 May 1993, he was identified by a boy who had reportedly had a fight with him a day earlier.[68] Chand Barkat, a bangle seller, was accused under Section 295-C in a case filed on 10 October 1991, by a competitor of his in the local market

66. *The Guardian* (6 November 1992)

67. U.S. Department of State *Country Reports on Human Rights Practices for 1994,* (U.S. Government Printing Office, February 1995) p. 1253; Mughal, Aftab Alexander "Freedom Without Fear" *Newsline,* December 1994

68. Shakoore, S. "Pakistan for all?" in *Frontier Post* (date unknown, probably December 1993 or January 1994) pp.30-31

who resented the success of Chand's stall.[69] The accusations of desecrating the Qur'an which led to the rioting in Shanti Nagar and area (see below) were thought by many to have been concocted by police officers who had been been accused of desecrating a Bible by some Christians in Shanti Nagar.

(c) Tahir Iqbal – *allegedly killed because of a charge of blasphemy*[70]

Tahir Iqbal was born into a Muslim family in 1959. In 1984 he became paralysed in his lower limbs, and was obliged to retire from his job as a mechanic with the Pakistan Air Force. He converted to Christianity and was baptized.

A First Information Report (FIR) was filed against him on 7 December 1990 by Peerzada Ali Ahmed Sabir.[71] He was immediately arrested and imprisoned in Kokhlapat Central Jail where he died on 19 July 1992.

According to the FIR, Tahir Iqbal had converted from Islam to Christianity; was coaching Muslim children free of charge and criticizing Islam to them; claimed that he could prove from the Qur'an that "illicit intercourse, drinking and sodomy are justified in Islam"; prepared a schedule mentioning various verses and chapters of the Qur'an "and he has marked and underlined those various verses according to his references"; abused Islam and the

---

69. Khwaja, Imrana "Guilty even if proven innocent" *The Friday Times* (27 Feb – 4 Mar 1992) p.5

70. First Information Report No. 297/90 Police Station South Cantonment, Lahore (7 December 1990); Ismail, Zafar, "Report on the Tahir Iqbal Case" (5 August 1992, unpublished)

71. First Information Report No. 297/90, Lahore Cantonment Police Station

Prophet Muhammad when he heard the call to prayer. Whilst offences against all three parts of Section 295 of the Pakistan Penal Code were listed in the FIR, the police charged him under Section 295B only (desecration of the Qur'an). The complainant himself offered coaching to children but he charged for his lessons.

Mullahs openly voiced threats against Tahir Iqbal's advocate and declared that they would kill Tahir Iqbal if he were released on bail. Local Christians felt that prison was the safest place for him, and Tahir Iqbal himself expressed this opinion.

While in prison, Tahir is reported to have continued to slander the religion of Islam and the prophet Muhammad. This resulted in additional charges being made against him under other sections of the Penal Code.[72]

The Christian community were not in favour of publicity for Tahir's case, feeling that this would lead to open confrontation with the mullahs and hence jeopardize his safety. It was, however, brought into the limelight by others: firstly by the Human Rights Commission of Pakistan when they decided to take the bail petition to the High Court (July 1991), then by the publication of an article in *The Economist* (October 5, 1991), then an article by the Western Christian news agency News Network International (December 12, 1991) and then a report by the Western Christian missionary organization Open Doors (June 1992). This publicity had exactly the effect which the Pakistani Christians had feared. The open involvement of the two Western Christian groups, News Network International and Open Doors, was interpreted by Muslims

---

72. Ismail, Zafar, "Report on the Tahir Iqbal Case" p.2

as a crusade against Islam.

In March 1992 Peerzada Ali Ahmed Sabir submitted an application to Additional Sessions Judge Sabah Mohyuddin that Tahir Iqbal be sentenced to death for apostasy from Islam. The case was heard on 23 April 1992 by Judge Sabah Mohyuddin, who dismissed the application, saying that the accused would only be sentenced to death if the prosecution could prove that he had defiled the name of Muhammad.[73]

Tahir Iqbal died some time during the night of 19-20 July 1992. There was no post mortem, but some of the Christian community believe that he was murdered.[74]

Tahir Iqbal's case illustrates a feature of several blasphemy cases against Christians, namely, that the accused is murdered before the due process of law has been completed. Other examples are given below. Another characteristic of Tahir Iqbal's case is that he made his situation worse than it needed to have been, in his case by continuing to make blasphemous remarks while in prison. In a minority of other cases, this has also appeared to happen – sometimes the blasphemer has been known to be mentally unbalanced. An example of this is Anwar Masih, a heroin addict who had converted from Christianity to Islam and then back to Christianity again, believed by

---

73. "Convert in Christianity dies mysteriously in prison" *The Friday Times* (30 July– 5 August 1992) p.3; *Raiwind Diocesan Newsletter* (September 1992)

74. "Christians feel insecure after prisoner's mysterious death" *The News*, Vol. 2 No. 227 (23 July 1992); "Bearing the Cross" *Newsline*, September 1992; Allen, Trevor "Report on the death of Tahir Iqbal" (undated MS reporting information he received on 7 October 1992 in Lahore)

his family to be insane, who had an FIR filed against him on 2 February 1993 under Section 295-C.[75] Mohammad Arshad Javaid, a Muslim from Bahawalpur, reportedly mentally unsound, was convicted of blasphemy and sentenced to death.[76] (He was eventually acquitted on appeal in January 1995, on the grounds of insanity.[77])

Tahir Iqbal's case also illustrates the link between apostasy and blasphemy (see below). While the former is a capital offence under the Shari'ah and the latter is considered much less serious, in Pakistani law the situation is reversed. Indeed, apostasy is not punishable at all according to the Pakistan Penal Code. His conversion to Christianity was the first offence listed against him in the FIR, but is not an offence under law, so he could not be charged with it. The blasphemy charge may have been, to a greater or lesser extent, a substitute for the apostasy charge which his accuser would have liked to make had it been available within the scope of the Pakistan Penal Code. It is significant that his step-mother, Hamida Bibi, who attended the court several times with the prosecution witnesses, had often condemned Tahir Iqbal for his apostasy, and asked the court to punish him according to Shari'ah.[78] However, it could be argued that blasphemy very often amounts to apostasy if committed by a Muslim (see below).

75. Mir, Anita "That way madness lies..." *The Frontier Post* (29 January 1994)

76. U.S. Department of State *Country Reports on Human Rights Practices for 1994* (February 1995) p. 1253

77. Dildar and Mughal op. cit. p.67

78. Shakir op. cit. p.123

(d) Shanti Nagar and area – *the first – and so far the only – example of mass rioting and large-scale destruction of property as a result of an accusation of blasphemy*[79]

The twin villages of Shanti Nagar and Tibba Colony (Bhoota Abad) lie about 12km east of Khanewal in the Punjab. Most Christians work on the land and are considered to be economically well off.

On 14 January 1997 three police officers raided the Shanti Nagar home of Raj Paul, a 60-year old Christian also known as Raji Baba, who was suspected of running a gambling den and an alcohol distillery. During the search one officer dropped a copy of the Bible on the floor. Raji Baba pleaded to be allowed to pick the Bible up. The officer forbade him to do so, and kicked the Bible. Raji Baba was taken to the police station.

Some residents of Shanti Nagar approached Khanewal Deputy Superintendent of Police Habib Ahmed Ghumman and another police officer named Azizur Rehman Dogar to seek Raji's release and the registration of a case of

---

79. Wafa, Gulzar (14 February 1997); *The Daily Dawn* (13 February 1997); *The Daily Khabren* (8 February 1997); Aftab, Fauzia (22 February 1997); *The Friday Times* (20-26 February 1997); *The Nation* (7 February 1997, 8 February 1997); Dean, George "Incident at Shanti Nagar, Pakistan, Feb 5th and 6th 1997"(8 February 1997); "Muslims blaming Christians burning Holy Qur'an" (unidentified Catholic source); Fazal, Asghar (teacher at St Joseph's Catholic School, Khanewal) (11 February 1997); Yusaf, Patras, Catholic Bishop of Multan in press release of 8 February 1997 issued by Caritas Pakistan; Ismail, Zafar (14 February 1997); *Daily Jang* (8 February 1997); Azariah, Bishop Samuel and nine other Christian leaders *Press Conference on the Desecration of Churches, the Holy Bibles, and the Houses of Christian in Khanewal and Shantinagar* (8 February 1997).

desecration of the Bible against the police officials concerned. The police responded by releasing Raji Baba but refused to register a case of desecration. The Christians increased their protest, and organized a protest procession on 17 January. This moved the senior police officials to suspend and order the arrest of the police officers involved in the incident. A First Information Report (FIR) was registered under Sections 452, 148 and 149 of the Pakistan Penal Code.[80] But before their arrest, the police officials arranged bail for themselves. They were not treated as accused persons, but were actually called on to go on duty during the elections of 3 February.

When Christians saw these police officers on duty again during the elections (3 February 1997), a huge Christian protest was organised against the civil authorities, demanding the immediate arrest of the police officers involved and the registration of another FIR under section 295-A. The Khanewal Deputy Commissioner, Mr. Haseeb Atthar, ordered the registration of the FIR and an immediate dismissal of the police officer who was chiefly involved in desecrating the Bible.

An announcement that torn or burnt pages of the Qur'an, with blasphemous statements written on them had been found near a bridge 6.5 km from Khanewal and 2.5 km from Shanti Nagar was made from Jamia Masjid Gapwal-Khanewal at 10.30 p.m. on 5 February. Both Christians and Muslims of Shanti Nagar denied the truth of the allegation. The announcement included the information that the desecration was blamed on a Christian

---

80. These Sections are concerned with trespass and armed rioting.

resident of Shanti Nagar known as Raji Baba. Afterwards
motorists and motorcyclists, equipped with megaphones,
rode around Khanewal spreading the news and urging the
Muslim inhabitants to gather for revenge. Several
announcements were made from mosques in and around
Khanewal, urging Muslims to assemble to march to Shanti
Nagar and other Christian localities to avenge the alleged
desecration.

A mob of several thousand Muslims assembled in
Khanewal the same evening and marched towards Shanti
Nagar and Tibba Colony. The police intervened and the
mob returned to Khanewal, setting fire to Christian
property on the way.

The following morning the number of Muslims involved
in the rioting had risen to between 20,000 and 30,000.[81]
More damage was done to Christian property in Khanewal,
while the largest section of the crowd attacked Shanti
Nagar. By 9.00 a.m. the Muslims had reached the village,
and the police withdrew. The rioters, led by Muslim clerics,
were armed with sticks, axes, stones, rocks, knives, firearms,
explosives and petrol bombs. Homes were looted and then
set on fire, resulting in the destruction of 785 of the 905
houses in Shanti Nagar, Tibba Colony and four other
settlements nearby. Telephone and electricity connections
were broken. Taps, water pumps and water tanks were
damaged, making it impossible to extinguish the flames.

---

81. Ahmed, Khaled "The sack of Shantinagar" *The Friday
Times* (20-26 February 1997) p.8; George, Sister Naseem and
Mughal, Aftab Alexander *Shantinagar's Incident: special report*
(Justice and Peace Commission of the Conference of Major
Religious Superiors in Pakistan, 13 February 1997);
"Shantinagar licks its wounds" in *Dawn* (February 13, 1997)
p.8

Cattle were driven away. A number of women and girls disappeared. Some later reported that they had been kidnapped. At least ten suffered attempts to force them to recite the Muslim creed (the implication of this for their marriages is described in chapter 4). They were threatened with violence. Some may have been raped, though families will not admit to such a dishonour.[82] Eventually the army intervened and the rioters left. Similar attacks were made on the Christian *basti* of Civil Lines in Khanewal, home to around 250 families. Sixteen houses, five shops and a church were burnt.[83]

---

82. *The Friday Times* (20-26 February 1997); *The Daily Dawn* (13 February 1997); *The Daily Khabren* (8 February 1997); Yusaf, Patras op. cit.; Ismail, Zafar (14 February 1997); Wafa, Gulzar (14 February 1997); Reuters in *Daily Jang*, (7 February 1997)

83. The total list of damaged buildings is as follows:
CHURCHES
1. Catholic Church and Priest's residence, Khanewal
2. COP Church and Pastor's house, Khanewal
3. Salvation Army Church, Khanewal
4. Baptist Church, Khanewal
5. Catholic Church and Priest's residence, Shanti Nagar
6. Salvation Army Church and Pastor's house, Shanti Nagar
7. Full Gospel Assemblies Church, Shanti Nagar
8. Calvary Baptist Church, Shanti Nagar
9. Salvation Army Church and Pastor's house, Tibba Colony
10. Full Gospel Assemblies Church, Tibba Colony
11. Catholic Church, Chak 81-82/10-R
12. COP Church, Chak 81-82/10-R
13. Catholic Church, Chak 83-85/10-R
14. COP Church, Chak 85-86/10-R
15. Catholic Church, Chak 87/10-R

The event appears to have been carefully planned and orchestrated, possibly by the suspended police officers. The date on which the accusations of desecration was made was the 27th of Ramadan, " the night of power", when the mosques were full and news could be spread quickly.

Investigation and interviews with district administration and police officials showed that the allegation against Raji Baba was completely baseless.[84] The two religious communities in the area had previously lived in peace, despite a strong presence of the Sipha-e-Sahaba in Khanewal.

---

16. COP Church, Chak 12, Rakh Kabirwala
DISPENSARIES
1. Salvation Army Dispensary, Khaniwal
2. Private Hospital of Dr. Izzat Jamal, near Shanti Nagar
3. Salvation Army Dispensary, Shanti Nagar
SCHOOLS AND HOSTELS
1. St. Joseph's High School, Khanewal
2. St. Joseph's Boys' Hostel, Khanewal
3. Salvation Army High School, Shanti Nagar
4. Christian Education Centre, Chak 81-82/10-R
PROPERTIES
1. Civil Lines, Khanewal: 5 houses and 15 shops, affected 26 families of 200 members
2. Shanti Nagar: 306 houses and 80 shops, affected 326 families of 5500 members
3. Tibba Colony: 285 houses and 25 shops, affected 305 families of 2874 members

Sources: Justice and Peace Commission (February 13, 1997); Asghar Fazal (February 11, 1997); Gulzar Wafa (February 14, 1997) all cited in Ismail, Zafar *Pakistan: Violence in Shanti Nagar – Khanewal February 5 and 6, 1997* (17 March 1997)

84. "Shantinagar licks its wounds" in *Dawn* (February 13, 1997) p.7

The lives of some Christian clergy in Khanewal were saved by their Muslim neighbours. Some of the Muslim religious leaders whose names were used to incite the crowd had themselves condemned the violence and declared the alleged desecration of the Holy Qur'an to be false. Some Muslim religious leaders attempted to defuse the situation and to calm the frenzied crowd.[85]

There is some suspicion that those orchestrating the riots may have sought help from the Sipah-e-Sahaba in Khanewal and Harakat-ul-Ansar, a militant group fighting for the liberation of Indian-occupied Kashmir.[86] The

---

85. These included Qazi Hussain Ahmad, the Amir of the Jama'at-e-Islami, appealed for peace, and condemned the desceration of the Qur'an and the arson that followed. He declared that Christians could not have been responsible for desecrating the Qur'an as minorities could not be involved in such a heinous act as they comprise downtrodden classes who are harmless. His statements had a degree of ambiguity since he went on to say that the act of an individual cannot be blamed on the whole community. He said it was the responsibility of Muslims to safeguard the life and property of minorities. Maulana Ajmal Qadiri, a leader of the Jamiat-Ulama-e-Islam, blamed the police for what had happened, and urged the president to ask the Christians for forgiveness. Muslim members of the local Peace Committee, Hakim Mohamad Alim, Mir Zahirul Hassan, Maulana Mohamad Abass Akhtar, Sufi Abdul Haq Rizivi, Fateh Mohamad Hamadi and Inam Ullah Qureshi, and two local leaders of the Jama'at-i-Islami, Sufi Mohamad Sabir and Aziz Latif, expressed that they were deeply grieved by the loss suffered by their Christian brothers, and expressed their willingness to assist them.

86. "Shantinagar licks its wounds" in *Dawn* (February 13, 1997) p.8; Howard, Roger "Wrath of Islam: the HUA analysed" in *Jane's Intelligence Review* (October 1997) pp.467-8

criminalization of Sipah-e-Sahaba as a terrorist organisation was confirmed by the police high command in Punjab through a press conference in which Sipah offenders confessed to bank robberies and other violent crimes.[87] Sipah-e-Sahaba is strengthened and given immunity by its offshoot Harakat-ul-Ansar, which the state authorities have to tolerate because of its participation in the Kashmir "*jihad*". Harakat-ul-Ansar has killed a number of Shi'a leaders in the province. In October 1996, Sipah-e-Jhangvi (another offshoot of Sipah-e-Sahaba) killed a Shi'a deputy commissioner, Ali Raza Kharal, in Khanewal. Leaders of both Sipah-e-Jhangvi and Harakat-ul-Ansar were members of the Punjab and National Assemblies after the 1993 elections and wielded considerable political influence in Khanewal.

These events illustrate the way in which an allegation of blasphemy or desecration could incite not just a few zealous individuals to seek out the alleged culprit and kill him or her, but tens of thousands of people to large-scale, well organized and well equipped attacks on any Christian property which they could find. That such a large number should take part in the violence indicates that many if not most of them must have ordinarily been moderate Muslims rather than extremists. The violence at Shanti Nagar also illustrates how the existence of the blasphemy law, which normally targets individuals, can impact communal relations on a much wider scale. At the time of writing this case is the only example of its kind. It remains to be seen if this pattern will be repeated in future blasphemy cases.

---

87. Ahmed, Khaled op. cit.

Misuse of the blasphemy law

The decision of the Federal Shariat Court in 1991 to prescribe a mandatory death sentence for derogatory remarks against the Prophet Muhammad made the blasphemy law a deadly weapon. The punishment was the most severe possible. Yet the crime was only a matter of spoken words; therefore an accusation was easy to make and hard to disprove. The accuser ran no risk in making the accusation. Many if not most accusations of defiling the Prophet's name appear to have been made by individuals who already had a grudge against the accused for some completely separate reason. Another important aspect is that once an accusation has been made, some extremist Muslims may see it as their duty to kill the person concerned, whether or not their guilt has been proven. Processions and calls for their death increase the popular feeling against the accused.

Naimat Ahmer, a Christian school-teacher, was accused of blasphemy against the Prophet and stabbed to death by Farooq Ahmed, who had read about the alleged blasphemy in an anonymous pamphlet (6 January 1992). Tahir Iqbal died in mysterious circumstances in jail after much publicity of his case (20 July 1992) – see above. Bantu Masih was stabbed by his accuser (May 1991) while in police custody. He never recovered from the stabbing and died on 23 October 1992.[88] Manzoor Masih was shot dead as he emerged from the Lahore High Court, having been granted bail on 5 April 1994.[89]

According to the Human Rights Commission of

---

88. Sarwar, Beena "God forbid..." *Frontier Post* (25 March 1993)

89. Sarwar "God forbid..."; *The Herald* (May 1994) p.52

Pakistan:

> The severity of the punishment apparently oversensitises
> weaker or more fanatical elements and makes them eager
> to become ready agents of the presumed divine wrath
> themselves. It also gives unscrupulous elements in society
> a handle to play their own prejudices against, or settle
> their scores with, individuals by easily alleging blasphemy
> and putting them in a difficult spot.[90]

The left-wing daily newspaper, *The Frontier Post*,
reported the concern of the Pakistan Law Commission over
the way Section 295-C is misused by the police and
sectarian organisations. The paper commented:

> It is no secret now that the law has been used to harass
> and persecute the minorities, particularly. A number of
> persons including children have been sent to jail under
> the law on the basis of allegations of questionable veracity
> to the effect that by some word or deed they had
> deliberately sought to insult the name of the Holy Prophet
> (PBUH). The environment of hysteria that is rapidly built
> up around such cases by the interested parties usually
> makes it very difficult for the victims to obtain relief from
> the courts. A central problem with the law is that the
> term 'defile' is open to all kinds of interpretation and, on
> the other hand, contrary to what is a major consideration
> in criminal law, it does not accord any room to the issue

---

90. "Blasphemy Laws Targeting Minorities: an inquiry"
Human Rights Commission of Pakistan Newsletter Vol.3 No.
2 (April 1992) p.28

of motive or intent. Even Section 295-B inserted by General Zia in 1982 makes wilfulness a crucial factor constituting offence. Other similar laws also accord due importance to motive and the issue of offence arises only when something is considered to have been deliberately done in order to insult religion or hurt someone's feelings.

The Law Commission is in favour of sending the law for further consideration to the Council of Islamic Ideology. The question is whether Section 295-C is really needed. As far as any deliberate insult to the name of the Holy Prophet (PBUH) is concerned such an offence is already covered under section 295 or 298. The CII should equally consider ways of tightening the law to bring to book those guilty of false accusations of blasphemy for ulterior, self-serving motives. Beyond that the media must be used extensively to inculcate a better understanding of religion and to prevent its use, so contrary to the spirit, as an instrument of repression against the weaker sections of our society.[91]

Anita Mir, a respected left-wing journalist, writing in *The Frontier Post* a few days earlier, asserted that the blasphemy law and the *Hudood* Ordinance "encourage some people to victimize other people". Religious minorities, she claimed, are seen as enemies inside the country, just as India and the West are seen as external enemies. "Christians are persecuted in this country because: 1) we have given people

---

91. "Misuse of blasphemy law" *The Frontier Post* (19 February 1994)

a law which invites them to make victims of Christians; 2) Pakistani Christians, though indigenous to the land, are seen to be connected with the white man (their shared religion). From here it is a short step to anger at the white man's dominance and revenge – taken out on local Christians."[92]

Apostasy Law

Introduction

Apostasy (*ridda* or *irtidad*) is often considered in Islam to be a *hadd* crime.[93] This puts it in the same category as adultery, false accusation of adultery, drinking alcohol, theft, and highway robbery (and in some lists rebellion against the government). The punishments specified for the five main *hudood* offences include death (by stoning, crucifixion or beheading), amputation of hands and/or feet, whipping and banishment.[94] There are detailed rules concerning the evidence required to prove a *hadd* offence – either voluntary confession, or the testimony of a certain number of adult male Muslim witnesses (four for adultery, two for the other offences), or indisputable circumstantial evidence.[95] The evidential requirements for apostasy vary

---

92. Mir, Anita "Citadels of difference?" *The Frontier Post* (16 February 1994)

93. The main alternative to a *hadd* offence is a *ta'zir* offence i.e. an offence whose punishment is not specified in the Qur'an or *Sunnah* but is left to the discretion of the legitimate authorities. Some discussion of whether apostasy is a *hadd* offence or a *ta'zir* offence is given in M.S. El-Awa *Punishment in Islamic Law: a comparative study* (Indianapolis: American Trust Publication, 1982) pp.54-6, 61-2

94. Sidahmad, Muhammad 'ata Alsid *The Hudud* (Petaling Jaya: Muhammad 'Ata al Sid Sid Ahmad, 1995) pp.219-254

95. Sidahmad op. cit. pp.146-208

according to different schools of law. Unsurprisingly, Hanafi Sunni law, which does not include apostasy among the *hudood*, has no mention of proving apostasy by the witness of others,[96] whereas some Shi'a statements include provision for not only confession[97] but also the witness of "two just and truthful men".[98]

Apostasy is listed as a *hadd* crime by the Shafi'i, Maliki and Hanbali schools of law. The Hanafi school separates it from the *hudood* crimes, but compares it to a *hadd* crime.[99] Unlike most of the *hudood* offences, there is no clear-cut penalty prescribed in the Qur'an for apostasy. Indeed, some interpreters consider that the Qur'an does not impose any earthly penalty at all, although the apostate is condemned to eternal damnation.

Nevertheless, the death penalty for apostasy is clearly specified in all four main schools of law,[100] and the reasoning which is sometimes given for such a punishment is the analogy with treason, for rejecting the Islamic religion is seen as equivalent to rejecting the Islamic state. This was the case for example, soon after the death of Muhammad, when many tribes apostatized from Islam and rebelled

---

96. The *Hedaya*, Vol. II pp. 225-246

97. "Apostasy is a glaring sin in Islam" *Kayhan International* (3 March 1986) cited in Appendix B of Syed Silas Husain and Ernest Hahn's translated and annotated *The Punishment of the Apostate According to Islamic Law* by Abul Ala Mawdudi (no publisher given, 1994) p.83

98. Khomeini, Ayatollah Imam *Tahrir al-Wassilah* vol. 2 p. 496 cited in *Kayhan International* (3 March 1986) in Mawdudi *The punishment of the apostate* p.83

99. Sidahmad op. cit. pp.36-40

100. except for women in the Hanafi school, *The Hedaya* vol. II p.227

against Muslim rule. It continues to be a key argument.[101] Some Muslim scholars, for example the renowned Pakistani jurist, S.A. Rahman, have argued that apostasy which is not accompanied by rebellion against the Islamic state should not be punished.[102] However, the distinction between on the one hand merely falling from faith, and on the other hand falling from faith accompanied by rebellion is not recognized in classical Islam.[103] Indeed, not only are those who leave the faith normally considered to be in rebellion against Islamic rule, but often those who rebel against Islamic rule are considered to have thereby proved themselves to be apostates.[104]

Khadduri draws a distinction between, on the one hand, individual apostates who have left Islam but with no intention of leaving the Islamic territory and, on the other hand, a group of apostates who have left the territory of Islam. The former are still to receive capital punishment, while the latter will find themselves the target of a *jihad*.[105]

---

101. Dr Suhaib Hasan, Secretary of the Islamic Shari'a Council (UK) uses this argument in a letter to *The Times* (27 May 1998) stating that "Apostasy is treated as a crime against the Muslim State, exactly like treason, and is punished accordingly."

102. Rahman, S.A. op. cit. pp.161-166

103. See, for example, Mawdudi *The Punishment of the Apostate* pp.46-52,61-64

104. For example, a Muslim who refuses to pay *zakat* (compulsory alms, one of Islam's five "pillars" – practical duties) is considered an apostate (though one who refuses to pay while acknowledging the obligation to do so is defined as a rebel). See Joel L. Kraemer "Apostates, rebels and brigands" *Israel Oriental Studies* 10 (1980) pp.36-7; Mawdudi *The Punishment of the Apostate* pp.26-27

105. Khadduri op. cit. pp.76-7, 149-152

How, it may be asked, can a Muslim who leaves Islam for one of the other God-ordained religions – Christianity and Judaism – be regarded as committing treason? In effect, all he is doing is entering a religion which already exists within Muslim society with the special protected *dhimmi* status. This, however, is not the Islamic view of an apostate's position. According to Islam, an apostate cannot be considered a *dhimmi* because he has not paid *jizya*, the obligatory payment by *dhimmi* to their Muslim rulers in return for their protection. An apostate is neither a Muslim nor a *dhimmi*, therefore an apostate is an infidel.[106] The *Hedaya* expressly forbids not only the imposition of *jizya* on apostates but also the acceptance of *jizya* from them.[107] An apostate is thus prevented from making any voluntary payment of *jizya* and has no way in which to be recognized as a *dhimmi*. Mawdudi asserts that it is a universal feature of human nature to distinguish between "one who was never affiliated and another who was affiliated and then severed the affiliation".[108]

Basis in Shari'ah

Islamic law (Shari'ah) , both Sunni and Shi'a, lays down that an adult male Muslim who chooses another religion should be killed. It was derived from the Qur'an and *ahadith* as follows. In the Qur'an there is an emphasis on God's punishment of apostates in the next life. "Anyone who, after accepting faith in God, utters disbelief – except under compulsion, his heart remaining firm in faith – but such as open their breast to unbelief, – on them is wrath from God,

106. The *Hedaya*, Vol. II pp.213,226; Khadduri op. cit. p.76
107. The *Hedaya* Vol. II p. 213
108. Mawdudi *The Punishment of the Apostate* pp.57-61

and theirs will be a dreadful penalty ... without doubt, in the hereafter they will perish" (S.16:106,109). Similar teaching is found in S.88:23,24; 3:86-91; 4:137 and 5:54).

Several controversial verses or passages are used by different interpreters to add weight to one or other side of the argument. These include:

S.2:217 speaks of those who die as unbelievers, but is sometimes mistranslated as a command that apostates should die for their apostasy.[109]

S.9.11-12 commands "fight ye the chiefs of unfaith", understood by Mawdudi[110] and by Muhammad Iqbal Siddiqi, a scholar who follows Mawdudi's school,[111] as a command to execute apostates but by some other commentators[112] as referring to pagans.

The "Sword Verse" S.9:5 states "Fight and slay the pagans wherever ye find them".[113] Taken at face value, this would appear to say that every non-Muslim (except those who had made a special arrangement with the Muslims), whether or not he has ever professed Islam, should be killed, but this has almost never been taken literally.

---

109. For example, Ath Tha'alibi, Fakhr-ud-Din-ar-Razi, also *Al-Khazan* commentary (used at Al-Azhar) which quotes from Malik ibn Anas, Ahmad ibn Hanbal and others, both cited in S.M. Zwemer *The Law of Apostasy in Islam* (London: Marshall Brothers, Ltd, 1924). p.34

110. Mawdudi *The Punishment of the Apostate* pp.18-19

111. Siddiqi, Muhammad Iqbal *The Penal Law of Islam* (Lahore: Kazi Publications, 1979) p. 97

112. For example, A. Yusuf Ali's commentary in *The Holy Qur'an: Text, Translation and Commentary* pp. 440-441

113. Mentioned in the context of apostates in *The Hedaya* Vol. II p.226

S.4:88-89 refer to the *munafiqun*, a group of Muslim dissenters led by Abdullah b. Ubayy, who deserted the rest of the Muslims at the Battle of Uhud in 625 and are to be killed. Some Muslim commentators consider the *munafiqun* to be apostates (as indeed they are described in S.63:3 and S.9:73-87), and extend the command to all apostates.[114]

S:2:256 "Let there be no compulsion in religion" is a verse whose meaning and applicability have been much debated. It is sometimes used as an argument against the death penalty for apostasy[115] but others believe that it merely means that no one can be forced into the Islamic faith.[116]

Many *ahadith* report Muhammad's words transmitted by Ibn 'Abbas and others, "Slay him who changes his religion" (e.g. Bukhari, Ibn Madja, Nasa'i). According to another *hadith* of Ibn 'Abbas and Aisha it is permissible to take the life of someone who "abandons his religion and separates himself from the community" (Bukhari, Muslim, Nasa'i). There are many reports in the form of a list of occasions when it is permitted to kill a Muslim, that is, in cases of adultery, murder and apostasy.[117] The question of

---

114. For example, Baidhawi, quoted in Zwemer op. cit. pp.33-4; al-Tabari *Gami' al-bayan fi tafsir al-Qur'an* ed. A.M. Sakir and M.M. Sakir (Cairo, 1954) IX p.18, cited in Kraemer op. cit. p.35; al-Zamakhshari *Al-Kashshaf* (Cairo, 1966) I p.551, cited in Kraemer op. cit. p.35; Marmaduke Pickthall *The Meaning of the Glorious Qur'an: text and explanatory translation* (Delhi: Taj Company, 1988) p.89 footnote

115. For example Rahman, S.A. p.160

116. Maududi, S. Abul A'la *The Meaning of the Quran* (Lahore: Islamic Publications (Pvt.) Limited, 13th edition, 1993) Vol. I p.186, note 285 p.186

117. Siddiqi *op. cit.* pp.99-101; Zwemer *op. cit.* pp.37-8; El-Awa op. cit. p.52

the correct method to be used in killing an apostate was given attention in various *ahadith* and commentaries, normally beheading.[118] There are also *ahadith* which report Muhammad himself ordering the execution of specific individual apostates, and not drawing the line at women.[119]

There are contradictory traditions concerning whether an apostate should be given a chance to repent. Some *ahadith* say that God will not accept the repentance of someone who has previously renounced Islam, while others say that even Muhammad forgave apostates.[120]

Mawdudi cites ten examples of the execution of apostates during the period of the Rightly Guided Caliphs, claiming that death was always the punishment for apostasy under these four caliphs. Mawdudi further adds the example of the first Caliph's *jihad* against apostates, and argues that the war was waged to counter apostasy, not to counter rebellion.[121]

Sunni Schools
All four schools agree on capital punishment for adult male apostates. A summary of Sunni laws on apostasy is given in Mohammed Al Abdari Ibn Hadj's legal treatise, *Al*

118. See, for example, Heffening W. "Murtadd" in C.E. Bosworth, E. van Donzel, W.P. Heinrichs and C. Pellat (eds.) *The Encyclopaedia of Islam*, new edition (Leiden: Brill, 1993) Vol VII p.635; "Apostasy from Islam" in T.P. Hughes *Dictionary of Islam* (Lahore: Premier Book House) p.16

119. For example, Baihaqi and Daraquini quoted in Siddiqi op. cit. pp.103-4

120. For examples and lists of *ahadith*, see "Murtadd" in Gibb, H.A.R. and Kramers, J.H. *Shorter Encyclopaedia of Islam* (Leiden: Brill, 1974) p.413

121. Mawdudi *The Punishment of the Apostate* pp.22-27

Madkhal: "As for apostates, it is permitted to kill them by facing them or coming upon them from behind, just as in the case of polytheists. Secondly, their blood if shed brings no vengeance. Thirdly, their property is the spoil of true believers. Fourthly, their marriage ties become null and void."[122]

(a) The Hanafi School

A list of criteria for recognizing apostasy is provided by the Hanafite scholar Shaykhzadeh in his *Madjma' al-anhur*. This list includes many details of doctrinal error and such actions as translating the Qur'an into another language or paying respect to a non-Muslim.[123]

The *Hedaya* lays down a procedure for dealing with apostasy. [124] Firstly the Islamic faith may be explained to the apostate, in the hope that this can persuade him of the rightness of Islam. (This step is desirable but not obligatory.) The apostate is to be imprisoned for three days, and if he has not returned to Islam by the end of that time he is to be killed. No penalty is incurred by anyone who kills an apostate before he has been given an exposition of the faith, even though such a premature killing is "abominable" (*makruh* i.e. disapproved and improper but not totally unlawful).

Women apostates are treated differently. They are not to be killed, but to be imprisoned until they recant. A boy

---

122. Ibn Hadj, Mohammed Al Abdari *Al Madkha*, (Cairo edition) vol. II, p.181 quoted in Zwemer op. cit. p.50

123. Shaykhzadeh *Madjma' al-Anhur* 1 pp.629-37 summarised in Peters, Rudolph and DeVries, Gert J.J. "Apostasy in Islam" *Die Welt des Islams* XVII, 1-4 (1976-7) pp.3-4

124. *The Hedaya Vol. II* pp.225ff.

who is a minor is also not to be killed, but imprisoned until he comes of age. If he has not returned to the faith by that time, he is then to be killed. Lunatics and drunkards are not held responsible for their act.

There are also detailed instructions in the *Hedaya* regarding other penalties for apostasy. A male apostate loses his right to choose how he disposes of his property; on death it can only be inherited by his Muslim heirs or go to the public treasury.[125] Any property transactions he may have in progress are suspended. He is immediately separated from his wife. The property of a female apostate will go to her heirs as normal, though her Muslim husband cannot inherit in normal circumstances.

The *Hedaya* also contains complex rules about the status of children and grandchildren of apostates. In general, the children are also regarded as apostates and may in some circumstances be "compelled" to become a Muslim, whereas an apostate's grandchild is considered "an original infidel and an enemy".

(b) Other Sunni schools of law

The other schools of law vary slightly in emphasis from each other, but perhaps the most important difference is that the Shafi'i[126], Maliki[127] and Hanbali schools require

---

125. Inheritance by Muslims from an apostate is a subject of complex argument and subtle reasoning because of the necessity to adhere to the rule that Muslims cannot inherit from infidels. See *The Hedaya* Vol. II p. 230.

126. mainly followed in Egypt, Syria, South India, Pakistan, East Africa, Malaysia, Indonesia, the southern part of the Arabian peninsula ("ash-Shafi" in Hughes op. cit. p.571; Goldziher, Ignaz *Introduction to Islamic Theology and Law*, transl. by Andras and Ruth Hamori (Princeton: Princeton

that female apostates, as well as male, should be put to death for apostasy.[128]   The Maliki school attaches importance to ascertaining whether the alleged apostate was formerly a true, practising Muslim.[129]   The Shafi'i school teaches that mere intention, thought or words spoken in jest can be evidence of apostasy as much as words in earnest or actions.[130]   The Hanbali[131] school places emphasis on the three-day period for repentance.[132]   Other variations between the different Sunni schools cconcern such details as the disposal of property or the definition of extenuating circumstances.

Shi'a law

Shi'a Islam remained in close contact with Sunni Islam during the development of the four Sunni schools of law. Consequently Shi'a law very much resembles Sunni law, differing no more from it than the four schools differ from

University Press, 1981) p.49; Zwemer op. cit. p.47)

127. mainly followed in North Africa, Egypt and West Africa ("Malik" in Hughes op. cit. p. 312, Goldziher op. cit. p.49)

128. Ruxton, F.H. "Convert's Status in Maliki Law" *The Moslem World* Vol. 3, no. 1 (1913) p.38

129. Peters and De Vries op. cit. pp.279-80

130. Nawawi *Minhaj-at-Talibin: A Manual of Mohammedan Law according to the School of Shafi'i* (French edition of A.W.C. ven dern Berg by E.C. Howard, District Judge, Singapore. London: Thacker, 1914) cited in Zwemer op. cit. p.47

131. mainly represented nowadays by the Wahhabis of Saudi Arabia ("ibn Hanbal" in Hughes op. cit. p.188; Goldziher op. cit. p.243)

132. From a *hadith* about the third caliph, narrated by Ahmad b. Hanbal, *Al-Saif al-Sarim* p.321 *al-Mughni* vol. 10 p.74, cited in Mawdudi *The punishment of the apostate* p.28

each other.[133]

The Shi'a law on apostates is very similar to Hanafi
Sunni law. A male apostate must be executed, his wife be
separated from him and his property confiscated. A female
apostate is imprisoned and "beaten with rods" at the prayer
times. A child born to apostate parents is also considered
an apostate; his murderer would not be punishable under
the law of retaliation.[134]

Contemporary debate
Many contemporary Islamic thinkers reinforce the
teaching of the Shari'ah on the punishment of apostates,
often basing this on the traditional argument that apostasy
is equivalent to treason. As capital punishment is often the
penalty for treason, so, according to this reasoning, it should
apply also for apostasy.[135]

Mawdudi considers that "the true position of an
apostate is that he by his apostasy provides proof that he
not only rejects the foundation for the order of society and
state but offers no hope that he will ever accept it in the
future". If such a person does not leave the country, argues
Mawdudi, he should be stripped of his rights of citizenship
or killed. According to Mawdudi the latter option is

---

133. Schacht, Joseph *An introduction to Islamic Law*
(London: Oxford University Press, 1964) p.16
134. A. Querry *Droit Musulman. Recueil de Lois
concernant Les Musulmans Schyites* Vol. II (Paris, 1872)
pp.528-533 quoted in Zwemer op. cit. pp.50-51
135. For example, Kurdi, Abdulrahman Abdulkadir
professor of Qur'an and Sunnah at Umm al-Qura University
in his *The Islamic State: A Study based on the Islamic Holy
Constitution* (London: Mansell Publishing Limited, 1984)
pp.52-3

preferable both from society's point of view and from the point of view of the apostate.[136]

Siddiqi counters the argument that the Islamic punishment for apostasy is too severe by pointing out that Islam is not merely a religion of the heart, but is externalized in politics, economics, law, international relations etc.

> In such circumstances it is quite obvious that when a person rebels against the Kingdom of Heaven within his heart, he commits high treason against the Kingdom of Heaven on earth, the visible and concrete expression of the Kingdom of Heaven within the heart. The persons who commit treason are always dealt with severely in every political order. A stern attitude is always adopted by all sane governments against rebels and disruptionists, and so is the case with Islam. There is nothing unusual in what Islam has done. In Islam religion is not a matter of private relationship between man and Allah, but is intertwined with society. So when he abandons Islam he in fact revolts against the authority of the Islamic State and society.[137]

Mohammad Asrar Madani confirms that the punishment for apostasy is death. The death sentence can be lifted if the apostate repents sincerely, unless he or she has also engaged in activities hostile to Islam, in which case forgiveness is not permitted.[138]

Execution for apostasy is not just directed against those

136. Mawdudi *The Punishment of the Apostate* pp.44 ff. especially pp. 49-52
137. Siddiqi op. cit. pp. 108-9
138. Madani op. cit. pp. 130-149 esp. pp. 131, 134-5

who have professed another faith. The definition of an apostate is widened by some authorities to include anyone who disagrees with what they consider to be orthodox Islam.[139] Given the historical divergence of view on questions of Islamic theology and law, there exists a broad range of Muslim belief, which until modern times was generally tolerated and accepted. However, some Muslims now find themselves classified as apostates according to the standards of certain governments or groups. Even if Muslim minorities are not executed for holding views that the government considers heretical, they may suffer discrimination, harassment and imprisonment. In Pakistan, Ahmadiyyas are officially classified as non-Muslims, in

---

139. For example Madani op. cit. (p.130) includes among a list of the acts which constitute apostasy, "repudiating any of Islam's basic and principal tenets" and " showing or expressing revulsion against the implementation of any of the laws of Islam".

140. Other examples include the execution of Mahmoud Muhammad Taha, leader of the Sudanese Republican Party, in 1985 partly for offences against the state and partly for apostasy. The charge of apostasy stemmed from his claim that the abrogation of the benign Meccan Qur'anic texts by the later and more intolerant Medinan texts should be reversed in modern times. See An-Na'im, Abdullahi Ahmed "The Islamic Law of Apostasy and its Modern Applicability: a Case from the Sudan" *Religion* Vol. 16 (1986) pp.197-221. Tunisians who adopted French nationality and thus became subject to French law were regarded as apostates by Tunisian nationalists on the grounds that they refused to judge or be judged by the Shari'ah. See Peters and De Vries op. cit. p.12. Sheikh Muhammad Ghazali of Al-Azhar University, Cairo, testified in court on 22 June 1993 that a Muslim who opposed the implementation of Shari'ah as an apostate "liable to be killed". See Human Rights Watch *Press Release* (10 July 1993)

contradiction to their own claim, and there is legislation specifically directed against them. (See above.)[140]

An alternative line is taken by some modernist scholars, who argue from the Qur'an and from the historical context in which the events recorded in the *ahadith* occurred, that an apostate should not be put to death unless he is also a danger to the Islamic state.[141] Thus they differ from the traditionalists in asserting the possibility of apostasy without rebellion. Following this line of argument, S.A. Rahman believes that there should be no punishment for apostasy, either as a *hadd* offence or as a *ta'zir* offence.

In the humble opinion of the present writer, such a consummation would be in conformity with the Qur'anic texts which remove punishment for disbelief, whether original or adopted, from the purview of the short span of human life on this earth and relegate it to the eternal life after death. The august practice of the Prophet of Islam is in no sense in conflict with this position.[142]

Another Pakistani, Fazlur Rahman, similarly believes that apostasy should not be confused with rebellion and should not be punished since "if apostasy had been considered a punishable crime in this world, the Qur'an would certainly have provided some punishment".[143] An additional argument against the death sentence was put forward by

---

141. Peters and De Vries op. cit. pp.14-15; the Lebanese scholar Subhi Mahmassani '*Arkan huquq al-insan*' (Beirut: Dar al-'ilm li'l-ma-layin, 1979) p. 123-124 cited in Mayer, Ann Elizabeth *Islam and Human Rights: Tradition and Politics* (Boulder: Westview Press, 1991). p.170

142. Rahman, S.A. op. cit. p.170

143. Rahman, Fazlur "Non-Muslim minorities in an Islamic State" *Journal of the Institute of Muslim Minority Affairs* Vol. 7 (1986) p.16

the Egyptian scholar Abd al-Muta'ali al-Sa'idi, deduced from the opinion of Ibrahim al-Nakha'i that the apostate should be asked indefinitely to repent. This implies that the point is never reached at which the apostate should be killed. It is interesting to note that, in addition to scriptural evidence, Al-Sa'idi places almost equal emphasis on upholding the principle of freedom of religion in Islam.[144] Another argument against the death sentence was put forward by Uthman Safi in 1970. Safi holds that man-made secular law i.e. law made by a constitutional legislator, takes supremacy over Islamic law. Writing in 1970, Safi believed that no Islamic country had laws which regarded apostasy as a penal offence; therefore, he argued, apostates could not be punished. Almost thirty years later, such laws do now exist in a number of Muslim countries,[145] but many apostates would still not be punished according to Safi, because the required criminal intention is often lacking.[146]

Development of the legislation
Although there is legislation which prevents an apostate from inheriting,[147] Pakistani law has no legislation to prohibit the conversion of Muslims to another faith. However,

---

144. 'Abd al-Muta'ali al'Sa'idi *al-Hurriyah al-diniyyah fi al-Islam*, 2nd imp. (Cairo: Dar al-Fikr al-'Arabi, no date but probably second half of 1950s) cited in Peters and De Vries op. cit. pp.15-16

145. Countries which have the death sentence for apostasy from Islam include Saudi Arabia, Qatar, Sudan and Iran.

146. Uthman Safi *Ala hamish naqd al-fikr al-dini* (Beirut: Dar al-Tali'ah, 1970) pp.87-93 cited in Peters and De Vries op. cit. p.14, footnote 37

147. Pearl, David *A Textbook on Muslim Personal Law,* 2nd ed. (1987) p.211 cited in Forte *op. cit.*, footnote 64

apostasy is sometimes punished in practice by the application of the blasphemy law.[148] The introduction of the *Hudood* Ordinances in 1979 was a point at which an apostasy law might well have been enacted. However apostasy was **not** included in the list of offences included in the *Hudood* Ordinances.

It is worth noting in this connection that in 1974 the National Assembly, under Z.A. Bhutto, unanimously passed a bill which declared that Ahmadiyyas were non-Muslims. In 1984 further legislation was passed under Zia ul Haq which prohibited Ahmadiyyas from calling themselves Muslim, or using any Islamic nomenclature, following any Islamic practices of worship or propagating their faith (Pakistan Penal Code Sections 298-B and 298-C).[149] While not strictly speaking condemning Ahmadiyyas as apostates, this reflects the general perception that the group as a whole have apostatized from Islam, hence they are severely harassed by Muslim extremists. They suffer more severe treatment than do Christians, who are *dhimmi*.

The Zikri sect in Baluchistan are also widely regarded as non-Muslims by orthodox Muslims. The Muslim religious parties of Baluchistan are calling for the Zikri to be declared non-Muslim, like the Ahmadiyyas.[150]

Case study – Esther John (formerly Qamar Zia) [151]
Qamar Zia was born on 14 October 1929 to a Muslim

---

148. See for example the case of Tahir Iqbal, described above, and analysed below specifically from this standpoint.

149. Human Rights Commission of Pakistan *State of Human Rights in 1995* p.81

150. ibid. p.83

151. Stacey, V. "Of whom the world was not worthy" *Missionary Fellowship* quarterly magazine of the Bible and

family living in Madras. At the age of about seventeen she had to leave the government school she had been attending and was sent instead to a Christian school. Here she began to study the Bible and then converted to Christianity. When she told her parents they were angry and took her away from the school.

Soon after the partition of India in 1947, the family moved to Karachi. Here a Christian missionary made contact with her and gave her a New Testament, which she read secretly for seven years, having no contact with any Christians. Then Qamar's parents began to take steps to arrange a marriage for her with a Muslim. She was not willing to disobey what she understood to be Christian teaching by marrying someone of another faith, so in June 1955 she ran away from home. She found some Christians who sheltered her and helped her to escape to Sahiwal, several hundred miles away.

In Sahiwal, Qamar was baptized in 1955 and took the name of Esther John. She completed her schooling and then attended the United Bible Training Centre in Gujranwala to train as an evangelist. During her studies there (1956-59) she returned twice to her family in Karachi during the holidays, who welcomed her and did not press her hard to renounce her Christian faith. In April 1959 she finished her course at Gujranwala and began to work as an evangelist in the villages around Chichawatni, under the supervision of missionaries from the American Reformed Presbyterian Mission.

Medical Missionary Fellowship (June 1960) p.34-5; White, Janet Ballantyne *Esther a Pakistani girl* (Bible and Medical Missionary Fellowship, 2nd edition, 1962); Wootton, R.W.F. *Jesus more than a prophet* (Inter-Varsity Press, 1982) pp.47-51

Her family in Karachi wrote to her, repeatedly pressing her to return home. She decided to visit them after Christmas 1959, but wrote to them, by registered mail, that she would return only on two conditions: that she be allowed to live as a Christian and that she should not be forced into marriage. She did not receive any reply to this letter.

On 1 February 1960 she was murdered in her bed in the missionaries' bungalow at Chichawatni. Her skull had been smashed by a heavy, sharp instrument. The police were unable to track down her assailant, but some believe it was one of her own brothers.

The case of Esther John has been documented in unusual detail, probably owing to her close association with Western missionaries. Any attempt to survey the persecution faced by Pakistani converts from Islam to Christianity can only be very superficial and partial, since there may be many individual converts whose sufferings are never known outside of their own family or perhaps their local church, let alone investigated and recorded with scholarly accuracy. Nevertheless it is useful to compare Esther John's case with what is known of others.

This author is aware of only one other case of a Pakistani convert in Pakistan being killed for apostasy from Islam. This was the case of Rahila Khanam, a 22-year old Muslim woman living in Lahore. She began attending Bible studies with a Christian friend at the home of a Christian pastor. When her family discovered what was happening, they quickly began to make arrangements for her to marry a Muslim. Rahila fled into hiding in a women's refuge. She was found by her family some weeks later and immediately shot by her brother (16 July 1997), who readily admitted his act, saying that he had done his religious duty by killing an apostate from Islam. He was arrested and charged with murder.[152]

The kind of problems more commonly faced by apostates in Pakistan have been documented by Syrjänen who interviewed 36 Pakistani converts from Islam to Christianity in 1973-4 and 1978. The most frequently reported problems were being beaten by their relatives and driven from the home. Other problems included threats from family and community (some vague, some specifically to shoot them), anger and insults from parents and community, having their water supply cut off by other villagers, being pensioned off from a job, and expulsion from school.[153]

More recent examples of similar attitudes include a *fatwa* issued by their local mosque in 1998 against three girls aged 11,13 and 15, who had allegedly converted from Christianity to Islam. It stated that if they returned to Christianity they would be "chopped into little pieces".[154] The National Commission for Justice and Peace also reports various cases of violence or threatened violence related to apostasy. One case concerns a Christian woman who married a Muslim man according to Islamic marriage rites. A few months later her husband converted to

152. Ismail, Zafar, interview with author (July 1997); Francis, Joseph *Update on Pastor Salim and Saleema Case* (Centre for Legal Aid Assistance and Development, undated but probably soon after 7 August 1997)

153. Syrjänen, Seppo *In Search of Meaning and Identity: Conversion to Christianity in Pakistani Muslim Culture* (Vammala: The Finnish Society for Missiology and Ecumenics, 1987) pp. 70-75, 205-227

154. Scott-Clark and Levy "Beyond Belief" op. cit. p. 36

Christianity, which caused her employer to tell her that if she did not leave her husband she would be taken to court. The reasoning behind this was that, having had an Islamic wedding, she was considered to have converted to Islam, so that her husband's conversion to Christianity meant that his marriage was dissolved because according to Islam a Christian man cannot be married to a Muslim woman.[155] In another example, a Christian man married a Muslim woman who converted to Christianity. Her two children by her previous marriage were baptised, according to their own wishes. In April 1997 she answered the door to an unknown man who shot her. This was believed by her husband to be in retaliation for her conversion to Christianity fourteen years earlier.[156] In October 1997 a young Muslim man from Faisalabad was shot and seriously injured by other Muslims who objected to him reading the New Testament and called him an apostate.[157] This sample of converts' experiences indicates that the murder of a convert such as Esther John or Rahila Khanam – though rare – is simply one end of a spectrum of reactions to apostasy which is chiefly characterized by anger and violence of varying degrees.

Links between the blasphemy law and the apostasy law

Blasphemy and apostasy are distinct terms with distinct meanings in the English language. However, the Arabic word *kafir* is often used to describe both a blasphemer and an apostate, thus closely linking the two issues in the minds

---

155. *Human Rights Monitor 97* p.11
156. ibid. pp.13-14
157. ibid. p.17

of Muslims. The word *kafir*, originally meaning "one who obliterates or covers [God's blessings]" i.e. ungrateful, later took on the sense of "infidel, unbeliever". *Kafir* includes not only infidels who have never been Muslim believers, but also Muslims who are deemed – by themselves or others – to have left the faith.[158] A Muslim can become a *kafir* in one of three ways:

(a)   by committing a serious sin i.e. by behaving like a *kafir;*

(b)   by denying (hiding) an essential truth of Islam, i.e. blasphemy; (Benazir Bhutto experienced this in 1992 when, criticising the Shari'at Court's ruling on the blasphemy law, she was declared by the Religious Affairs Minister to be a *kafir*. Doubtless she would have profoundly disagreed with his assessment.)

(c)   by apostasy (*ridda* or *irtidad*)

Thus a blasphemer and an apostate are both *kafir*. This overlap of terminology may explain why in some cases of blasphemy, it appears that the offence is linked with apostasy. Anwar Masih, accused of blasphemy in February 1993, had converted from Christianity to Islam and then back to Christianity again.[159] This makes him an apostate from Islam.

The FIR about Tahir Iqbal stated "He has disowned Islam and embraced Christianity." When his lawyers moved

---

158. Björkman, W. "Kafir" in Bosworth, C.E., van Donzel, E., Lewis, B. and Pellat, Ch. (eds.) *Encylopaedia of Islam* (Leiden: Brill vol. IV (1978) pp.407-8; "Blasphemy" in Hughes op. cit. p.43

159. Mir "That Way Madness Lies"

an application for bail it was dismissed. The judge, Mr Zia-ur-Rahman, additional sessions judge, Lahore, had repeatedly asked the lawyers to withdraw the application for bail, and after five months issued his formal order refusing bail (order dated 8 July 1991). This refusal was based on Tahir Iqbal's conversion to Christianity, despite the fact that this is not illegal.

> Learned Counsel for the petitioner has conceded before me that the petitioner has converted himself as Christian. With this admission on the part of petitioner's Counsel, there is no need to probe further into the allegation as contained in the FIR because learned DDA (Deputy District Attorney) has disclosed that charge has already been framed by the Illaqa Magistrate and the accused is facing trial. Since conversion from Islam to Christianity is in itself a cognisable offence involving serious implication, hence I do not consider the petitioner entitled to the concession of bail at this stage. This application is accordingly dismissed.[160]

It should be emphasized that the judge was **in error** when he stated in his order that conversion from Islam to Christianity is a cognizable offence.

Tahir Iqbal's next bail petition was moved in the high court before Mr Justice Izar Nisar. The complainant appeared in court, saying that since Tahir Iqbal's crime was liable to capital punishment he should not be granted bail. Others who had also come to attend the hearing demanded the death punishment for him without further trial, so that the judge decided that it was better for Tahir Iqbal's safety

---

160. Order of Judge Zia-ur-Rahman, dated July 8, 1991, quoted in Shakir op.cit. p.122

to keep him in prison.

The complainant moved an application to the effect that since Shari'ah had been declared to be the supreme law of the land by the Enforcement of Shari'ah Act 1991. there was no need to try Tahir Iqbal under the Pakistan Penal Code. According to the complainant, since the Shari'ah punishment for apostasy is death, the trial should be stopped and Tahir Iqbal should be awarded the death penalty. This application was argued by the various counsels, and then dismissed by Mr Sabah Mohyuddin, Additional Sessions Judge, on the grounds that so far there was no law for blasphemy in place other than Sections 295 and 298 of the Pakistan Penal Code.[161]

Later the complainant agreed (at the request of Christian leaders and others) to drop his case against Tahir Iqbal on condition that Tahir Iqbal made a declaration in court stating that he was still a Muslim and was not a Christian. Tahir Iqbal refused to do this (13 July 1992)[162] and died a week later, probably poisoned.

Mohammad Ijaz Hussain of Faisalabad converted from Islam to Christianity on 26 November 1978. When his family learnt of his conversion, his elder brother, a general in the Pakistan army, had him implicated in a blasphemy case. He was arrested on 19 January 1979 under sections 295-A and 295-B of the Pakistan Penal Code and spent the next seventeen years (or more[163]) in prison.[164] In this case, it appears that the family, unable to have him arrested

161. Shakir op. cit. pp.122-3
162. ibid. pp. 124-5
163. At the time of writing he was still in prison.
164. Centre for Legal Aid Assistance and Development, Lahore *Update of Cases from 1st July – 31st December 1996*

for apostasy which is not a legal offence, used the charge of blasphemy instead.

Another clear example of confounding blasphemy with apostasy is the case of Salman Rushdie, whose allegedly blasphemous novel, *The Satanic Verses,* resulted in his condemnation as an apostate, even after his own claim to have re-converted to Islam.[165]

Conclusion

Pakistan's blasphemy legislation in Section 295 of the Penal Code, made potent by the crucial addition of Section 295-C in 1986, has become a convenient weapon for the settling of personal disputes. Although the Muslim majority are also affected, it is minorities such as Ahmadiyyas and Christians who are most vulnerable. The rioting in Shanti Nagar in February 1997 indicated that not only individuals but whole communities may be targeted by those with a grievance against one or more Christians. It is also a convenient way for aggrieved Muslims to punish those who have caused offence not at a personal level such as local politics (for example, Gul Masih) or commercial competition (for example, Tahir Iqbal, Chand Barkat), but in a religious context. Examples of this include Christians who have converted from Islam (for example, Tahir Iqbal, Muhammad Ijaz Hussain) and Christians who are active in evangelism (for example, Daniel Scot). Neither conversion from Islam nor the proselytizing of Muslims are offences under Pakistani law. Yet they are banned in many Muslim countries and are commonly held to be unacceptable by Muslims. Apostasy from Islam is particularly important in this respect, given the clear

---

165. Kharroufah op. cit. passim

teaching of the Shari'ah that it should be punished by death.

As well as the blasphemy legislation itself, with its lack of requirement to prove criminal intent and (since 1991) mandatory death sentence, a number of other factors combine and interact to make this law one of the greatest causes of fear to the Christian community. The most important of these factors are: the method of investigation of complaints, which is biased in favour of the accuser; the Islamic tradition of confounding blasphemy with the capital crime of apostasy; the Islamic tradition of private individuals enforcing death sentences for crimes against Islam; the influence of local mullahs in rousing popular sentiment against alleged blasphemers. Thus, as demonstrated in the case studies, innocence of blasphemy is of minimal use in the courts, and of no use at all in the context of society at large. Those accused have spent long periods in prison, with three being found guilty before being acquitted on appeal. More importantly some – apparently innocent – have been killed by Muslim zealots.

The fear which this law causes throughout the Christian community in Pakistan is thus well-founded. Even Muslim political leaders who may consider it harsh or unjust seem powerless to change the situation, as Benazir Bhutto found. The legislation cannot be amended because of threats by religious extremists. Even if it were to be amended, it would be unlikely to lessen the influence of local Islamic leaders who could call for the death of a named individual, such as Gul Masih, or the destruction of a named community, such as Shanti Nagar.

SIX

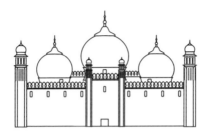

Christian responses
to Islamization
and discrimination

Introduction

The response of Pakistani Christians to the influence of
Islamization and discrimination has been characterized by
lack of co-ordination, planning or unity. A series of
initiatives – usually completely separate from one another
– have come from individuals in the church hierarchies and
from Christian politicians. In most cases these have had
little or no mandate or support from the Christian
community. These initiatives have varied widely as will be
described below. A particular area of difference has been
over whether or how much to liaise with the West in the
form of expatriate missionaries to Pakistan and Western-
based advocacy and human rights organizations.

Christians at the grass-roots have been little involved in

such initiatives. One obvious reason for this is that they generally need to concentrate their whole energy on simply surviving. The low level of literacy also hampers an active engagement in intellectual and political debate. But another reason has been suggested arising from the psychology of the Christian community as an oppressed minority, which leads to a submissive apathy. Munawar Rumalshah, the Church of Pakistan Bishop of Peshawar, writes:

> The psyche of the church is very parochial. It is a church that continually wants sympathy for being "sinned against", in this case for being at the harsh end of an Islamic dominance where mere survival is taken as a matter of triumph.[1]

A clear example of this attitude occurred in the Bishop's own diocese a few months after he spoke. Nine members of a Christian family in Nowshera were murdered on the night of 17-18 November 1998. Christians assumed that it was a sectarian attack by Islamic extremists and would not co-operate with the police investigation for fear of reprisals. However, a Christian human rights group which investigated concluded that the attack was probably made for personal reasons, not sectarian.[2] A very similar observation on Christian attitudes comes from a Muslim source, namely, the prestigious Human Rights Commission of Pakistan who wrote in their 1998 report that "Christians generally nursed a feeling of not being equal citizens with the majority population."[3]

---

1. Rumalshah "Hear the cry" p.41
2. Francis, Joseph M. *Christian massacre in Nowshera* CLAAS (30 November 1998) passim
3. *State of Human Rights in 1998* (Lahore: Human Rights

It is perhaps understandable that few Pakistani Christians should have cared to put on record comments like those of Bishop Rumalshah.[4] It is also understandable that few comments of this nature have been made in recent decades by non-Pakistanis, since sociological and political sensitivities militate against such sentiments in an age when independence and self-sufficiency are highly valued. Yet earlier there were many observations of the same phenomenon from Westerners living in Pakistan (or India). In the 1950s Comfort spoke of the Christian community's "inferiority complex growing out of long dependence on others for help and guidance".[5] This dependence of the Pakistani Christian community pre-dated the creation of Pakistan and the advent of Muslim *zamindars* (see chapter 4). Before partition the Christians depended on Hindu and Sikh *zamindars*. Before that, i.e. before their Chuhra forefathers converted to Christianity in the mass movements of the late nineteenth and early twentieth centuries, the community had been Hindus of the lowest possible social strata. Phillips comments that they "think of themselves as naturally dependent upon others... This tendency has been engrafted in them for 1000 years, and is now part of their very nature."[6] Pickett describes them as having been "trained by centuries of exploitation and servility to avoid the acceptance of responsiblities that may

---

Commission of Pakistan, 1999) p.157

4. Another who was willing to do so was Aftab Pervaiz, a Christian school teacher, who said that Christians should "stop waiting around for handouts... Crying doesn't change anything" quoted in Balchin p.14

5. Comfort op. cit. p.6

6. Philipps, Godfrey E. *The Outcast's Hope* (London: Church Missionary Society, 1912) p. 16

prove burdensome..."[7]

It might be thought that the observations of Westerners can only be of limited value, since their association with the colonial powers is likely to have affected the way in which people behave to them. Yet these observations are in line with the conclusions of Heinrich's careful study *The Psychology of a Suppressed People*, which compares the behaviour of African Americans with that of the scheduled castes of India. He describes a number of abnormal patterns of behaviour which result from continued oppression of a community including "apparent submissiveness and acquiescence".[8] He also comments on "the suggestion of [the Indian Christian's] own inferiority constantly conveyed by the dominating position of the European missionary and the Mission" as well as by the abnormal behaviour (in the sense used above) of other Indian Christians and of his own low caste (if applicable).[9]

Heinrich identifies another characteristic of suppressed peoples, namely, a "craving for superiority that finds expression in the minimizing and undervaluation of others".[10] This he says is most common amongst groups which are beginning to emerge from their oppression, for example the Christian descendants of scheduled castes show it more strongly than their Hindu ancestors did.[11] Self-assertion and "a conflict attitude" are also characteristics of a depressed group which sees some hope of improving its lot.[12] This is manifested in division and

7. Pickett op. cit. pp.217-8
8. Heinrich op. cit. pp.2-3, 77
9. ibid. pp.66,74
10. ibid. pp.39-41
11. ibid. p. 60-1.
12. bid. p.57

mistrust between Christians. Streefland comments on how village Chuhras look down on Chuhras who have moved to the towns.[13] The few in the towns who have managed to gain a respectable job look down on those in the towns who work as sweepers.[14] The Christians from non-Chuhra origins look down on all the Chuhra Christians,[15] some refusing to eat or drink with them, just as Muslims refuse to do so.[16]

Christians are well aware of the divisions amongst them.[17] Some blame their denominationalism on the Western missionaries.[18] But there are many other divisions apart from between denominations. The Church of Pakistan Bishop of Sialkot, Samuel Pervez, rebuked the destructive criticism of his diocesan committees and boards, and his pastors who were concentrating on "politicking" to the neglect of their duties.[19] The press reported a dispute over the appointment of a pastor between Full Gospel

---

13. Streefland op. cit. p.6

14. ibid. p.21

15. Moghal *Human Person in Punjabi Society* p.47; Streefland op. cit. pp.28,30,34

16. Streefland, op. cit. p.32; Deedes,W.F. and Combe,Victoria "Christians and the Cross" *The Daily Telegraph* (29 March 1999)

17. "The Christian Church in Pakistan: a vision for the 21st century" final statement of a seminar held at the Pastoral Institute, Multan, 7to 11 April 1997 published in *Al-Mushir* Vol.39 no. 2 (1997) p.82

18. One such is Philip Lall, quoted by Deedes and Combe op. cit. as claiming that the caste system is "alive and well" in Pakistan, practised even by bishops, with churches for untouchables although they are not named as such.

19. Minutes of the 24th annual meeting of the Sialkot Diocesan Council held on May 06 and 07, 1996 pp.7-8

Assembly Christians in Lahore in 1998 which resulted in the closure of their church.[20]

Development of the Christian community is severely hampered by the *biradari* culture and the divisions which result from it. It is normal for loyalty to one's *biradari* (network of related extended families) to be paramount over the needs of the community as a whole.[21] According to Moghal:

> A person lives and dies for his/her [*biradari*] and in *(sic)* most occasions of his/her life remains faithful to the *biradari*... This concept basically trains a person to help his close relatives obtain advantageous positions even if they are not capable of holding these positions. The welfare of the family is considered far more important than the "common good"...[22]

Campbell comments: "From the beginning of the mass movement churchmen and particularly western churchmen saw that the *biradari* was a competitor of the idea of church and Christian community."[23]

McClintock elaborates on the implications of the *biradari* system for the church, also noting the "double standards" whereby the *biradari* system is resented by those who are suffering because of it, but exploited by the same people

20. Gul, Muhammad Shan "Christians versus Christians" *Friday Times* (6-12, February 1998) p.4

21. Syrjänen, Seppo "Bradri – Millat – Ecclesia: the interrelationship of faith and community" *Al-Mushir* Vol. XV Nos. 11-12 (Nov-Dec 1973) pp.362-3

22. Moghal *Human Person in Punjabi Society* pp.65-6

23. Campbell op. cit. p.43, see also pp.44-7

when they have opportunity to do so.

Social identity is so enmeshed in this web of relationships that other duties and responsibilities – to friends, patrons, employers, religious sects, and the state – become subject to the interests of the *biradari*.

The leaders of the various denominations and parachurch organizations in Pakistan are subject to these same familial pressures. They are expected to use their positions within the church to provide economic and political support to their immediate family and to other members of their *biradari* as well. If they ignore the requests of relatives for jobs or other material aid their relationships with other members of the *biradari* become very strained. Yet, if they do respond positively to some of these requests for aid from their relatives, they will be heavily criticized by other leading members of the church for practising nepotism. Should any of these critics have a similar opportunity to use their own positions within the church to secure economic benefits for their own relatives, however, they probably would not hesitate to exploit it.[24]

Therefore the *biradaris* compete with each other at the expense of the community as a whole.[25] A few Christian *biradaris* control most of the Christian institutions and the benefits tend to be channelled primarily to their own relatives. Similarly, the government's donations towards the economic development of Christian communities find their way mainly to the relatives of the four Christian MNAs. When the office-holders of the Christian school boards were

---

24. McClintock op. cit. pp.349-350

25. Tebbe, R.F. "Education in Pakistan: a minority perspective, 1982" *Al-Mushir* Vol. XXV No. 3 & 4 (Autumn and Winter 1983) p.184

negotiating with the government over the nationalization of the Christian educational institutions (see chapter 4), they gave preference to their family's own interests over the interests of the community as a whole. Thus they sought to have total control of the schools given back to them and their relatives, and would not accept the government's compromise offer of a Christian headteacher and a minimum percentage of Christian staff and students at each school. Because of their leaders' refusal to negotiate on this, the Christian community lost even the offer regarding head, staff and students. This would have been much more advantageous for the Christian community as a whole than the system which the government chose in the end which excluded the Christians from management completely and provided no quotas for Christian pupils. One Christian engineer described Christian leaders as "the biggest robbers", meaning that they did not help their community.[26]

Even Muslims criticize the Christian community for its divisions[27] and poor leadership. A Muslim judge rebuked some bishops who were willing to have their case heard on 1st January, a day on which the Christian community traditionally held New Year services, rather than postpone it as the judge suggested. The bishops told the judge they

---

26. Vivian John, quoted in Balchin op. cit. p.14

27. For example, Rev. Gerald Mall, professor of Old Testament at St Thomas' Theological College, Karachi, speaking at Gujranwala Theological Seminary (28 January 1999). He told of a Muslim judge who rebuked Christians for bringing him a case challenging the election of the Bishop of Karachi and told them to settle their disputes among themselves, as commanded in the New Testament.

would make other arrangements so that he could hear their case, but the judge attacked them as bad shepherds who did not care for their sheep.[28] In this context it is less than surprising that Christians do not speak with a united voice when they respond to Islamization and discrimination.

Political engagement

Pakistan's Christians have commonly been viewed by others[29] and by themselves[30] as meekly accepting their situation, without attempting to remedy it. As Alexander Malik the Church of Pakistan Bishop of Lahore, states, they have "shunned participation in the political life of the country"[31] or, in the words of Charles Amjad-Ali, "more or less abdicated our responsibility in this debate".[32] This meekness and apathy are often attributed to the influence of missionaries. Moghal asserts that because the missionaries, as foreigners, could not be active in politics, they taught the Pakistani Christians similarly to eschew political involvement and to concentrate their hopes on the next life.[33] Certainly the evangelical Western "mother-

---

28. Rev. Gerald Mall, professor of Old Testament at St Thomas'Theological College, Karachi, speaking at Gujranwala Theological Seminary (28 January 1999)

29. For example Khan, Aamer Ahmed "BearingTheir Cross" *The Herald Annual* (January 1993) p.99

30. for example Aftab Pervaiz quoted in Balchin p. 15

31. Rt Rev. Alexander Malik, Bishop of Lahore and Moderator of the Church of Pakistan, paper given at a Christian consultation (title unknown) in Lahore (September 1988) p.5

32. Amjad-Ali, Charles "Religion and Politics" in Miller, Roland E. and Mwakabana, Hance A.O. *Christian-Muslim Dialogue: Theological and Practical Issues* (Geneva: Lutheran World Federation, 1998) p.127

33. Moghal, Dominic "Alienation of the local people: the

churches" of some Pakistani denominations (for example, Brethren, Baptists and Presbyterians) had a tradition in their country of origin of avoiding political and social involvement. Another line of reasoning considers that a generation of "mission compound" Christians developed the habit of non-involvement in politics, and this continues today. In the context of the mission compound there were two reasons why the Pakistani Christians tended to be passive and uninvolved in politics. Firstly, the missionaries took on the role of looking after the converts and Christians and this included interacting with the authorities on their behalf. It was a logical division of labour given that the educated, confident and relatively invulnerable Westerners were likely to have greater success and at a lower risk than were the indigenous Christians. Secondly, the missionaries would often actively discourage or prevent the Pakistani Christians in their compound from political involvement because any antagonism the Christians might inadvertently produce could have resulted in the missionaries losing their visas.[34] They were "indoctrinated to abstain from politics as if it was the 'forbidden tree'."[35]

When Zia proposed the system of separate electorates, the Christians, who were effectively without political leadership from their own community, turned to the clergy for guidance. The clergy endorsed Zia's proposal, a fact

future of religious minorities in Pakistan" *Al-Mushir* Vol. 37 No. 2 (1995) p.39

34. Ismail, Zafar, interview with the author (2 July 1999)

35. Akhter, Salamat *Tehrek-e-Pakistan ke Gumnam Kirdar* [The anonymous heroes of the Pakistan Movement] (Rawapindi: Christian Study Centre, 1997) p.21 quotation is translated from the Urdu text

which is now bitterly resented by many Christians today.
Some consider it a short-sighted bargaining ploy in response
to Zia's suggestion of returning to clergy control the
Christian schools which had been nationalized in 1972 by
Bhutto.[36] Christian political parties today are divided on
the issue of separate electorates.

The introduction of separate electorates ensured that
four Christians would be members of the National
Assembly but severely curtailed Christian political power
(see chapter 4). At least sixteen Christian political parties
quickly developed, nine of which openly supported Zia's
martial law regime. The first four Christian MNAs, elected
in the 1985 elections – a businessman, a lawyer, a retired
army colonel and a headmaster[37] – all supported Zia. The
goals of Christian politicians were mostly limited to seeking
to provide Christian communities with sewerage,
electricity, metalled roads and clean water. Christians
continued to avoid substantial involvement in politics.[38]

Christian leaders now are painfully aware of the isolation
– political and social – of their community. A seminar for
Christians and other non-Muslims held at the Christian
Study Centre in Rawalpindi in 1996 included the following
paragraph in their final statement:

We shall try to come out from our isolation and alienation.
We shall leave our ghettoized mentality and try to be a
part of the main stream. For this purpose we shall blend
and merge with others. We shall try to get the full support

36. Khan, Aamer Ahmed "Bearing their cross" pp.99-101
37. Tebbe, James "Interviews with Christian Members of
the National Assembly" pp.93-103
38. Khan, Aamer Ahmed "Bearing their cross" p.111

of those Muslim groups who believe in the full rights of citizenship of the non-Muslims in Pakistan. This means that we shall join those political parties which will struggle for the full rights of non-Muslims in Pakistan.[39]

Christian political parties and politicians[40]

There is little co-operation between the Church establishment and the Christian political parties. Originally just four, there is now a multiplicity of Christian parties which prevents the Christian community from speaking with a unified voice, and leaves it vulnerable to manipulation by the larger political parties in power.

Two months before partition, in June 1947, the Punjab branches of the original four Christian parties – the All India Christian Association, the All India Christian League, the Catholic Association and the All India Anglo-Indian Association – merged to become one body, known as the Pakistan Joint Christian Board. This was re-named the All Pakistan Christian League in 1949. It was closed down in 1958, along with all the other political parties in the country, under the military rule of Ayub Khan, but then re-established in 1964 as the Pakistan Masihi League (PML), under the leadership of Chaudhury Chandu Lal. The decision to re-establish this party was in part at least a reaction to a motion proposed in the first National Assembly elected under the 1962 constitution. This motion, proposed by an MNA called Sheikh Abdul Aziz,

---

39. Final Statement of national seminar on "Religious Minorities in Pakistan: struggle for identity" p.106

40. A detailed history of the elections and parties will not be attempted here, but the most significant and characteristic points will be mentioned.

declared that "Christians are like cylinders of poisonous gas, polluting our atmosphere. Their missionary and educational activities should be brought under strict control."[41] The PML stood for more representation of Christians in local politics, for economic development for Christians in rural areas including the allocation of land to them, and for religious tolerance, resisting the anti-Christian aspirations of the mullahs and Islamic extremists. It was very active in protesting against the nationalization of the schools in the early 1970s. It was closed down again when General Zia took power in 1977 and closed all the political parties, but re-opened on his death in 1988.[42]

The introduction of separate electorates resulted in the blossoming of a multitude of new Christian parties as well as a number of independent candidates. The numbers are indicated by the fact that in the February 1997 elections, there were 30 Christian candidates for the National Assembly and 38 for the Punjab Provincial Assembly.[43] Unlike the PML, the policies of most of these parties and individuals could be described as "the politics of survival" – their foremost concern was simply the survival of the Christian community. With little in the way of ideology, they were very much dependent on the personalities of their respective leaders. Amidst the plethora of current Christian parties, some of the more significant are:

• The Pakistan Masihi Party, led by Tariq C. Qaiser, who
  polled the most Christian votes in the 1997 elections.

41. quoted in Akhter op. cit. p.180
42. Akhter op. cit. pp.179-180
43. Their names are listed in "Minority NA candidates" *The Nation* (1 February 1997) p.2

This party is mainly supported by upper class and middle class Christians.

- The Pakistan Christian National Party, led by Joseph Francis. This party is closely allied to Benazir Bhutto's Pakistan People's Party, who assist with funding. It is supported by Christians who are sympathetic to the PPP's secularist stance.

- The Pakistan Liberation Front, led by Shabaz Bhatti. This is a relatively new party, supported mainly by younger Christians. Its candidate, Simon Jacob, was elected to the National Assembly in 1997 in fourth place.

It will be noticed that, of the four significant parties described above (the PML and the three newer ones), only two currently have their own MNAs. The other two Christian seats in the National Assembly were won by independent candidates, Rufin Julius and Peter John Sahotra. These are both Roman Catholics, and stand as independents because Catholic teaching forbids clergy to stand for election. There is therefore no Catholic political party in Pakistan, as the natural leadership of such a party is not allowed to take on this role.[44] Despite this handicap, many Catholic bishops manage to be closely involved in politics through their relatives.

The whole Christian political system is not unlike the classic *millet* system[45] of the Ottoman empire, whereby the Muslim rulers permitted their religious minority communities to be self-governing, and controlled them

---

44. Akhter op. cit. pp.179-180; "EC notifies results of minority communities" *The Nation* (14 February 1997) p.11
45. Syrjänen "Bradri – Millat – Ecclesia" p.368

through the minority leaders rather than directly communicating with the ordinary non-Muslims.[46] The separate electorates system created the same gap between the minorities and the government, bridged only by their elected leaders. Even prior to the establishing of the separate electorates, General Zia tended to work through the bishops and other church leaders in a similar way, by-passing those Christians who had been elected to political leadership. The church leaders' willingness to embrace the separate electorate system is perhaps indicative of their understanding of the enormous personal power they would have forfeited if they had lost their role in liaising between their people and the government. The Finnish scholar of Pakistani Christian society, Seppo Syrjänen, asserts that the *millet*-like character of the Christian community in Pakistan has affected the quality of Christian leadership, producing leaders who are more concerned with external dignity than with spirituality, just as tend to be found in other *millet* systems.[47]

Rallies and protests

Beginning in 1972 when the Christians schools were nationalized, Christians have organized rallies and public gatherings to draw attention to their grievances. This method of expression was halted from 1977-88 under General Zia's martial law, but resumed again once

46. Kymlicka, Will *Multicultural citizenship* (Oxford: Clarendon Press, 1995) p.157; Bowen, Harold and Gibb, H.A.R. *Islamic Society and the West* Vol 1 Islamic Society in the eighteenth century part II (London: Oxford University Press, 1957) pp.212-213; Syrjänen "Bradri – Millat – Ecclesia" pp.364-5

47. Syrjänen "Bradri – Millat – Ecclesia" p.368

democracy was restored. Like the earliest rallies which protested about the nationalization of the schools, many rallies focused on particular topical issues. Many were held, for example, towards the end of November 1992 to protest about the proposed religion column to be added to identity cards.[48] Two years later, nationwide protests were organized by Rt Rev. John Joseph, the Catholic Bishop of Faisalabad, when Manzoor Masih was shot dead by Islamic extremists as he left the court building following his trial for blasphemy with two other Christians.[49] In February 1997 a rally was held in response to the mass violence at Shanti Nagar.[50] In 1998, following Bishop Joseph's own protest suicide over the death sentence for another Christian accused of blasphemy, Christians demonstrations were held across the Punjab on 15 May.[51] Some rallies had a more general purpose, for example that held on 11 August 1998, organized by the Christian Liberation Front but attended by Hindus and Sikhs as well as Christians. This gathering had the dual purpose of giving voice to the minorities' problems and expressing solidarity with all Pakistanis.[52]

Other ways of drawing public attention to certain issues or events are also used, such as press conferences and

48. Khan, Aamer Ahmed "Bearing Their Cross" p.99

49. "Bishop Commits Suicide in Pakistan" Associated Press Report, (6 May 1998)

50. "Christians rally demands Blasphemy Law's repeal" *The Muslim* (16 February 1997)

51. "Police brutalise Christians protesters" *The News* (16 May 1998); "Bishop's death: Christians protest across Punjab" *Dawn* (16 May 1998)

52. "Minorities plan solidarity rally on Aug 11" *Dawn* (23 July 1998) p.8; "Minorities to hold rally for national solidarity" *The News* (23 July 1998) p.3

statements. For example, ten prominent individuals, both Christians and human rights activists, issued a joint statement at a press conference on the violence at Shanti Nagar in February 1997.[53]

A special mention must be made in this section of Julius Salik, a former MNA, who made himself notorious by the dramatic gestures he used to highlight the plight of the Christians. These included a hunger strike, setting fire to all his furniture in front of the Punjab Assembly building, and tying himself to a cross.[54] Although dismissed as a madman by some, he was recommended for the Nobel Peace Prize by Prime Minister Benazir Bhutto, who included in her commendation "his courageous defence of the rights of Pakistani Christians".[55]

Human rights advocacy

Pakistan has a very influential non-sectarian advocacy

53. *Press conference on the desecration of churches, the Holy Bibles and the houses of Christian* (sic) *in Khanewal and Shantinagar*, a statement addressed to journalists and signed by Bishop Samuel Azariah, of the Church of Pakistan Diocese of Raiwind, Mr Joseph Francis of the Centre for Legal Aid, Assistance and Settlement, Hina Jilani of the Human Action Forum, I.A. Rehman, director of Human Right of Pakistan, Group Capt (retd.) Cecil Chaudhury of St Anthony's School, Robert Taylor, territorial commander of the Salvation Army, Amjad Saleem Mehnaz of Punjab Nojawan, Younas Rahi of the Pakistan Christian National Party, Chaudhury Naeem Shakir of the Committee for Justice and Peace, and Shahtaj Qasilbash of the Joint Action Committee

54. Khan, Aamir Ahmed "Protest resignations are a family trait" *The Herald* (November 1992) pp.61-63

55. Letter from Benazir Bhutto to the Chairman of the Nobel Peace Prize Committee (10 April 1996)

body, the Human Rights Commission of Pakistan. But in addition the Roman Catholic community have been active in engaging the Muslim community in this way. Because of their size and their inherent unity, coupled with the courageous and outspoken leadership of Bishop John Joseph, they have been able to develop two human rights advocacy organizations, both based in Lahore, and with an emphasis on helping minorities, especially Christians.

One was established in 1984 by the Catholic Bishops' Conference of Pakistan and is called the National Commission for Justice and Peace. It is a very well respected and was chaired, until his suicide, by Bishop John Joseph. It describes its objectives as:

1. To organise and conduct seminars, workshops on human rights education and training on para-legals and human rights activism.
2. To provide legal aid and paralegal assistance to the victims of injustice, especially the victims of discriminatory laws.
3. To organize fact finding missions on cases of gross violation of human rights.
4. To keep a record of such cases, arrange studies on these cases and issues of national importance especially those relating to minorities.
5. To publicize such reflections/reports, for awareness and advocacy purpose, through newsletter, pamphlets, books etc.
6. To network and collaborate with like-minded organization, *(sic)* Church based or non-government in accordance with the objective of NCJP.[56]

The other organisation is called Centre for Legal Aid Assistance and Settlement (CLAAS), also based in Lahore. It was founded in 1996 and is directed by Joseph Francis, a respected human rights activist who is also the chairman of the Pakistan National Christian Party. It describes itself as:

> a multi-religious organisation which works to address human rights issues faced by religious minorities; women and children. The twin focus of its activities are: Legal aid assistance and settlement. Its activities reinforce and strengthen the human rights issues in Pakistan. In this context CLAAS seeks cooperation and close working relationship *(sic)* with other human rights organisations and groups to advance human rights for everyone.[57]

CLAAS publishes regular updates on the human rights cases it is dealing with. It has recently opened an office in London.

Research and documentation

The most significant organization concerned with researching the situation of Christians in the Islamic context of Pakistan is the ecumenical and international[58] Christian Study Centre (CSC) in Rawalpindi, which was established under this name in 1967, but had been developing in stages since 1951. Its purpose is to promote good relations between Christians and Muslims in Pakistan.[59] Research,

---

56. *Human Rights Monitor 97* p.64
57. *Human Rights Today* (Jan-Feb 1997) p.5
58. Kraan, J.D. "Muslim-Christian relations and Christian Study Centres" *Al-Mushir* Vol. XXVI Nos. 3 & 4 (1984) p.176

teaching and seminars focus primarily on Christian-Muslim relations, Islam, minorities in Pakistan and developing contextual Christian theology. Secondary foci are human rights, women's issues and democratization.[60] A journal, *Al-Mushir,* is published by the CSC in English and Urdu (varying in frequency).

Pakistani Christians have at various times and using various media made efforts to communicate the fact that they have significantly contributed to their country in many different ways. A three-day seminar was held in 1978 on the theme of "The Role of Minorities in National Development".[61] One of the resolutions contained in the final statement from the seminar on religious minorities in Pakistan held at the CSC in 1996 was that "we shall document the contribution of the non-Muslims for the creation and development of the country".[62] Christians ask for their positive role in the formation of Pakistan to be remembered, as well as Christians who have been prominent in politics,[63] law, the armed forces, and other fields.[64] It must be acknowledged

---

59. *Christian Study Centre Rawalpindi Annual Report 1997* p.1; introductory leaflet produced by Christian Study Centre (1996) p.1

60. "Study Islam in Pakistan" leaflet produced by Christian Study Centre (undated but not earlier than 1995)

61. *The Role of Minorities in National Development* – papers from a seminar held 27-29 April 1978 under the auspices of the Institute of Political and Social Studies of Forman Christian College, Lahore

62. Final Statement of a national seminar on "Religious Minorities in Pakistan" p.106

63. For example, Herbert Fernandes, President of the Catholic Association, speaking in May 1997 and reported in "Minorities role" *The Nation* (15 May, 1997) p.7

64. For example, Michael Javed, a Christian member of the

that, in recent years, there have been various public statements by prominent Muslims, also affirming the contribution of Christians to Pakistan's formation, development and prosperity. Special mention is often made of Christian contributions to education, health, sports and culture.[65] When Lahore Cathedral celebrated its centenary in 1987, President Zia himself commended the patriotism of Pakistani Christians as a whole and the specific role of the cathedral in education, health and social welfare.[66] Nawaz Sharif, then chief minister of the Punjab, also praised the cathedral's work in education and social welfare.[67]

Sometimes particular issues have prompted the publication of related materials, with a view to making the situation more widely known. A typical piece of work of this kind is a 17-page photocopied booklet produced by the National Affairs Commission of the National Council of Churches in Pakistan after the murder in 1992 of Naimat

---

Sind Provincial Assembly reported in "Christians urged to help in country's progress" *Dawn* (15 September 1997) p.2; Ansari op. cit. p.4

65. For example, Prime Minister Nawaz Sharif reported in "Muslims, Christians enjoy complete harmony:PM" *Dawn* (23 December 1997) p.6; Hidayatullah Khan Chamkan, acting governor of the North West Frontier Province, reported in "Chamkani praises minorities' role in country's prosperity" *The Nation* (30 December 1997) p.4; Saleem Zia, Law Minister of Sind reported in "Christians urged to help in country's progress" *Dawn* (15 September 1997) p.2

66. President's message in Phailbus, Theodore (ed.) *The Cathedral Church of the Resurrection Lahore 1887-1987* (Lahore? Allied Press Limited, 1987) p.4

67. Message from Nawaz Sharif in Phailbus, Theodore (ed.) *The Cathedral Church of the Resurrection Lahore 1887-1987* (Lahore? Allied Press Limited, 1987) p.10

Ahmer, a Christian accused of blasphemy. More than half the pages are simply reproductions of other reports on the incident.[68]

Engaging the international arena

Having recognized that the government of Pakistan, its structures and institutions seem unlikely to change merely from pressure within the country, some Christian leaders have in the last few years appealed to the international community and particularly the West to apply pressure on the Pakistani government to make the desired changes. This came about at an opportune moment in the early 1990s, after the fall of Communism in Europe and the Soviet Union, when the Church internationally became aware of the situation of Christians in Muslim-majority countries and began to develop an interest in religious liberty in Islamic contexts. Bodies such as the World Evangelical Fellowship created religious liberty commissions, and various para-church agencies in the West that were initially engaged in other tasks added religious liberty in the Islamic world to their portfolios. Through their campaigning this was to impact heavily on Western governments and institutions. A two-way process developed in which Western organizations approached Pakistani Christians offering help in advocacy. In turn, Pakistani Christians realized the potential of utilizing these and other bodies outside their country to bring pressure on their own government, and began to initiate approaches of their own to such bodies.

---

68. *Brutal murder of Christian teacher Naimat Ahmer under the garb of the blasphemy law* (Lahore: National Affairs Commission of the National Council of Churches in Pakistan (no date but probably late January 1992)

Bishop Munawar Rumalshah of the Church of Pakistan Diocese of Peshawar has in particular played a key role. He made four proposals for the international context, which, if implemented, would in his view affect the Pakistani situation:

1. The setting up of a type of UN of religious bodies. This would offer an open platform where major issues, especially those of conflict or harmony, could be discussed.
2. The setting up of a Religious Prominent Persons' Group. This means a group of prominent religious leaders, who would go to places of religious conflict and bring about reconciliation.
3. The teaching of all religions, either through schools or through some other organised way, so that people do not grow up in a monochrome religious environment.
4. The issue of a Bill of Rights for religious minorities. This is of utmost importance in situations where even the civil rights of the minority are in danger of being swallowed up by the majority religion.[69]

The growing Christian indignation concerning the blasphemy law has been the main issue aired in the international arena. In particular the mass violence at Shanti Nagar in February 1997 and the protest suicide of Bishop John Joseph in May 1998 – both resulting from the blasphemy

---

69. Rumalshah, Munawar "Contemporary Challenges to the Religious World in Pakistan" *Al-Mushir* Vol. 39 No. 2 (1997) p. 53. The same points were first offered by Bishop Rumalshah at an inter-religious conference in 1990 in a paper entitled "South Asia: Cradle of Religious Conflict".

law – drew international coverage and appeared to spur many organizations and individuals to speak out and act.

The events at Shanti Nagar drew a particularly strong response from British Pakistani Christians, many of whom have relatives in Shanti Nagar. They were also supported in this by some indigenous British Christians and by some British Pakistani Muslims. David Smith, the Anglican Bishop of Bradford, whose diocese has one of the highest concentration of British Muslims, responded to the destruction of Christian property in Shanti Nagar with a strongly worded letter of protest to the Acting Pakistani High Commissioner in London. It was signed not only by the Bishop himself but also by three other Christian leaders and five Muslim leaders.[70] The Bishop went on to visit Pakistan in November 1997, also as a response to the events in Shanti Nagar nine months earlier.[71] Another response to Shanti Nagar came from a large church of Pakistani-

---

70. Letter dated 19 February 1997 to Mr Moin Jan Naim, Acting High Commissioner for Pakistan, signed by Rt Rev. David Smith, the Bishop of Bradford and Rev. Canon Peter Maguire, representing the Catholic Bishop of Leeds, Councillor Mohammed Ajeeb, ex-Lord Mayor of Bradford, Rev. Geoff Reid, representing the Rev. Peter Whittaker, Chairman of the Methodist Church West Yorkshire District, Sher Azam, ex-president of the Bradford Council for Mosques, Mr Andrayas Khan, Pakistan Christian Action Group, Faqir Mohammed, general secretary of the Bradford Council for Mosques, Khadim Hussain, President of the Bradford Council for Mosques, and Ishtiaq Ahmed, director of Bradford's Racial Equality Council

71. *The human family and the duty of religion* Address by the Archbishop of Canterbury at the International Islamic University, Islamabad, Pakistan, visit to Pakistan 4-7 December 1998 p.2 p.8

origin British Christians meeting at Walthamstow, east London, who wrote to the Prime Ministers of Britain and Pakistan to express their concern asking for practical steps to be taken to ameliorate the suffering and insecurity of Christians in Pakistan.[72] A sympathetic reply was received from the British Foreign and Commonwealth Office, indicating their continued concern about the human rights of Christians in Pakistan and violence against individual Christians.[73] In the United States, Pakistani Christians held a protest demonstration outside the United Nations and the Pakistani Consulate.[74]

The anniversary of the day on which Jinnah made his famous speech on 11 August 1947 to the Constituent Assembly promising freedom and equality for all faiths in the new country of Pakistan has become a symbolic date for Christian protests. Thus on 11 August 1997, a large demonstration was held in Faisalabad against the death sentence for blasphemy. But the Christians of Pakistan were not the only ones marking this day in this way. On the same day, Austrian Christians demonstrated in Vienna for the same cause, under the auspices of Christian Solidarity International, a Western advocacy and human rights organization.[75]

---

72. Letter dated 17 February 1997 to Rt Hon. John Major from Shaheen Zar, secretary of the Asian Christian Church (London)

73. Letter dated 25 March 1997 from S. Horner of the South Asian Department of the Foreign and Commonwealth Office to Shaheen Zar, secretary of the Asian Christian Church, Walthamstow

74. "Pak Christians protest in US" *The Nation* (1 March 1997); "Pakistani Christians demonstrate at UNHQ" *Dawn* (1 March 1997)

75. Joseph, John Bishop of Faisalabad *Vienna rally against*

Christians in Pakistan were encouraged by a state visit from George Carey, the Archbishop of Canterbury, to Pakistan in December 1997. He spoke of the prejudice towards minorities and called for tolerance and specifically for amendments to the blasphemy law and an improvement in the situation regarding Christian schools.[76] His statements on the blasphemy law caused a furious outcry from Muslim religious leaders.[77] In a speech at the International Islamic University in Islamabad on 5 December 1997 about the status of religious minorities, specifically Muslims in Britain and Christians in Pakistan, he spoke of the need for a better kind of "tolerance" than "being allowed to exist on sufferance". He called for a tolerance that involved mutual respect and true security for the minority groups.[78] He also listed five areas for practical action: places of worship and education, freedom to convert, mutual understanding, freedom to participate in public life, and valuing the gifts of the minorities. He deplored the tendency of minorities to "retreat into enclaves".[79] His visit, made at the invitation of the Church of Pakistan, succeeded in bringing not only encouragement

---

death sentence in blasphemy law (unpublished paper, dated 11 August 1998)

76. "Pakistan urged to amend blasphemy law" *The Nation* (5 December 1997) "Archbishop stresses need for tolerance" *Dawn* (7 December 1997) p.7; "Archbishop's remarks resented" *The Muslim* (9 December 1997) p.2

77. Ali, Mayed "Pakistani religious leaders respond angrily to Carey's suggestion for rethink on blasphemy law" *The News* (8 December 1997); Iqbal, M.M. "Blasphemy law" *The News* (22 December 1997) p.7

78. Carey *The human family* p.2

79. ibid. pp.7-8

to Pakistani Christians but also prominence to their problems.[80] It was well reported in the Pakistani press and sparked some lively debate amongst Pakistani Muslims, and even in the National Assembly. Responding to a motion tabled by four MNAs that the Archbishop had caused public resentment by his comments about propagating religion, the Federal Minister for Religious Affairs, Raja Zafar-ul-Haq, made a statement in the National Assembly that the Archbishop's remarks had not been anti-Muslim, and affirmed the freedom of all to propagate their own religion.[81]

On 6 May 1998, Roman Catholic Bishop John Joseph shot himself dead in protest following the pronouncement of a death sentence for Ayub Masih, a Christian found guilty under the blasphemy law. This stirred international interest for a short time, and Pakistani Christians inside and outside of their country took every opportunity to draw attention to their situation. Michael Nazir-Ali, Anglican Bishop of Rochester, spoke of how the blasphemy laws had "poisoned" relations between faiths in Pakistan.[82] The Pakistan Christian Welfare Organisation (UK) met with the Pakistani High Commissioner in London, Mian Riaz Samee, and the Speaker of Pakistan's National Assembly, Elahi Bux Sumro, on 13 May 1998 to discuss the problems

---

80. Nazir-Ali, Michael, Bishop of Rochester, quoted in "Dr Carey appeals for Pakistani Christians" Church of England Newspaper (12 December 1997)

81. "The Archbishop's remarks are not anti-Muslim" *Daily Jang* (12 December 1997)

82. "Pakistan: WCC urge repeal of blasphemy law" circular issued by the Anglican Communion News Service (22 May 1998)

which Christians in Pakistan faced, especially from the blasphemy laws.[83] The following day another group of British Pakistan Christians visited the Prime Minister's office and the Pakistan High Commission.[84] On 25 May 1998 Pakistani Christians in Britain held a protest march in London, organized by the Pakistan Christian Alliance in Europe.[85]

Support in the aftermath of Bishop Joseph's suicide was also voiced by Christians from other countries, by Muslims and by politicians. The World Council of Churches, representing 322 Protestant and Orthodox churches world-wide, called on the Pakistan government to repeal Section 295-C of the Pakistan Penal Code in a letter to Ambassador Munir Akram, Pakistan's permanent representative at the United Nations, made public on 13 May 1998.[86] Petitions were raised. Christian Solidarity Worldwide, a British advocacy and human rights organization, collected 4,000 signatures and presented them to the Pakistani High Commissioner in London in

83. David, Dr P.J. and Shams, Qamar, (president and general secretary respectively of the Pakistan Christian Welfare Organisation) letter to Mr Elahi Bux Sumro, speaker of the National Assembly of Pakistan and Mian Riaz Samee, High Commissioner of Pakistan (13 May 1998); *Feedback from meeting on 13 May 1998 – Pakistani High Commission* notes taken by Stone, Rev. Christopher (representing the Bishop of Rochester at the meeting)

84. Dean, Dr George, fax letter to the author (undated, but some time between 7 and 13 May 1998)

85. "Protests to Pakistan Government" *Baptist Times* (28 May 1998)

86. Brown, Stephen "World Council of Churches urges Pakistan to repeal blasphemy law" *ENI Bulletin* No. 10 (27 May 1998) p.7

May 1998.[87] The Barnabas Fund, an international Christian relief and development charity, collected 31,410 signatures from 26 countries covering every continent on a petition calling for the repeal of Sections 295-B and 295-C. The petition was presented to the military secretary to the President of Pakistan in Islamabad in January 1999.[88] The Minorities Council of India issued a statement on 11 May 1998 through their leader, Prof. Iqbal Ansari (a Muslim), which expressed serious concern over the events which led to the bishop's suicide and urged Pakistan to bring their law and practice into conformity with human rights standards.[89] The persecution of Christians in Pakistan was raised in the British House of Commons, and the British High Commission in Islamabad led a European Union *demarche* to the Pakistan authorities on 14 May 1998 about the situation of religious minorities, in particular the death penalty imposed on Ayub Masih.[90] This was followed by a visit to Pakistan by Derek Fatchett, the Secretary of State for Foreign and Commonwealth Affairs, in February 1999 during which he raised the issue of the treatment of religious minorities with Pakistan's Law Minister. Senior officials from the British Foreign Office held discussions with their Pakistani counterparts in Islamabad in May 1999,

---

87. "Protests to Pakistan government" *Baptist Times*, 28 May 1998

88. "Pakistan Blasphemy Petition Update No. 3" produced by the Barnabas Fund (19 March 1999)

89. "Aligarh minorities' body deplores 'religious intolerance' in Pakistan" *The News International*, London edition (12 May 1998)

90. Fatchett, Derek, Secretary of State for Foreign and Commonwealth Affairs, House of Commons Hansard written answers for 23 June 1998 column 470)

which included the subjects of religious persecution and the blasphemy laws. Furthermore the UK development programme for Pakistan, run by the Department for International Development (with an annual budget of about £25 million) places an emphasis on funding projects which will improve human rights and in particular to create greater justice for marginalized groups – this would directly benefit Christians.[91]

The blasphemy law – particularly cases involving Christians – has been raised repeatedly at the United Nations Commission on Human Rights. The Special Rapporteur, Bacre Waly Ndiaye, submitted an urgent appeal in September 1993 concerning the death sentences passed on Salamat Masih (aged 13 at the time of his alleged offence), Rehmat Masih and Manzoor Masih.[92] In 1994 he raised the murder of Manzoor Masih outside the court by Islamic militants, and also a number of other blasphemy cases pending (not only of Christians).[93] In 1995 David Littman, representing the Indian Institute for Non-Aligned Studies, raised the issue again at the UN Commission on Human Rights, making particular reference to Christians

---

91. Hoon, Geoffrey, UK Minister of State, Foreign and Commonwealth Office (House of Commons Hansard debates for 9 June 1999 column 611)

92. Report by the Special Rapporteur, Mr Bacre Waly Ndiaye, submitted pursuant to commission on human rights resolution 1993/71, Commission on Human Rights, 50th session (1994), E/CN.4/1994/7 (7 December 1993) p.107

93. Report by the Special Rapporteur, Mr Bacre Waly Ndiaye, submitted pursuant to Commission on Human Rights resolution 1994/82, Commission on human rights 51st session (1995), E/CN.4/1995/61 (14 December 1994) p.78

accused and murdered because of the law.[94]   Later the same year, another UN Special Rapporteur, Abedlfattah Amor, visited Pakistan and presented a report on the status of religious minorities to the UN Commission on Human Rights in January 1996. This report expressed concern about the blasphemy law and many other areas of legislation affecting minorities.[95]   The pressure has continued, with a quick response to the suicide of Bishop John Joseph in the form of an appeal by Littman and his colleague René Wadlow of the Association for World Education to Mary Robinson, the United Nations High Commissioner for Human Rights, calling for the repeal of Sections 295-B and 295-C of the Pakistan Penal Code.[96]

Having had their problems highlighted by Bishop Joseph's death, Christians in Pakistan continued to organize events to keep their grievances in the public eye.   On 21 June 1998 the Christian Liberation Front organised a conference for minorities on the subject of discrimination against them and solidarity among them. The conference was attended not only by political leaders and other minority leaders from within Pakistan but also by delegations of Pakistanis living abroad.[97]   A rally was held in Lahore on 11 August 1998 organised by the Christian Liberation Front of Pakistan to protest about the problems

---

94. Statement by Representative David Littman on 6 February 1995 to the United Nations Commission on Human Rights, Geneva (30 January – 10 March 1995)

95. Rehman, I.A. "UN advice on minorities" *The News* (12 July 1996)

96. Littman, David and Wadlow, René, Association for World Education, letter to Mary Robinson (8 May 1998)

97. "All minorities parties conference on 21st" *The News* (15 June 1998) p.3

of the minorities. Similar rallies were held on the same day in the United States, Canada and Britain.[98]

Though Christians in Pakistan marked the first anniversary of Bishop Joseph's suicide on 6 May 1999,[99] internationally much of the public and media interest had waned within a few weeks of the bishop's death. Significantly, the debates in the British House of Commons, which had been so concerned for Pakistani Christians in May and June 1998, in the following twelve months mentioned the problems of Pakistani Christians only as an adjunct to those of Indian Christians[100] and of Pakistani Ahmadiyyas.[101] (Nevertheless, the Foreign and Commonwealth Office was active behind the scenes, as mentioned above.)

Some Pakistani Christian leaders have taken the opportunities provided by overseas travel to speak of the difficulties faced by Christians in Pakistan to audiences they would not normally be able to address. On 27 April 1998 Joseph Coutts, the Roman Catholic Bishop of Hyderabad, addressed a meeting of Asian bishops at the Vatican and spoke of the suffering caused to Asian churches by Islamic "intolerance, militancy and oppression".[102] Bishop

---

98. "Minorities plan solidarity rally on Aug 11" *Dawn* (23 July 1998) p.8

99. Akkara, Anto "Pakistani Christians remember bishop's 'ultimate' sacrifice for tolerance" *ENI Bulletin* No. 9 (21 May 1999) pp.17-18

100. House of Commons Hansard debates for 10 February 1999 column 443-4

101. House of Commons Hansard debates for 9 June 1999 column 605-611

102. "Pakistani bishop denounces Islamic 'intolerance'" *The News International*, London edition (29 April 1998) p.12

Munawar Rumalshah testified before the U.S. Senate Foreign Relations Committee on 17 June 1998 on the subject of "Being a Christian in Pakistan"[103] In this speech, Bishop Rumalshah gave a frank and strongly worded description of the problems facing Christians in Pakistan. Mohan Lal Shahani travelled to the United States and Britain, hoping to "create awareness in the West about the plight of Christians and other religious minorities in Pakistan".[104]

Various Western Christian human rights organizations (such as Jubilee Campaign and Christian Solidarity International / Worldwide) have taken up the causes of Pakistani Christians, and they have also become a regular focus of some Christian news agencies, such as Compass Direct, which has a part-time Pakistani reporter based in Pakistan. These are helping to remind the international community that the problems which led to the violence at Shanti Nagar and the death of Bishop John Joseph remain basically unchanged.

Inter-faith dialogue and links

As Charles Amjad-Ali notes with regret, there are few organized attempts at building relationships the Muslim and Christian communities. Christians are sycophantic towards Muslims in public but denigrate them in private. Muslims largely ignore the Christian community except when they attack them and their faith in sermons and literature.[105]

---

103. Rumalshah *Being a Christian in Pakistan*
104. "Interview with Mohan Lal Shahani" in *Rutherford International* Vol. 2 Issue 8 (August 1998) p.2
105. Amjad-Ali, Charles "Political and Social Conditions in Pakistan" in Miller, Roland E. and Mwakabana, Hance A.O. *Christian-Muslim Dialogue: Theological and Practical Issues* (Geneva: Lutheran World Federation, 1998) p.341

This lack of contact is a development since the process of Islamization began under Zia; formerly there were more contacts between the two communities.[106]   Khurshid Ahmad, who had been one of major players in dialogue with Western Christians while living in Britain,[107] describes as "threadbare" the discussions which parliamentary committees in Pakistan had with Catholic and Church of Pakistan leaders,[108] which would seem to indicate a lack of determination in pursuing dialogue with Pakistani Christians.

The main promoter of Christian-Muslim dialogue has been Father Archie deSouza, working in Karachi, whose efforts have extended over many years, including weekly study sessions for Muslims and Christians with the aim of understanding each other.[109]   A one-day conference attended by *ulema* from various Islamic schools and Christians from various denominations was held in May 1998. The aim of the meeting, organised by the former Christian MNA Julius Salik, was to build good relations between the two communities.[110]

---

106. Kraan "Muslim-Christian relations and Christian Study Centres" p.176

107. Some of Khurshid Ahmad's appointments and activities in the UK and the West are listed in Siddiqui, Ataullah op. cit. p.125

108. Unpublished interviews with Ataullah Siddiqui, Leicester (22 April 1991) quoted in Siddiqui, Ataullah op. cit. pp.134-5

109. Jillani, Shahzeb "Choosing to stay with his people" *The News* (21 December 1997) p.28

110. "Joint meeting calls for unity among Muslims and Christians" *Dawn* (28 May 1998); "Muslims, Christians should jointly foil designs of vested interests" *Pakistan Observer* (20 May 1998)

Other public initiatives to promote good relations with Muslims are few in number. One was included in the final statement of the seminar for religious minorities held at the CSC in Rawalpindi in 1996. This included a resolution to "strengthen existing networks of support and create new links in order to share our resources with one another in our common struggle with other Muslim fellow citizens, of discerning our identity as equal citizens of Pakistan".[111] Levrat's study of Christian study centres in Muslim countries (including the one at Rawalpindi) makes the interesting point that the existence of such study centres in itself promotes dialogue with Muslims if Muslims are encouraged to use them as well as Christians.[112]

In 1997 a seminar was held at the Pastoral Institute, Multan, attended by representatives of the Presbyterians, Salvation Army, Catholic Church and Church of Pakistan. The final statement arising from this seminar called for the urgent formation of an inter-denominational, inter-faith theological group.[113] As a result a "Muslim-Christian dialogue group", organised by Father James Channon, now meets monthly at a Dominican centre in Lahore. Meetings are attended by 70 to 80 Muslim and Christian theologians, lawyers, academics and journalists.

---

111. Final Statement of national seminar on "Religious Minorities in Pakistan: struggle for identity" p.106

112. Levrat, Jacques *Une Expérience de Dialogue. Les Centres d'Etude Chrétiens en Pays Musulmans* (Thèse de Doctorat présentée à la Faculté de Théologie de Lyon, 1984) reviewed in Kraan "Muslim-Christian relations and Christian Study Centres" pp.176-7

113. "The Christian Church in Pakistan: a vision for the 21st century" p.83

A group describing themselves as "liberal Muslims of Pakistan" formed the Muslim-Christian Solidarity Council of Pakistan, based in Karachi in 1998 with the aim of strengthening understanding between Muslims and Christians, to safeguard religious freedoms and to solve problems facing minorities in Pakistan.[114] It is interesting to note that this Muslim group, which invited co-operation and collaboration from "all peace and human loving persons", was formed as a result of a message sent by Cardinal Francis Arinze, president of the Pontifical Council for Interreligious Dialogue, at the end of Ramadan in 1998. The message spoke in generalizations of the importance of "religious values" and educating the young to respect other people's faiths. It ended with the statement "It may be necessary for Christians and Muslims to meet together more often in order to search together, before God, for answers to these questions."[115]

A pertinent comment on the subject of contemporary inter-faith dialogue and the possible dangers for minorities involved is made by Avril Powell who observes that Pakistani society is far more homogeneously Islamic now than when the state was created. Minority comments on religious issues, she concludes, "when perceived to be in conflict with the ideology of the Islamic state, can certainly

---

114. Letter dated 8 April 1998 from A.H. Zameer Ahmed Binyamin, convener / chief executive of the Group of Liberal Muslims, on behalf of the Central Organising Council of the Muslim-Christian Solidarity Council of Pakistan to the Bishop of Peshawar (copy supplied to the author by the addressee)

115. Letter from Cardinal Francis Arinze, president of the Pontifical Council for Religious Dialogue, to Mr A.H. Zameer Ahmed, chief executive of the Group of Liberal Muslims, Lahore (undated but received 18 February 1998)

not be engaged in safely in a public arena in the 1990s".[116]

Affirmation of Muslim aspirations

A very small number of Christians have firmly identified with Muslim aspirations for Pakistan. As mentioned previously, Dominic Moghal of the Christian Study Centre, would like to see Pakistan becoming an Islamic state under Shari'ah. If few Christians would go as far as desiring a true Islamic state, many had been active in the pro-Pakistan movement before partition, supporting the calls for the formation of Pakistan.[117] The lack of recognition given to this fact by the Muslim majority is a long-standing grievance of the Christian community.[118]

Dr Frank Khair Ullah, principal of Murree College, Sialkot, took a middle position, affirming the central nature of Islam in Pakistan without seeking an Islamic state. He wrote of the need for Pakistani Christians to "identify ourselves with the aspirations of the people and do all that we can for the achieving of this goal". He had earlier in the same sentence written of the search by Pakistani leaders for "a common basis of life for the translation of the ideology of Pakistan into practical form", the ideology being Islam and the search being chiefly the search for a consensus on the place of Islam in Pakistan.[119]

---

116. Powell, Avril "Contested Gods and Prophets: Discourse among minorities in late nineteenth-century Punjab" *Renaissance and Modern Studies* (December 1995) p.59

117. Sada, Mehboob "The cheating of history" *Al-Mushir* Vol. 38 No. 3 (1996) p.119

118. For example, Akhter op. cit. passim

119. Khair Ullah. "The future of Christians in Pakistan" p.1

Calls for the arming of the Christian community

Considerable publicity was given to the suggestion of the Christian community arming itself, which was made by Rt Rev. Alexander Malik, Church of Pakistan Bishop of Lahore. His warning was given in the aftermath of the protest suicide of Bishop John Joseph. Addressing a press conference, Bishop Malik spoke of the possibility of a Sipah-e-Masiha (Guardians of the Messiah) being formed if the violence and discrimination against Christians continued. The name cited by the bishop made a clear comparison with the Sunni Muslim militant group Sipah-e-Sahaba (Guardians of the Friends of the Prophet) which has been linked to many sectarian killings, mainly of Shi'a Muslims, and was perhaps involved in the Shanti Nagar violence.[120]

The suggestion was apparently a reaction to Bishop Joseph's suicide and the idea has not been adopted by anyone else, or even pursued by Bishop Alexander himself. Nevertheless, it is worth noting that in other countries where Christians suffer regular violence at the hands of Muslims, the previously passive Christian community has recently in certain areas started to arm itself or actually to retaliate.[121]

---

120. "Lahore Bishop warns of establishing 'Sipah-e-Masiha" *The News* (13 May 1998); "Bishop rejects govt claim on blasphemy law" *Dawn* (13 May 1998); "Pakistan Christian Militant Group Forms*" Daily News Brief from Catholic World News* (13 May 1998); Goldenberg, Susan "Fear among reviled believers breeds Christian soldiers" *The Guardian* (11 June 1998) p.17

Withdrawal from mainstream society

The majority of Pakistani Christians live in small groups of their co-religionists either in Christian *bastis* or colonies within a mixed settlement or in Christian-majority villages. In some cases this situation has arisen because missionary societies have bought plots of land and leased it to Christians. In other cases it is because, considered "untouchables", the Christians were prevented by social pressure from living close to anyone else and therefore had to live with each other.

Furthermore, most urban Christians are isolated from Muslims in that they follow Western customs at the major rites of passage, such as birth, marriage and death. Some Christian men adopt Western dress, particularly in urban contexts and for Christian ceremonies such as attending church worship services or weddings.[122] This strongly proclaims a Western identity, since Muslims going to mosque would all wear the traditional *shalwar kameez*. Since Zia's time it has been compulsory for civil servants to wear *shalwar kameez* at work. Goan and Anglo-Indian Christians[123] put a strong emphasis on using Western table manners (eating with cutlery rather than fingers, for example) and following Western food customs such as the consumption of alcohol and pork. These cultural choices are of course permitted but not necessary for Christians; they create barriers for social intercourse with Muslims. Christians in rural areas tend to remain closer to Pakistani customs and culture.[124]

---

121. For example, Nigeria, Indonesia
122. Heinrich op. cit. p.115
123. Jamshaid, Arif "The people time forgot" *The News* (15 June 1997) p.25

Because of the socio-economic status of the Christian community, the church establishment is very dependent financially on foreign mission agencies.[125] An example which demonstrates this clearly is the budget for the Church of Pakistan Diocese of Peshawar. Figures are given below for the years 1995 (actual) and 1996 (expected) in rupees.[126]

Year	Donations from Western Christian organizations	Income from Pakistan	Bank interest	Total	% Western sources
1995	5,680,442	3,631,758	145,500	9,457,700	60.1
1996	4,488,875	4,912,700	100,000	9,501,575	47.2

From this it can be seen that Western sources accounted for over 60% of the diocesan budget in 1995 and were expected to amount to almost 50% of the 1996 budget. It should be noted that both years the diocese was running at a deficit.

Migration

Some Christians respond to feelings of alienation from society by migrating. Anglo-Indians in particular (who usually prefer to focus on their European heritage rather

---

124. McClintock op. cit. pp.348-9

125. Malik, Alexander paper given at a Christian consultation (September 1988) p.4

126. Figures calculated from Ghauri, Sardar Hassan (Diocesan Treasurer) *Diocese of Peshawar Church of Pakistan*

than on their Asian heritage) left the country in large numbers in 1960s for Australia, the United Kingdom and the United States. Many young Anglo-Indians would still like to leave Pakistan but find it difficult because of stricter immigration laws in their would-be destination countries.[127]

In other cases migrants are the Christians of greatest ability and intellectual prowess who have been offered jobs in the West. It has become very difficult for Christian hospitals in Pakistan to find Christian Pakistani doctors for their staff, as most such doctors have emigrated.

A third category of migrants are those Christians who have been accused of blasphemy and acquitted by the courts. Because of the continuing danger to their lives from Islamic militants, some have been granted asylum in the West, for example Salamat Masih and Rehmat Masih in Germany.[128] Others have escaped before trial, for example Daniel Scot to Australia.[129] In the context of Gul Masih (see chapter 5), Shaukat Masih, advisor to the Chief Minister of Baluchistan, wrote of the likelihood that Christians would have to seek "political asylum" in other countries.[130]

Pakistan's Christian community are conscious that many are emigrating from their community to the West. While no comprehensive figures are available, Christians believe that emigration is increasing.[131] DeSouza estimates that

---

Budget for 1996
127. Jamshaid op. cit. p.25
128. Moghal "Alienation of the Local People" p.34
129. See the case history in chapter 5
130. Masih, Shaukat letter to Benazir Bhutto, published in *Jaudat International* Vol. 5 no. 40 (April 1995) pp.25-26
131. Moghal "Alienation of the local people" p.28

the Christian population of Saddar, Karachi, which had numbered 15,000 to 18,000 in 1947, was reduced to 7,000 or 8,000 by 1997. Most of this he believed to be due to emigration to the United States, Canada and the United Kingdom in the previous 25 years, and in particular since the process of Islamization had begun under Zia in the late 1970s.[132] Amongst those emigrating were all deSouza's own relatives, he himself staying only because of his responsiblities as a priest to his people.[133]

Emigration is a costly option in terms of finance and is therefore normally open only to those of substantial means. (An exception to this is individuals accused of blasphemy whose high-profile cases have gained them financial support from Western human rights organizations.) Moghal points out that the first Christians to emigrate were the Goans, who were economically better off than most other Pakistani Christians.[134] DeSouza states that most of the Christians who emigrated from Saddar were financially secure. (Indeed, they were mainly Goans and Anglo-Indians, that is the wealthiest and most Westernized of Pakistani Christians.) In other words, these Christians were not primarily economic migrants.

The emigration of the relatively more prosperous members of the community – usually the better educated – is obviously detrimental to the wellbeing of the community as a whole, leaving them poorer and more vulnerable over all.[135]

---

132. Father Archie deSouza of St Patrick's Church, Saddar, quoted in Askari, Hussain "A departure from the past" *The News* (25 May 1997)

133. Jillani, Shahzeb op. cit.

134. Moghal "Alienation of the local people" p.28

135. Yusuf, Zohra "The apartheid card" *The Herald* (November 1992) p.60

Calls for the creation of a Christian state

The possibility of a separate independent state for Pakistani Christians – to be called Takistan[136] – has sometimes been suggested. Arguments used to support this are the comparable population size of various European countries (3-4 million) and the logical parallel with the creation of Pakistan itself as a homeland for the Muslim minority in India.[137] Moghal suggests that the need for a separate homeland would be triggered by Pakistan becoming a theocratic state, i.e. with Shari'ah dominant over secular law, as proposed in the Fifteenth Constitutional Amendment Bill of 1998.[138]

The idea of Takistan first emerged following the nationalization of the Christian schools in 1972. It is a concept familiar to all educated Christians, who mostly consider it an unattainable ideal and do not expect it ever to become a reality. A marginally more feasible suggestion is that made by Pitras Ghani, the leader of a Christian party called Aqliati Haq Parast Party, who suggested soon after the suicide of Bishop John Joseph, that if Section 295-C of the Pakistan Penal Code was to remain on the statute books, Christians should be allocated a separate province within Pakistan.[139] There are six adjoining districts of Punjab where Christians are most densely concentrated. These are Lahore (190,169 Christians), Faisalabad (164,415), Sialkot (118,992), Sheikhupura (108,922), Gujranwala (109,659) and Kasur (75,611); together they have 58.9%

---

136. literally "vineyard" – a biblical allusion
137. Moghal "Alienation of the local people" p.35
138. Moghal "The right of dual vote" p.76
139. quoted in "Redress of Christians' grievances demanded" *The News* (14 May 1998)

of the total Christian population of Pakistan. Yet this still amounts to only 4.4% of the total population of the six districts, making it very unlikely that they could ever be made into a specifically Christian province.[140]

An interesting comment was made at the time of the first elections with separate electorates (1985) by one of the victorious Christian candidates who spoke of the need for unity and a single political party for Christians. He compared the Christians of Pakistan with the Palestinians, saying that the Palestinian Liberation Organisation's leader Yasir Arafat, was considered a head of state, though there was no Palestinian state. "So it can be with the Christians of Pakistan."[141]

Conclusion

For the first 50 years of their country's existence, Pakistani Christians had two self-imposed handicaps in responding to their problems. The first was an apathy born of self-pity and missionary influence and the second was their disunity. Furthermore, the ablest of their community tend to emigrate so that the best leadership is unavailable to lead. Thus the many disparate efforts in politics, research, publicity, dialogue etc. have had little effect in stemming the effects of Islamization as they impinge on Christians.[142] Social reaction has mainly involved a withdrawal from

---

140. Figures derived from the 1981 District Census Reports as presented in Addleton op. cit. pp.40-45

141. Emmanuel Zafar quoted in Tebbe, James "Interviews with Christian Members of the National Assembly" p.102

142. with the exception of the successful protests about the proposed religion column on national identity cards (see chapter 4)

contact with the majority community, and efforts at dialogue with Muslims have been few and far between.

Christians feel increasingly that they have no place in Pakistan and are unsure whether their identity as Christians is compatible with being Pakistanis. In the February 1997 elections, the Muslim League's slogan ran: "If you are a Muslim then join the Muslim League". The Jama'at-i-Islami and other Islamic parties had the slogan: "What is the meaning of Pakistan? – There is no God but Allah and Muhammad is His Apostle!" A sympathetic Muslim journalist of repute commented: "The atmosphere pervading the entire country is so completely Muslim in its ambience and impact that a non-Muslim appears to be something alien and out of place."[143] Moghal reports feelings of desperation such as "non-Muslims have no place in Pakistan and now it is totally a country of the Muslims" or "they have to leave this country in order to retain their religious identity".[144]

Some indeed do leave the country while others drop their Christian names (for example, "Masih", meaning "Messiah") and adopt Muslim names or give their children Muslim names in an attempt to integrate more successfully.[145] A Christian audio engineer, who was known by the Muslim name Sohail, described how useful it was to be generally thought a Muslim. In the middle of filming a scene, "all of a sudden I heard the director calling my real name [Christofer]. He didn't call me Sohail. It was only then that I realised that people had recognised me, and

---

143. Rahman, Hafizur "Minorities in our midst" *Dawn* (23 September 1998) p.21

144. Moghal "Alienation of the Local People" pp.25,28

145. Yusuf op. cit. p.60; Jacob, Noshin op. cit. p.26

were only too willing to beat me up. I wished my director had used Sohail to call me. You see, it helps." Interestingly, his Muslim name had been given him by a school-teacher who found the word "Christofer" too difficult to say.[146] Although not his own initiative, he still valued the concealment of his religious identity in this way.

A seminar on the subject of the "struggle for identity" faced by religious minorities in Pakistan was held at the CSC in 1996. The final statement of the seminar included the following comment, indicating the realization of the minorities that the Muslim majority may also be unclear about their identity:

> We realized that our identity in the country is confused. We want to be equal and wish to play a positive role but the legal and political processes in the country had (sic) cut us from the national main stream.[147]

The extreme and dramatic events of the destructive rioting at Shanti Nagar in 1997 and Bishop John Joseph's suicide the following year have had a marked effect, apparently radicalizing Pakistani Christians and lifting them from their previous lassitude to greater efforts and more courageous outspokenness. This has applied not only to Pakistani Christians within Pakistan but also to those in the diaspora. However the problem of disunity remains. The Christian community is fragmented along ecclesiological and theological lines, and further along biradari and family lines. In addition there are divisions because of socio-

---

146. Shirvanee op. cit. p.29
147. Final statement of the National Seminar on Religious Minorities in Pakistan p.104

economic status and the remnants of the caste system, the rural-urban differences, and the fact that the community is scattered geographically. It is hard to see how the Christians can unite to confront Islamic ideology together.

A further problem concerns the fact that their Western links and history of influence by Western missionaries have resulted in a Christian community which is by and large not trained in how to approach Islam. Its leaders have mainly been educated according to Western patterns only and are therefore ill-equipped to communicate and argue with the *ulema*. Christian leaders[148] tend to protest and complain, making uncompromising Western-type demands for human rights, in a way that is unlikely to convince the *ulema*, but could even push the *ulema* to the extreme of actually declaring Christians to be *dhimmi*. A better method would appear to be to negotiate with the *ulema*, reasoning from appropriate Islamic teachings and traditions, to find a middle ground acceptable to both sides. This, however is an unrealistic expectation because the current leadership generally lacks the necessary skills.

In the light of so many problems caused by Western links, it is ironic that perhaps the greatest immediate hope for Pakistani Christians comes from international pressure, which has developed greatly since the Shanti Nagar rioting in February 1997. Bishop John Joseph's suicide note (May 1998) said that his death would be the first "sacrifice" in a renewed campaign to get the blasphemy law repealed. So indeed it has proved to be. The day before his death Bishop

148. A good example is Alexander J.Malik, Bishop of Lahore, who makes frequent use of the words "human rights" and often refers to the United Nations, when he speaks about the difficulties which face Christians.

Joseph had released to the press a letter he had addressed to the people of Pakistan, calling for action to have Sections 295-B and 295-C repealed. He said that this required unity and co-ordination, including bishops inside and outside Pakistan, Parliamentarians, Muslims, Christians and Hindus, Pakistani NGOs and foreign NGOs, and urged contact with other governments who could act through their embassies in Pakistan.[149] It is interesting to note how many of these groupings have indeed got involved (though without much co-ordination and collaboration) since the Bishop's death and mainly as a direct result of his death. The Muslim initiative on behalf of Christians that was created in 1998 in response to a friendly message of greetings from Cardinal Arinze in the Vatican is also of interest.[150] Despite the years of pleading from Pakistani Christians in Pakistan, it was in the end a mildly worded Western approach which resulted in sympathetic action by Pakistani Muslims. It must also be noted that the American decision to withdraw aid from countries with a poor record on religious liberty[151] give a financial edge to international opinion which seems certain to increase the concern of the Pakistani government to earn the good opinion of that country at least.

---

149. "The final step against 295-C" Open letter dated 5 May 1998 from Dr John Joseph, Bishop of Faisalabad; Jillani, Anees "Blasphemy laws and the minorities" *The News* (14 May 1998)

150. Arinze, Cardinal Francis op. cit.

151. The International Religious Freedom Act of 1998 passed by the U.S. Senate on 9 October 1998, see for example "Senate Passes Religious Persecution Bill" *Daily News Brief from Catholic World News* (9 October 1998)

SEVEN

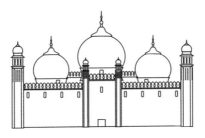

CONCLUSION

This study has sought to demonstrate the growing marginalization and oppression of the Christian community in Pakistan since independence. The beneficial effects of increasing urbanisation and education during this period have been counteracted by the process of Islamization, which has led to changes in the religious, cultural and political fabric of Pakistan that have had severe effects on the minority Christian community. As Bishop Michael Nazir-Ali noted in 1987, "The life of the Church of Pakistan is lived out today in a context which is becoming more and more difficult. There is cause for concern, and even for fear."[1] The situation has continued to deteriorate as the

---

1. Nazir-Ali, Michael *Frontiers in Muslim-Christian Encounter* (Oxford: Regnum Books, 1987) p.91

inequalities have increased.

Many Pakistani Christians feel they have been repeatedly betrayed. To start with the British Raj viewed Pakistan principally from a Hindu-Muslim basis, ignoring the existence of Christianity, and therefore made no provision or guarantees for the safety, security or status of Christians in the newly emergent state of Pakistan. Subsequently they felt betrayed by the West. For example, the USA supported and armed Islamic extremists as a by-product of its policies in Afghanistan, which added immensely to the difficulties of Pakistani Christians. The missionaries, whose faithful service had brought so many into the Christian faith, failed significantly to prepare the Christian community they had created for the political and inter-religious realities they were to face, in particular the encounter with Islam that lay ahead. As the years passed the worldwide Christian denominations of which the Pakistani Christians were a part failed to appreciate fully the difficulties facing their adherents in Pakistan; rather they saw their relationships on the international stage as being principally with Islam, both in the inter-faith context and in the context of Pakistani immigrants in the "home countries" of the denominations.

A clear example of this occurred in the weeks after the terrorist attack on the World Trade Centre and the Pentagon on September 11th 2001, which was followed by the launch of American-led air attacks on Afghanistan. Christians in Pakistan were subjected to retaliation from Muslims seeking vengeance on supposed allies of the Americans. Meanwhile in Britain, the US and other western countries, church leaders, media and government spoke out strongly in support of Muslim minorities, but said nothing in support of vulnerable Christians, such as the beleaguered Christian minority of Pakistan. While senior British bishops asserted that they were "standing shoulder to shoulder" with British Muslims, they said nothing of any solidarity with or concern for the defence of their Christian counterparts in Pakistan.[2] The Muslim population in Britain is approximately the same in percentage terms as the Christian population in Pakistan but, although every effort was made by Christian leaders in Britain to protect Muslims in Britain, they were silent on the plight of Christians in Pakistan. It is to the credit of General Musharraf and his government that he pledged to defend Christians in Pakistan in the wake of the events of September 11th and took action to curb Islamic leaders who were inciting violence against Christians.

Pakistani Christians feel betrayed not only by their co-religionists but also by their Muslim compatriots in Pakistan. Jinnah promised that all Pakistani citizens would be treated equally, irrespective of religion, but the erosion of this ideal began less than two years after independence. Broadly speaking, legislators favour Muslims, as do the law-enforcement agencies. Muslim leaders, whether political or religious, tend to behave as if a second-class status for Christians is natural and right.

It is easy to argue that, without the benefit of hindsight, no one at the time could have predicted the degree to which Pakistan would be transformed from Jinnah's ideals, that is a tolerant, kind and benevolent Muslim state where all minorities would be equal, to the intolerant, unequal Pakistan of Zia and post-Zia. Nevertheless betrayal is perhaps the most concise term to describe what the

---

2. Wynne-Jones, Jonathan "Bishops stand 'shoulder to shoulder' with Muslims" *The Church of England Newspaper* (21 September 2001)

Christian community in Pakistan has faced.

Implications of the two-nation theory

The rationale for the creation of Pakistan was the "two-nation theory", according to which it was impossible for Indian Muslims to continue to share a state with Hindus. Pakistan's founder, Muhammad Ali Jinnah, firmly embraced this argument. Nevertheless, he stated clearly that all citizens of the new state were to be equal, irrespective of their religion or caste. Less than two years after the creation of Pakistan, and just months after Jinnah's death, the first concrete step was taken in a process which would eventually negate Jinnah's expressed ideals of equality. This step was the adoption of the Objectives Resolution in March 1949, later to be incorporated into the various constitutions. It was the fruit of a debate begun in the early years of the decade as to the place Islam should have in Pakistan when it was later to come into existence.

Non-Muslims were immediately alarmed at the influential position given to Islam within the Objectives Resolution. But perhaps even more significant, though few realized it at the time, was that it drew a distinction between Muslims and non-Muslims. As Joshua Fazl-ud-Din pointed out, "There is a clear picture of two peoples, the Muslim majority and the non-Muslim minorities. With regard to both these communities the State has clearly assumed definite duties which have naturally got to be different and distinct from each other."[3] The Muslims of the new state of Pakistan had separated themselves from "two-nation"

---

3. Fazl-ud-Din, Joshua "Separate electorates – the life-blood of Pakistan" reproduced in Grover and Arora, op. cit. p. 176

India only to find that there were two "nations" in Pakistan, though this time the Muslims were the majority.

To distinguish between Muslims and non-Muslims is far more than a mere statement of fact. From its very inception Islam has been acutely conscious of its relations with non-Muslims. The vast majority of Islamic teaching – in early times the whole of it – assumes that the political, social and military dominance of Muslims over non-Muslims is the normal state; where this does not obtain, it must be sought. Modernist interpretations of Islam do not follow this pattern, so that distinguishing Muslims from non-Muslims would have little or no significance in such a context. But, as this study has shown, the overall trend in Pakistan is persistently towards conservative Islam. Given this fact, to distinguish Muslims from non-Muslims is to imply superiority and inferiority respectively. Three chapters (chapters 3, 4 and 5) have been devoted to examining the way this is worked out in Pakistan today with respect to Christians. Some aspects of discrimination are enshrined in the legislation, for example, the separate electorates system and the laws of evidence for the Islamic legal system. The dreaded "blasphemy law" does not specifically target Christians but can be, and has been, so easily mis-used by Muslims against Christians that it seems in practice to be discriminatory. Most aspects of the inferiority of non-Muslims arise not from legislation but from the choice and practice of individuals. As well as Islam there are other contributory factors, most notably the *jajmani* system in rural areas, the fact that the majority of Christians are descended from the despised low-caste Chuhras, and early missionary policies which hampered the political development of the Christian community. It is notable that, both in legislated discrimination and in the discriminatory choice and practice of individuals, discrimination is not limited to the specific requirements of the Shari'ah but extends more broadly. With respect to the choice and practice of individuals there is a great diversity of forms of discrimination and humiliation. It is small wonder that when the radical Islamic group Tanzeem-i-Islami protested against the government's proposal to give non-Muslims a dual vote, its complaint was that the government was "trying to wipe out differences between Muslims and minorities".[4]

Particular mention should be made here of the role of the police. If they chose to enforce and uphold the existing legislation many of the problems of Christians would be eliminated, for example bonded labour, physical violence, seizure of their property, etc. This could even be extended to discrimination in education and employment. However, the police commonly not only turn a blind eye to crimes against Christians but also very often exhibit the same prejudices themselves. Hence the frequent reports from Christians about visiting the police station to report a crime of which they were the victim and finding themselves beaten up by the police, not to mention the other examples of injustice described in chapters 3 and 4.[5] Christians are not the only ones who commonly fail to receive justice from the police; the poor of any religion are liable to suffer the same kind of treatment. But poor Christians tend to be treated worse than poor Muslims and furthermore their

---

4. "Protest against dual vote right" *Dawn* (12 March 1996) p.6

5. A detailed study of police corruption and malpractice is given in Chaudhry, M.A.K. *Policing in Pakistan* (Lahore: Vanguard Books (Pvt) Ltd, 1997)

poverty is itself to some extent a result of discrimination. It is interesting to note that one of the projects funded by the UK development programme for Pakistan is a training scheme for senior police officers.[6]

Having established that it is intrinsic within Islam that Muslims should have a higher status than non-Muslims, it seems with hindsight inevitable that a state founded on the basis of Islam should be unable to hold long to its founder's promise of equality irrespective of religion. Chapters 2 and 3 describe how the process of official Islamization developed by means of law and constitution, slowly at first, and then gathering momentum when General Zia gained power in 1977.

Considerable space has been devoted to the various constitutions of Pakistan. This subject is far from irrelevant to ordinary Pakistani Christians. Writing in 1973, when the Christian community was still shocked by the nationalization of its schools the previous year, Dr Frank Khair Ullah discussed the importance of the constitution for Christians. "Our interest in the constitution-making process and in the end product of it, that is the permanent constitution, is very vital to us. Our future, our life and death, will be determined by the type of document that would finally emerge."[7] "If the permanent constitution does not give us a real and honourable protection, we are doomed."[8] Similarly, Joshua Fazl-ud-Din wrote of the non-Muslim minorities that "their main source of strength lies in the fact that in the last resort they can always fall

6. Hoon, Geoffrey (House of Commons Hansard Debates for 9 June 1999 part 15, column 610)
7. Khair Ullah "The future of Christians in Pakistan" p.3
8. ibid. p.6

back on the constitution as their mainstay."[9] The very fact that Pakistan struggled so long with constitution-making, a pre-occupation decried by the right-wing political analyst, Z.A. Suleri,[10] was an indication of the enormous importance of the issue and the vastness of the gulf which existed between Westernized Pakistanis and the religious (i.e. Muslim) establishment.[11] Khair Ullah recognised the theoretical possibility that a constitution might be framed which would relegate Christians, as *dhimmis*, to the status of second-class citizens. He discussed the possible logical developments by which Christians, left unprotected by a faulty constitution, might even lose the right to profess, practise and propagate their religion, or that Muslims might lose the freedom to convert to Christianity. However, he finishes his discussion with the comment that he "cannot conceive in this enlightened age such a thing would happen in Pakistan".[12] Yet exactly quarter of a century later in 1998 the Prime Minister of Pakistan was proposing just such a measure, a constitutional amendment which could deprive the constitution of all power to protect non-Muslims. At the time of writing this proposed legislation has not been rejected by Parliament but merely set aside with no decision having been reached.

The role of Islam

The place and role of Islam in Pakistan has been an area of continuing controversy since before partition. The *ulema*

---

9. Fazl-ud-Din "Separate electorates" op. cit. p. 182

10. Suleri, Z.A. *Politicians and Ayub* (Rawalpindi: Capital Law and General Book Depot, 1965) p.7

11. Khair Ullah "The future of Christians in Pakistan" p.2

12. ibid. p.6

strove to give Islam a place superior to all man-made institutions and documents and make Pakistan a theocracy.[13] Politicians resisted this, and for many decades the *ulema* had to accept the position of opposition rather than supremacy.[14] In 1991 the Shari'ah was made the supreme law, though this had no practical effect because the constitution remained independent. The Fifteenth Constitutional Amendment Bill proposed in 1998 would, if passed, give to Islam the long-sought supra-constitutional status. Theoretically the implications of this for Christians could be enormous, relegating them to *dhimmi* status with no legal way to reassert their former rights, though optimists would remind themselves that most of the more extreme measures in the law and constitution have never yet been put into practice.

Mention must also be made of militant Islamic groups, many of which are closely linked with the religious schools.[15] As yet they do not enjoy massive political backing in Pakistan as a whole, nor are they even united.[16] In rare cases they have a direct effect on Christians, one example of this being the destructive rioting at Shanti Nagar and Khanewal in 1997, which appears to have been orchestrated with the help of Sipah-e-Sahaba and Harakat-ul-Ansar. Mostly, however, their activities are directed at

---

13. Khan, Mohammad Asghar "Pakistan's Geopolitical Imperatives" in Khan, Mohammad Asghar ed.. *The Pakistan experience: State and religion* (Lahore: Vanguard Books Lrd, 1985) p.236

14. Pirzada op. cit. pp.26-47

15. Malik, Jamal *Colonialization of Islam: Dissolution of traditional institutions in Pakistan* (Lahore: Vanguard Books (Pvt) Ltd, 1996) pp.303-6

16. Hyman op. cit. p.4

other targets, particularly the forces of secularism and opposing Islamic sects or schools. Nevertheless, there is an indirect effect on Christians in that an increasing number of Muslims in public office feel that their own security (both physical and occupational) requires them to be seen to be thoroughly Islamic. This can result in them showing bias against non-Muslims. The validity of these concerns is illustrated by the fact that when a judge acquitted on appeal Christians who had been accused of blasphemy he was himself threatened and eventually assassinated. It is difficult to speculate about Nawaz Sharif's motives, but it is interesting to note that his Fifteenth Constitutional Amendment Bill of 1998, which was to greatly increase his personal political power, would also have made the Qur'an and *Sunnah* the supreme law. If the latter measure was intended to sweeten the pill, it would nevertheless have had dire consequences for non-Muslim minorities.

First generation converts from Islam form only a very small percentage of the Pakistani Christian community, yet the subject of apostasy from Islam must also be included here. Pakistan has no law against this, and yet so strong is the conviction amongst Muslims that those who convert away from Islam should be punished that sometimes the blasphemy law is used for this purpose. Here is another example of Christian suffering caused not by laws and institutions but by biased and faulty interpretation, apparently due to prejudice. While numbers affected are small the problems for those involved can be enormous, even leading to death. Many converts lose their jobs or homes, and therefore there are some who keep secret from the Muslim community their change of faith.[17]

Christian identity

In a nation created as a homeland for Muslims, Christians have an identity problem (chapter 6). Three months before Pakistan came into being, Muhammad Asad wrote:

> we – we alone in the modern world – can, if we but want it, bring again to life that glorious vision which arose over the sands of Arabia nearly fourteen centuries ago: the vision of an *ummah* of free men and women bound together not by the accidental bonds of race and birth, but by their free, conscious allegiance to a common ideal.[18]

Asad's dismissive attitude to race and birth may not have been unrelated to the fact that he himself was European; nevertheless his writings carried great influence. He considered that Islam, the "common ideal", was the only acceptable qualification to gain a place in the new nation of Pakistan.

Nearly four decades later Jameel Jalibi, the Vice Chancellor of the University of Karachi, addressed the issue of Pakistani culture without considering that there were any non-Muslim Pakistanis at all:

> It is a fallacy to expect unity among different parts of Pakistan to remain established simply by virtue of the fact that their inhabitants are all Muslims. Unity among

---

17. Ismail, Zafar various interviews with the author (June 1999); confidential unpublished thesis (January 1999)

18. Asad, Muhammad "What do we mean by Pakistan?" (May 1947) reproduced in abridged form in *Impact International* (September 2001) p.9

them can be maintained only on the basis of culture; and culture, as I will explain later on, comprehends a religion, beliefs, customs, social living, material resources and needs and, indeed, all societal factors.[19]

Jalibi considers religion – meaning Islam – to be an intrinsic part of Pakistani culture and devotes more than a quarter of his book to the subject of the link between them. This is a widespread attitude which seems to have increased with the process of Islamization over the years. Christian Pakistanis are considered to be semi-Westerners as it were, following what is held to be a Western faith.

Many Pakistani Christians struggle hard to demonstrate that they are not Western-orientated. A complicating factor is that most Christians in Pakistan today are descended from converts made by Western missionaries. The fact that there was a Christian community in Pakistan which pre-dated Islam and existed alongside Islam for some time before being apparently eliminated is not widely acknowledged by Muslims. Amongst Christians, however, this fact is very precious and hence the space devoted to it in chapter 1. The other message which Christians try to communicate is that they are not immigrants or the descendants of immigrants, but "sons of the soil" and as such are loyal citizens of Pakistan.

The crisis of identity is not helped by self-generated confusion on the part of some Pakistani Christians. In rural areas there is much syncretism amongst the Christians and many add elements of Islam and Hinduism to their faith.

---

19. Jalibi, Jameel *Pakistan: the identity of culture* (Karachi: Royal Book Company, 1984) p.12

These Christians possibly feel less of an identity crisis than urban Christians as they are more sure about their identity as Pakistanis although less sure about their identity as Christians. In urban contexts, a contrasting problem exists – some Christians adopt Western cultural practices, unrelated to the Christian faith. This tends to reinforce to themselves their religious identity as Christians but blurs their cultural identity as Pakistanis.

It is primarily this identity crisis – as opposed to economic motives – which leads many better off Christians to emigrate to the West, while those who remain dream of a separate homeland for Christians of the sub-continent. The secession of minorities is not unknown in today's world and Bangladesh set a local precedent in 1971. However, the demographics of the Christian community make this unrealistic, as they are nowhere concentrated enough to be anything but a small minority within a Muslim majority. This also is the conclusion of Mordechai Nisan, of the Hebrew University of Jerusalem, as he surveys the situation of minorities in the Middle East (a term to which he gives a broad meaning):

> The logic of separation remains a latent possibility in the political equation. Where state-level compromise and conciliation do not exist or do not succeed … separating peoples by possibly decomposing multinational states is the obvious resolution of such a political problem. Life for the minority may be unbearable and meaningless without a collective self-assertion of national rights. But across the region, aside from the successful instance of Bengali separation from Pakistan in 1971, the possiblity of minority separation seems slim.[20]

The future

If secession is an impossibility, then what does the future hold for Pakistan's three million Christians? Campbell[21] writing in 1961 and Webster[22] writing in 1976 were both very optimistic about the future of the Church. But this was before Zia began to increase the pace of Islamization in 1977, at a time when few were alert to the signs of Islamization which had already taken place or had any concept of how things might develop. It is perhaps also significant that both authors were Westerners, a factor which could possibly dull their appreciation of the pressures and handicaps which Pakistani Christians faced.

Previous safeguards in law and constitution (see chapter 3) have been gradually eroded and were on the brink of being overridden altogether if the Fifteenth Amendment Bill had been passed. As a largely poor and uneducated community, it is hard for Christians even to avail themselves of the existing safeguards in a society where bribery and anti-Christian prejudice are the norm. The majority of Punjabi Christians were loyal supporters of the creation of Pakistan, some of whose community leaders made a positive decision to be part of the new Muslim-majority state rather than remain within India. As early as 1949 Joshua Fazl-ud-Din expressed their sense of betrayal with respect to the fact that there were no Christian representatives in the Constituent Assembly and therefore no Christian voice in the framing of the Constitution. "All

---

20. Nisan, Mordechai *Minorities in the Middle East: a history of struggle and self-expression* (Jefferson, North Carolina: McFarland and Company, Inc, 1991) p.24
21. Campbell op. cit.
22. Webster op. cit.

deputations and appeals of the community have failed to move the Central Government, although the promise of 'fair and generous treatment' towards the minorities has never been doubted by the Christians".[23] Fazl-ud-Din urged Christians to replace their attitude of suspense with one of optimism.[24] Yet hopes for positive change continue to be disappointed.

The Christians' disappointment is understandable, but perhaps their hopes of equality in a Muslim homeland had been unrealistic, given the nature of Islam. It is unlikely that Jinnah's promise of equality could have been kept for long, as non-Muslims cannot be equal citizens with Muslims in an Islamic context. Their perceived "betrayal" was almost inevitable.

Although the human desire for equality will always remain, realistically speaking it would seem doubtful whether calls for equal status with Muslims will ever be completely effective. However, from this study of the process of Islamization in Pakistan it would appear that there are some practical possibilities for improving their condition which could realistically be attempted by the Christian community.

One possible way forward might be to work for the proper enforcement of the existing laws and constitution and their protection from being over-ridden by the proposed fifteenth amendment to the constitution. If this could be achieved it would give Christians at least access to justice to right many of the wrongs committed against them by individuals, including false accusations under the

23. Fazl-ud-Din *Future of Christians in Pakistan* p.10
24. ibid. p.144

blasphemy law. In seeking this, Christians would have the support not only of other non-Muslim minorities who would benefit too, but also of many secular Muslim organizations, notably the Human Rights Commission of Pakistan, who are already advocating this. It would be a difficult but not impossible task. The police force has very little to recommend it at the moment, but with the judiciary the picture is somewhat better. Incidents of gross injustice towards Christians do occur, for example the case of Gul Masih who was found guilty of blasphemy because the one person who testified against him was a bearded Muslim. On the other hand there are many judges who are courageous and fair-minded and willing to over-rule unjust decisions made at a lower level. Thus Gul Masih was later acquitted.

A second possible realistic goal to aim for would be an amendment to the electoral system so as to give Christians more political power. This is supported by the Pakistan People's Party. Like the first goal, it would be difficult in that there is much opposition from the Islamic parties, but it need not be considered impossible, especially given the fact that many other Muslim-majority countries have equal voting rights for all their citizens.[25]

A third possible achievable goal might be to change the attitude and behaviour of Christians themselves. Naturally there are exceptions, but generally speaking the Church is

---

25. Since completing this book, there has been an important change in the situation regarding separate electorates in Pakistan. On 16th January 2002 the Government of Pakistan announced that the system of separate electorates would be abolished. However, at the time of going to press (March 2002), there is still much dispute from both Christian and Muslim parties as to the best way forward.

severely weakened by disunity and particularly by selfish leadership arising principally from the *biradari* system. William Young, a former Bishop of Sialkot, who studied Church-State relationships in the East up to 820 AD, drew from his studies a number of lessons for minority churches today, concluding:

> This brings us to our final point. For the spiritual health of the Church, and to ensure its security and respect in a non-Christian State, it is absolutely essential that Christians lay to heart the importance of avoiding in-fighting or inter-denominational conflicts. Where visible union is possible, it is not only desirable but right; where it is not possible, at least the various churches should co-operate with one another and aim at unity of spirit.[26]

Effective Christian response is also emasculated by a self-pitying apathy. Again, there are many valiant exceptions to this, notably the protest suicide of Bishop John Joseph in May 1998. Also, it is only to be expected that an impoverished and poorly educated community, for whom mere existence is a struggle, trained two or three generations back to avoid political involvement, should be fairly passive. Help has been sought in recent years from abroad, but there would appear to be more which Christians could be doing for themselves if they so wished.

Some have argued that Pakistani Christians might be well advised to try to accept that it is doubtful whether they will ever have equality with Muslims. Unpalatable though it may be, acceptance of this probable outcome, so the argument runs, could help the Christian community to learn

26. Young *Patriarch, Shah and Caliph* p.182

to live as an unequal minority in a society where the majority
has been conditioned by history to be especially nervous
and suspicious of them. There are areas in which they
already have advantages over traditional *dhimmi*, for
example the freedom from paying *jizya* (although they do
have to do military service), and the legal freedom to erect
churches (albeit there are often difficulties in practice, and
it is not possible in the NorthWest Frontier Province). Also
relevant is the freedom for Muslims to convert to
Christianity. On the other hand there are areas in which
they are deprived beyond the traditional restrictions on
dhimmis, for example, the violence to person and property
which affects Christians disproportionately and for which
they find it so hard to get redress. *Dhimmi* status is not as
high as Muslim status but nevertheless carries many rights
which are not available to all minorities in Muslim contexts
today. Some believe that Pakistani Christians might be able
to improve their situation by arguing from the teachings of
Islam itself to seek for themselves the full rights of *dhimmi*
where these are lacking, although this runs the risk of losing
the "extra" benefits which they already have. These extra
benefits would need to be safeguarded to ensure that the
Christians did not end up worse off than at present. Another
possibility would be to argue for *mu'ahid* status, which is
free of the need to pay *jizya*. It is possible to draw a parallel
with the experience of Muslim feminists who have tended
to make better progress for the rights and freedoms of
women when working within the Islamic paradigm (such
as in Saudi Arabia and Iran) than outside it.[27] At a more
hopeful time than the present, Dr Khair Ullah, though

27. Yamani, Mai (ed.) *Feminism and Islam: legal and literary
perspectives* (Reading: published for Centre for Islamic and

reluctant to believe that Pakistani Christians **would** ever find themselves relegated to second-class status, wrote:

> If we are officially considered as *dhimmis*, we, at least, would like to know what are our rights and duties. What would be worse still is to be merely tolerated as a minority, without any special privileges but surrounded with many invisible and intangible handicaps.[28]

However, this would seem to be a counsel of despair. Pakistani Christians have an advantage over many other Christian minorities in Muslim contexts in that their rights are are at least partially safeguarded in law and constitution, albeit these are rarely put into effect. They need not accept the second-class status of *dhimmi*. They have the constitution and much of the law of the land, as well as Pakistan's signature on the United Nations Universal Declaration of Human Rights, on their side in their struggle for equality. Though they may never achieve complete equality, still they can work towards it, and every step gained is an advantage.

Although this study has shown that Islamization has had a seriously detrimental effect on the Christian community in Pakistan, it should in theory be possible for the process, at least as it affects Christians, to be halted or even reversed. The modern era has the example of Kemal Atatürk's Turkey, a secular state created from the last remnants of the Ottoman Empire and still determinedly secular after nearly 80 years.[29] However, the argument that the methodology most likely to be effective in achieving this

---

Middle Eastern Law SOAS by Garnet, 1996) passim
  28. Khair Ullah "The future of Christians in Pakistan" p.6
  29. An excellent study on this subject is Mango, Andrew *Atatürk* (London: John Murray, 1999)

reversal is by using Islamic principles is fundamentally flawed. Islam will never grant more than *dhimmi* status to non-Muslims, unless it undergoes a reformation. At the time of writing, President Musharraf has done much to counteract the power of the *ulema* in a matter of weeks in late 2001, not acting from an Islamic stance but from a secular-liberal stance based on the national interest. On seizing power he declared his intention of being another Atatürk,[30] and this he has now begun to live up to, as a strong leader who has imposed his will on his people, taking the first small steps in reversing the Islamization trend.

The overall conclusion to be drawn is that Christian minorities in Muslim-majority contexts are intrinsically vulnerable. There seems to be a one-way process towards oppression that has rarely been reversed. It is in the very nature of Islam to discriminate against non-Muslims. Equality with the majority would be the first choice of a minority. If this fails, then *dhimmi* status offers at least some rights and protection. However, today's Islam is in turmoil, and even *dhimmi* status cannot be guaranteed. As this study has shown Christians in Pakistan suffer in many ways additional to the restrictions traditionally imposed on *dhimmi*. The protection element of *dhimmi* status seems to have been lost, leaving only the restrictions. But there is no international outcry on their behalf. Neither is there much to be heard about the suffering of Christians in other Muslim contexts. Christian minorities are defended neither by their own governments nor by their fellow Christians in freer contexts. Their cries and protests go unheeded and they can only watch helplessly as the seemingly inexorable process of Islamization engulfs them.

---

30. 12 October 1999

GLOSSARY

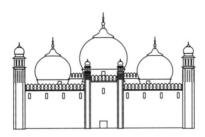

ahl al-kitab — people of the book (i.e. Jews and Christians)

basti — slum-like settlement

biradari — network of related extended families

comity — in a Christian missionary context, the division of territory between different denominations or mission societies

dhimmi — non-Muslims in an Islamic society. The term implies protection and subjugation. Strictly speaking it means non-Muslims who have been conquered by Muslims

din

religion, in its practice

diyat

financial compensation for injury or homicide

fatwa

a published decision concerning religious doctrine or law

hadd (pl. *hudood*)

fixed punishment for a crime as specified in the Qur'an or *ahadith* e.g. amputation for theft, flogging for drinking alcohol, stoning or flogging for adultery

hadith (pl. *ahadith*)

a tradition recording a precedent set by Muhammad or his early followers

ijma

consensus of opinion of the recognized religious authorities at any given time concerning the interpretation and application of the teaching of the Qur'an in any particular situation

ijtihad

literally "exertion"; a logical deduction on a legal or theological question by a *mujtahid*, as distinguished from *ijma*, which is a collective opinion. Most Sunni Muslims believe that "the door of *ijtihad* has closed", whereas Shi'a Muslims believe *ijtihad* can still be practised.

irtidad apostasy from Islam

jajmani system of land ownership and economics which exists in rural Pakistan, based on the power of small numbers of *zamindars* who own most of the land

jihad literally "an effort"; a holy war; understood by some Muslims literally as military action to expand or defend Islam, and by other Muslims in spiritual or moral terms as self-improvement

jizya tax payable by *dhimmi*, as a sign of their subjugation to Muslims

kafir (pl. *kafirun*) unbeliever, infidel, non-Muslim

millet non-Muslim minority community ruled by the Ottoman empire; the minority communities were permitted to be self-governing and were controlled by the Ottomans through the minority leaders.

muhajirun	Muslims who migrated to Pakistan from India at partition
mujtahid	literally "one who strives to obtain a high position and learning"; a very learned religious teacher; one who practises *ijtihad*
nizam-e-mustafa	literally "order of the Prophet" but used to mean "Islamic system"; a political rallying call of some Islamic parties
qisas	retaliation for injury or homicide
qiyas	analogous reasoning
rayah	the term used in the Ottoman empire to mean *dhimmi* i.e. non-Muslim subject
ridda	apostasy from Islam
Shari'ah	Islamic law
Shi'a	Muslim sect which believes that the rightful successor to Muhammad was Ali, his closest relative. They are a minority in Pakistan
shirk	associating anyone with Allah as a co-deity. The worst sin in Islam.

Sunnah	literally "a trodden path" i.e. a custom or practice; the words and actions of Muhammad and his early followers who knew him personally.
Sunni	literally "one of the path"; orthodox Islam as distinguished from Shi'a Islam; the majority who follow the successors of Muhammad by election
ta'zir	a discretionary punishment for a crime (in contrast to *hadd*)
ulema	group of Islamic theologians
umma	the whole community of Islam, the totality of all Muslims
ushr	a tithe given to the Islamic state
zakat	alms due from every Muslim
zamindar	powerful land-owner in rural parts of Pakistan, wielding huge influence in local society and politics
zina	adultery

BIBLIOGRAPHY

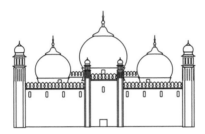

Books (including sections within books)

Ahmad, Khurshid ed. and transl. of Maududi, S. Abul A'la *The Islamic Law and Constitution*, 7th edition (Lahore: Islamic Publications Ltd, 1980)

Ahmed, Aziz *Islamic Modernism in India and Pakistan 1857-1968* (London: Oxford University Press, 1967)

Ahmed, Ishtiaq *The Cconcept of an Islamic State in Pakistan: an analysis of ideological controversies* (Lahore: Vanguard Books Ltd, 1991)

Akhter, Salamat *Tehrek-e-Pakistan ke Gumnam Kirdar* [The anonymous heroes of the Pakistan Movement] (Rawapindi: Christian Study Centre, 1997)

Alavi, Hamza "Pakistan and Islam: Ethnicity and Ideology" in Halliday, Fred and Alavi, Hamza (eds.) *State and Ideology in the Middle East and Pakistan* (London: Macmillan, 1988)

Ali, A. Yusuf *The Holy Qur'an: Text, Translation and Commentary* (Leicester: The Islamic Foundation, 1975)

Ali, Chaudhri Muhammad *The Emergence of Pakistan* (Lahore: Research Society of Pakistan, University of the Punjab, 1996)

Amin, Mohammad *Islamization of Laws in Pakistan* (Lahore: Sang-e-Meel Publications, 1989)

Amjad-Ali, Charles "Political and Social Conditions in Pakistan" in Miller, Roland E. and Mwakabana, Hance A.O. *Christian-Muslim Dialogue: Theological and Practical Issues* (Geneva: Lutheran World Federation, 1998)

Amjad-Ali, Charles "Religion and Politics" in Miller, Roland E. and Mwakabana, Hance A.O. *Christian-Muslim Dialogue: Theological and Practical Issues* (Geneva: Lutheran World Federation, 1998)

Amjad-Ali, Christine "The Literary Evidence for Thomas in India" in Rooney, John (ed.) *St Thomas and Taxila: A Symposium on Saint Thomas* (Rawalpindi: Christian Study Centre, 1988)

Amjad-Ali, Christine and Charles *The Legislative History of the Shariah Act* (Rawalpindi: Christian Study Centre, 1992)

Anderson, J.N.D. "Pakistan: an Islamic state?" in Code Holland, R.H. and Schwarzenberger G. (eds.) *Law, Justice and Equality* (London: Sir Isaac Pitman & Sons, Ltd, 1967)

An-Na'im, Abdullahi Ahmed *Toward an Islamic Reformation: Civil Liberties, Human Rights and International Law* (Syracuse: Syracuse University Press, 1990)

Anwarullah *The Islamic Law of Evidence* (Lahore: Research Cell, Dyal Singh Trust Library, 1992)

Arkoun, Mohammed "The Notion of Revelation" in Havemann, Axel and Johansen, Baber (eds.) *Gegenwart als Geschichte: Islamwissenschaftliche Studien* (Leiden: Brill, 1988)

Asad, Muhammad *ThePrinciples of State and Government in Islam*, new edition (Gibraltar: Dar Al-Andalus Limited, 1980)

Attwater, Donald *The Dissident Eastern Churches*, (USA, The Bruce Publishing Company, 1937)

Barrett, David B. (ed.) *World Christian Encyclopedia* (Oxford: Oxford University Press, 1982)

Bat Ye'or *The Dhimmi: Jews and Christians Under Islam* revised and enlarged English edition (London: Associated University Presses, 1985)

Bat Ye'or *The Decline of Eastern Christianity Under Islam: From Jihad to Dhimmitude* (London: Associated University Presses, 1996)

Björkman, W. "Kafir" in Bosworth, C.E., van Donzel, E., Lewis, B. and Pellat, Ch. (eds.) *Encylopaedia of Islam, Vol. IV* (Leiden: Brill, 1978)

Bosworth, C.E., E. van Donzel, W.P. Heinrichs and C. Pellat (eds.) *The Encyclopaedia of Islam*, new edition, vols issued at intervals (Leiden: Brill, 1979 – 1997)

Bowen, Harold and Gibb, H.A.R. *Islamic Society and the West,* Vol 1 Islamic Society in the eighteenth century part II (London: Oxford University Press, 1957)

Burke, S.M. and Quraishi, Salim Al-Din *Quaid-i-Azam Mohammad Ali Jinnah: His personality and his politics* (Karachi: Oxford University Press, 1997)

Butt, M. Rafiq *The Constitution of the Islamic Republic of Pakistan, 1973* (Lahore: Mansoor Book House, 1991)

Cahen, C. "Dhimma" in *Encyclopaedia of Islam* Vol. II (Leiden: Brill, 1983)

Campbell, Ernest Y. *The Church in the Punjab* (place of publication not stated, perhaps Nagpur: National Christian Council of India, 1961)

Cantwell Smith, Wilfred *Modern Islam in India*, 2nd Indian edition (London: Victor Gollancz Ltd, 1946)

Cantwell Smith, Wilfred *Pakistan as an Islamic state* (Lahore: Shaikh Muhammad Ashraf, 1951)

Caroe, Sir Olaf *The Pathans* (Karachi: Oxford University Press, 1958)

Chaudhry, M.A.K. *Policing in Pakistan* (Lahore: Vanguard Books (Pvt) Ltd, 1997)

Choudhury. G.W. *Constitutional Development in Pakistan* (London: Lowe and Brydone, 1971)

Choudhury, Golam W. *Pakistan: Transition from Military to Civilian Rule* (Essex: Scorpion Publishing Ltd, 1988)

Choudhury, Golam W. *Islam and the Modern Muslim World* (Kuala Lumpur: WHS Publications Sdn Bhd, 1993)

Code Holland, R.H. and Schwarzenberger G. (eds.) *Law, Justice and Equality* (London: Sir Isaac Pitman & Sons, Ltd, 1967)

Comfort, Richard O. *The Village Church in West Pakistan: Report of a Consultation held under the auspices of the West Pakistan Christian Council, November 10, 1956 to April 1, 1957* (printed for private use, no date given)

Contemporary Forms of Slavery in Pakistan (New York: Human Rights Watch/Asia, 1995)

Dar, Saifur Rahman "Gondophares and Taxila" in Rooney, John (ed.) *St Thomas and Taxila: A Symposium on Saint Thomas* (Rawalpindi: Christian Study Centre, 1988)

Dawood, Jan Mohammed *The Religious and Political Dilemma of Pakistan* (Karachi: Hasan Publisher, 1993)

De Young, Chris *The Pakistan Educational Survey* (place and publisher unknown, possibly Illinois? and the American Presbyterian Mission, 1955)

Dildar, Peter Jacob and Mughal, Aftab Alexander *Section 295-C Pakistan Penal Code: A Study of the History, Effects and Cases Under Blasphemy Laws in Pakistan* (Faisalabad: National Commission for Justice and Peace Pakistan, February 1995)

Doi, Abdul Rahman I. *Non-Muslims under Shari'ah* (Maryland: International Graphics, 1979)

Dumont Louis *Homo Hierarchicus: the caste system and its implications,* translated from the French by Mark Sainsbury, Louis Dumont and Basia Gulati (London, 1970)

Edwardes, S.M. and Garrett, H.L.O. *Mughal Rule in India* (New Delhi: Asian Publication Services, 1979)

El-Awa, M.S. *Punishment in Islamic Law: a comparative study* (Indianapolis: American Trust Publication, 1982)

Esposito, John L. "Pakistan: Quest for Islamic Identity" in John L, Esposito (ed.) *Islam and Development* (Syracuse: Syracuse University Press, 1980)

Fattal, Antoine *Le Statut Légal des Non-Musulmans en Pays d'Islam* (Beirut: Imprimerie Catholique, 1958)

Fazl-ud-Din, Joshua *Future of Christians in Pakistan* (Lahore: The Punjabi Darbar Publishing House, 1949)

Fazl-ud-Din, Joshua *Pakistani Revolution and the Non-Muslims* (Lahore: The Punjabi Darbar Publishing House, 1960)

Fazl-ud-Din, Joshua "Separate electorates – the life-blood of Pakistan" reproduced in Grover, Verinder and Arora, Ranjana (eds.) *Pakistan Fifty Years of Independence* (New Delhi: Deep and Deep Publications, 1997)

Fortescue, Adrian *The Orthodox Eastern Church* 3rd edition (London, Catholic Truth Society, 1911)

Gibb, H.A.R. and Kramers, J.H. *Shorter Encyclopaedia of Islam* (Leiden: Brill, 1974)

Goldziher, Ignaz *Introduction to Islamic Theology and Law,* translated by Andras and Ruth Hamori (Princeton: Princeton University Press, 1981)

Government of Pakistan Ministry of Law *The Constitution of the Islamic Republic of Pakistan* (Karachi, Manager of Publications, the Government of Pakistan, 1956)

Grover, Verinder and Arora, Ranjana (eds.) *Pakistan Fifty Years of Independence* (New Delhi: Deep and Deep Publications, 1997)

Hakim, Khalifa Abdul *Islamic Ideology: the fundamental beliefs and principles of Islam and their application to practical life,* 8th edition (Lahore: Institute of Islamic Culture, 1994)

Halliday, Fred and Alavi, Hamza (eds.) *State and Ideology in the Middle East and Pakistan* (London: Macmillan, 1988)

Halliday, Fred "'Islam is in danger': Authority, Rushdie and the Struggle for the Migrant Soul" in Hippler, Jochen and Lueg, Andrea (eds.) *The Next Threat: Western Perceptions of Islam* translated by Laila Friese (London: Pluto Press, 1995)

Hamidullah, M. *Status of non-Muslims in Islam* Publication no. 40 (Islamabad: Da'wah Academy, International Islamic University, 1989)

Havemann, Axel and Johansen, Baber (eds.) *Gegenwart als Geschichte: Islamwissenschaftliche Studien* (Leiden: Brill, 1988)

The Hedaya: Commentary on the Islamic Laws, translated by Charles Hamilton, Vol. II, 1791 (New Delhi: Kitab Bhavan, reprinted 1985)

Heffening W. "Murtadd" in C.E. Bosworth, E. van Donzel, W.P. Heinrichs and C. Pellat (eds.) *The Encyclopaedia of Islam*, new edition, Vol. VII (Leiden: Brill, 1993)

Heinrich, J.C. *The Psychology of a Suppressed People* (London: George, Allen and Unwin, 1937)

Hennecke, E. *New Testament Apocrypha* (Philadelphia: Westminster Press, 1965)

Hippler, Jochen and Lueg, Andrea (eds.) *The Next Threat: Western perceptions of Islam,* transl. Laila Friese (London: Pluto Press, 1995)

Hoke, Donald (ed.) *The Church in Asia* (Chicago: Moody Press, 1975)

Horner, Norman A. *A guide to Christian Churches in the Middle East* (Elkhart, Indiana: Mission Focus Publications, 1989)

Hughes, T.P. *Dictionary of Islam* (Lahore: Premier Book House, 1885)

Human Rights Commission of Pakistan *The 'Blasphemy' Episodes: An HRCP inquiry* (Lahore: Human Rights Commission of Pakistan, no date)

Human Rights Commission of Pakistan *State of Human Rights in Pakistan 1993* (Lahore: Human Rights Commission of Pakistan, 1994?)

Human Rights Commission of Pakistan *State of Human Rights in 1998* (Lahore: Human Rights Commission of Pakistan, 1999)

Human Rights Monitor 97: a report on the religious minorities in Pakistan (Lahore: National Commission for Justice and Peace, Catholic Bishops' Conference of Pakistan, 1998)

Humphreys, R. Stephen *Islamic History* (London: I.B. Tauris, 1991)

Hussain, Asaf *Islamic Movements in Egypt, Pakistan and Iran: an annotated bibliography* (London: Mansell Publishing Ltd, 1983)

Ibn Hadj, Mohammed al Abdari *Al Madkhal,* vol. ii (Cairo edition)

Iqbal, Afzal *Islamisation of Pakistan* (Lahore: Vanguard Books Ltd, 1986)

Iqbal, Javid *Ideology of Pakistan* (Lahore: Ferozsons Ltd., 1971)

Jalibi, Jameel *Pakistan: the identity of culture* (Karachi: Royal Book Company, 1984)

James, M.R. *The Apocryphal New Testament* (Oxford: Clarendon Press? 1972)

Janin, Père Raymond *The Separated Eastern Churches,* transl. by P. Boylan (London: Sands & Co., 1933)

Johnstone, Patrick *Operation World,* 5th edition (Bulstrode: WEC Publishing, 1993)

Joshua, P.N. *A Manual of Laws for Christians* (Lahore: Punjab Religious Book Society, 1957)

Kennedy, Charles *Islamization of Laws and Economy: case studies on Pakistan* (Islamabad: Institute of Policy Studies, 1996)

Khadduri, Majid *War and Peace in the Law of Islam* (Baltimore: The Johns Hopkins Press, 1955)

Khan, Mahmood Hasan *Underdevelopment and Agrarian Structure in Pakistan* (Lahore: Vanguard Publications Ltd, 1994)

Khan, Mohammad Asghar ed.. *The Pakistan experience: state and religion* (Lahore: Vanguard Books Lrd, 1985)

Khan, S.A. *Manual of Christian Laws* (Lahore: Mansoor Book House, 1995)

Kharroufah, Prof. Dr Ala'ul Deen *The Judgement of Islam on the Crimes of Salman Rushdie "Death Sentence Still in Force"* (Kuala Lumpur: Percetakan Sentosa (KL) Sdn. Bhd., 1991)

Khuri, Fuad I. *Imams and Emirs: state, religion and sects in Islam* (London: Saqi Books, 1990)

Klein, F.A. *The Religion of Islam*, new edition (London: Curzon Press Ltd, 1979)

Korson, Henry (ed.) *Contemporary problems of Pakistan* (Leiden: E.J. Brill, 1974)

Kurdi, Abdulrahman Abdulkadir *The Islamic State: A Study based on the Islamic Holy Constitution* (London: Mansell Publishing Limited, 1984)

Kymlicka, Will *Multicultural Citizenship* (Oxford: Clarendon Press, 1995)

Lambton, Ann K.S. *State and Government in Medieval Islam: an introduction to the study of Islamic political theory: the jurists* London Oriental Series, Vol. 36 (Oxford: Oxford University Press, 1981)

Little, Donald P. (ed.) *Essays on Islamic Civilisation* (Leiden: E.J. Brill, 1976)

Lodhi, Naheed Jehan *Pakistan Religious Minorities and Adultery (Muslim Laws)* (Lahore, date unknown, between 1995 and 1998)

Lucas, E.D. and Thakur Das, F. *The Rural Church in the Punjab* (Lahore: Forman Christian College, 1938)

Madani, Mohammad Asrar *Verdict of Islamic Law on Blasphemy and Apostasy* (Lahore: Idara-e-Islamiat, 1994)

Mahmassani, Subhi '*Arkan huquq al-insan*' (Beirut: Dar al-'ilm li'l-ma-layin, 1979)

Mahmood, Safdar *Constitutional Foundations of Pakistan* (Lahore: Publishers United Ltd, 1975)

Mahmood, Shaukat *The Constitution of Pakistan 1962* (Lahore: Pakistan Law Times Publications, 1962)

Mahmood, Shaukat *The Constitution of Pakistan (as amended upto date)* (Lahore: The Pakistan Law Times Publications, 1965)

Malik, Alexander John, Bishop of Lahore *Serving Community* (Lahore: Tanzeem-i-Nau, no date but before April 1982)

Malik, Iftikhar H. *State and Civil Society in Pakistan: politics of authority, ideology and ethnicity* (Basingstoke: MacMillan Press, 1997)

Malik, Jamal *Colonialization of Islam: dissolution of traditional institutions in Pakistan* (Lahore: Vanguard Books (Pvt) Ltd, 1996)

Mar Thoma, Alexander *The Mar Thoma Church: heritage and mission* (Tirvalla, 1985)

Maududi, Abul A'la *Jihad in Islam* a version of a speech delivered on Iqbal Day 13 April 1939 at Lahore Town Hall (Kuwait: International Islamic Federation of Student Organisations, no date)

Mawdudi, S. Abul A'la *The Process of Islamic Revolution* (Lahore: Islamic Publications Ltd, 1970)

Maududi, S. Abul A'la *The Islamic Law and Constitution* translated and edited by Khurshid Ahmad, 7th edition (Lahore: Islamic Publications Ltd, 1980)

Maududi, S. Abul Ala *Purdah* (Lahore: Islamic Publications Ltd, 1981)

Maududi, S. Abul A'la *Rights of Non Muslims in Islamic State* (sic), 7th edition (Lahore: Islamic Publications Ltd, 1982)

Maududi, S. Abul A'la *The Meaning of the Quran,* 13th edition (Lahore: Islamic Publications (Pvt.) Limited, 1993)

Mawdudi, Abul Ala *The Punishment of the Apostate According to Islamic Law,* transl. and annotated by Syed Silas Husain and Ernest Hahn (publisher unknown, 1994)

Mayer, Ann Elizabeth *Islam and Human Rights: Tradition and politics* (Boulder: Westview Press, 1991)

Medlycott, A.E. *India and the Apostle Thomas* (London: David Nutt, 1905)

Mehdi, Rubya *The Islamization of the Law in Pakistan,* Nordic Institute of Asian Studies, Monograph Series No. 60 (Richmond: Curzon Press Ltd, 1994)

Miller, Roland E. and Mwakabana, Hance A.O. *Christian-Muslim Dialogue: Theological and Practical Issues* (Geneva: Lutheran World Federation, 1998)

Moffett, Samuel Hugh *A History of Christianity in Asia,* Vol. 1 *Beginnings to 1550* (San Francisco: HarperSanFrancisco, 1992)

Moghal, Dominic *Changing Realities and Churches' Response* (Rawalpindi: Christian Study Centre, 1997)

Moghal, Dominic *Human Person in Punjabi Society: a tension between religion and culture* (Rawalpindi: Christian Study Centre, 1997)

Moghal, Dominic and Jivan, Jennifer (eds.) *Religious Minorities in Pakistan: Struggle for Identity* (Rawalpindi: Christian Study Centre, 1996)

Mughal, Dr Justice Munir Ahmad "Foreword" to Anwarullah *The Islamic Law of Evidence* (Lahore: Research Cell, Dyal Singh Trust Library, 1992)

Munir, Muhammad *From Jinnah to Zia*, 2nd ed.(Lahore: Vanguard Books, Ltd, 1980)

"Munir Report" i.e. *Report of the Court of Inquiry constituted under Punjab Act II of 1954 to enquire into the Punjab disturbances of 1953* (Lahore: Government Printing, Punjab, 1954)

Nawawi *Minhaj-at-Talibin: A Manual of Mohammedan Law according to the School of Shafi'i* (French edition of A.W.C. ven dern Berg by E.C. Howard, District Judge, Singapore. London: Thacker, 1914)

Nazir-Ali, Michael *Frontiers in Muslim-Christian Encounter* (Oxford: Regnum Books, 1987)

Nazir-Ali, Michael *From Everywhere to Everywhere* (London: Collins, 1991)

Nisan, Mordechai *Minorities in the Middle East: a history of struggle and self-expression* (Jefferson, North Carolina: McFarland and Company, Inc, 1991)

Nizami, Muhammad Mazhar Hassan *The Pakistan Penal Code with Commentary and Shariat Criminal Laws* (Lahore: PLD Publishers, 1998)

Parwez, Ghulam Ahmed *Islam: a challenge to religion*, 3rd edition (Lahore: Asmat Alam Press, 1996)

Patel, Rashida *Islamization of laws in Pakistan?* (Karachi: Faiza Publishers, 1986)

Phailbus, Theodore (ed.) *The Cathedral Church of the Resurrection Lahore 1887-1987* (Lahore? Allied Press Limited, 1987)

Philipps, Godfrey E. *The Outcast's Hope* (London: Church Missionary Society, 1912)

Pickett, J. Waskom *Christian Mass Movements in India* (New York: The Abingdon Press, 1933)

Pickthall, Marmaduke *The Meaning of the Glorious Qur'an: text and explanatory translation* (Delhi: Taj Company, 1988)

Rabbani, M. Ikram *Introduction to Pakistan Studies: Seceondary, Intermediate, 'A' & GCE 'O' Level* (Lahore, Caravan Book House, 2001)

Rahman, Fazlur "Islam and the new constitution of Pakistan" in Korson, Henry (ed.) *Contemporary problems of Pakistan* (Leiden: E.J. Brill, 1974)

Rahman, Fazlur "Some Islamic Issues in the Ayub Khan Era" in Little, D.P. *Essays on Islamic Civilisation* (Leiden: E.J. Brill, 1976)

Rahman, S.A. *Punishment of apostasy in Islam,* 2nd revised and enlarged edition (Lahore: Institute of Islamic Culture, 1978)

Rashid, Ahmad *Taliban: Islam, Oil and the New Great Game in Central Asia* (London and New York: I.B. Tauris & Co. Ltd, 2000)

Rashiduzzaman, M. *Pakistan: A Study of Government and Politics* (Dacca: Ideal Library, 1967)

Report of the Court of Inquiry constituted under Punjab Act II of 1954 to enquire into the Punjab disturbances of 1953 often called the Munir Report (Lahore: Government Printing, Punjab, 1954)

Rooney, John *The Hesitant Dawn* (Rawalpindi: Christian Study Centre, 1984)

Rooney, John *Shadows in the Dark* (Rawalpindi: Christian Study Centre, 1984)

Rooney, John *Into Deserts: A History of the Catholic Diocese of Lahore, 1886-1986* (Rawalpindi: Christian Study Centre, 1986)

Rooney, John (ed.) *St Thomas and Taxila: A symposium on Saint Thomas* (Rawalpindi: Christian Study Centre, 1988)

Rushdie, Salman *Imaginary Homelands* (London: Granta Books, 1992)

Ruthven, M. *A Satanic Affair* (London: Hogarth, 1991)

Sadullah, Mian Muhammad (compiler) *The Partition of the Punjab 1947* Vol. II (Lahore: National Documentation Centre, 1983)

Schacht, Joseph *An Introduction to Islamic Law* (London: Oxford University Press, 1964)

Schimmel, Annemarie *And Muhammad is His Messenger: the veneration of the Prophet in Islamic piety* (Lahore: Vanguard, 1987)

Schmidt, C. *Die Alten Petrussakten im Zussamenhang der Apocryphen Apostelliteraure* (Leipzig, 1903)

Shaban, M.A. *The Abbasid Revolution* (Cambridge: Cambridge University Press, 1970)

Shafi, M. and Shari, P. *Labour Code of Pakistan,* 13th edition (Karachi: Bureau of Labour Publications, 1999)

Sharif, Nawaz, message in Phailbus, Theodore (ed.) *The Cathedral Church of the Resurrection Lahore 1887-1987* (Lahore? Allied Press Limited, 1987)

Sharma, Sri Ram *The Religious Policy of the Mughal Emperors* (first published Calcutta, 1940, reprinted Lahore: Panco Press, 1975)

Sheridan, Sharon *Hear the cry! Standing in solidarity with the suffering Church* Report of a consultation organised by the Episcopal Council for Global Mission, New York, April 1998 (New York: Anglican and Global Relations, 1998)

Sherif, Faruq *A guide to the contents of the Qur'an* (London: Ithaca Press, 1985)

Sidahmad, Muhammad 'ata Alsid *The Hudud* (Petaling Jaya: Muhammad 'Ata al Sid Sid Ahmad, 1995)

Siddiqi, Muhammad Iqbal *The Penal Law of Islam* (Lahore: Kazi Publications, 1979)

Siddiqui, Ataullah *Christian-Muslim Dialogue in the Twentieth Century* (Basingstoke: Macmillan Press Ltd, 1997)

State of Human Rights in 1998 (Lahore: Human Rights Commission of Pakistan, 1999)

Stewart, John *Nestorian Missionary Enterprise: the story of a Church on fire* (Trichur: Mar Narsai Press, 1961)

Stock, Frederick and Margaret *People Movements in the Punjab: with special reference to the United Presbyterian Church* (Bombay: Gospel Literature Service, 1975 copyright by the William Carey Library)

Streefland, Pieter H. *The Christian Punjabi Sweepers: their history and their position in present day Pakistan* (Rawalpindi: Christian Study Centre, 1974)

Suleri, Z.A. *Politicians and Ayub* (Rawalpindi: Capital Law and General Book Depot, 1965)

Syrjänen, Seppo *In Search of Meaning and Identity: conversion to Christianity in Pakistani Muslim culture* (Vammala: The Finnish Society for Missiology and Ecumenics, 1987)

Thomas, P. *Christians and Christianity in India and Pakistan* (London: George Allen and Unwin Ltd, 1954)

Tinker, Hugh *India and Pakistan: a political analysis,* 2nd ed., revised, (London: Pall Mall Press Ltd, 1967)

Tritton, A.S. *The Caliphs and their Non-Muslim Subjects: a critical study of the Covenant of Umar* (London: Oxford University Press, 1930)

U.S. Department of State *Country Reports on Human Rights Practices* (Washington: U.S. Government Printing Office, published annually)

Usman, Muhammad *Islam Pakistan Mein* (Lahore: Maktab-i-Jadid, 1969)

Uthman Safi *Ala hamish naqd al-fikr al-dini* (Beirut: Dar al-Tali'ah, 1970)

Watt, W. Montgomery *Muhammad at Medina* (Karachi: Oxford University Press, 1981)

Webster, John C. *The Christian Community and Change in Nineteenth Century North India* (Delhi: The Macmillan Company of India Limited, 1976)

Wellhausen, Julius "Muhammads Gemeindeordnung von Medina" *Skizzen und Vorarbeiten* (Berlin: G. Reimer, 1884-99) Vol. IV (1889)

West Pakistan Christian Council *Survey Report of the*

Church in West Pakistan: A Study of the Economic, Educational and Religious Condition of the Church 1955-1959 (Lahore, West Pakistan Christian Council, 1960)

Wheeler, Richard S. *The politics of Pakistan: a constitutional quest* (Ithaca and London: Cornell University Press, 1970)

White, Janet Ballantyne *Esther a Pakistani girl,* 2nd edition (Bible and Medical Missionary Fellowship, 1962)

Wootton, R.W.F. *Jesus more than a prophet* (Inter-Varsity Press, 1982)

Wright, W. *Apocryphal Acts of Apostles* (London, 1871, re-printed Amsterdam: Philo Press, 1968)

Yamani, Mai (ed.) *Feminism and Islam: legal and literary perspectives* (Reading, published for Centre for Islamic and Middle Eastern Law SOAS by Garnet, 1996)

Young, William G. *Handbook of Source Materials for Students of Church History,* (Madras: The Senate of Serampore College and the Christian Literature Society, 1969)

Young, William G. *Patriarch, Shah and Caliph: A study of the relationships of the Church of the East with the Sassanid Empire and the early Caliphates up to 820A.D. with special reference to available translated Syriac sources* (Rawapindi: Christian Study Centre, 1974)

Zafar, S.M. *Awam, Parliament, Islam* (Lahore: Aeina-i-Adab, 1980)

Zia ul Haq, message in Phailbus, Theodore (ed.) *The Cathedral Church of the Resurrection Lahore 1887-1987* (Lahore? Allied Press Limited, 1987)

Zwemer, S.M. *The Law of Apostasy in Islam* (London: Marshall Brothers Ltd, 1924)

Articles (including newspaper articles where author given)

Abbas, Azhar "Standing apart" *The Herald* (February 1997)

Abbasi, Ansar "SC withdraws order granting minorities right to joint electorate" *The News* (5 October 1993)

Addleton, Jonathan S. "A Demographic Note on the Distribution of Minorities in Pakistan" *Al-Mushir* Vol. XXVII no. 1 (Spring 1985)

Ahmad, Eqbal "Sectarianising national identity" *Dawn* (18 October 1992)

Ahmad, Mirza Mahmood "A.R. Cornelius a giant among mortals" *The News International* (28 December 1991)

Ahmad, Mubarik "Woes of the minorities" *The News International* (11 March 1997)

Ahmad, Riaz "Non-Muslims in an Islamic State" *Dawn* (16 November 1979)

Ahmad, Salah-Ud-Din "Ijtihad" reprinted in *All Pak. Legal Decisions* Vol. XXXII (1980) Journal 1

Ahmed, Khaled "The sack of Shantinagar" *The Friday Times* (20-26 February, 1997)

Ahmed, Manzooruddin "Islamic Aspects of the New Constitution of Pakistan" *Islamic Studies* Vol. II (1963)

Ahmed, Manzooruddin "Sovereignty of God in the Constitution of Pakistan: a study in the conflict of traditionalism and modernism" *Islamic Studies* Vol. IV, No. 2 (1965)

Ahsan, Ijaz "A religious civil war" *The Nation* (2 March 1997)

Akkara, Anto "Pakistani Christians remember bishop's 'ultimate' sacrifice for tolerance" *ENI Bulletin* No. 9 (21 May 1999)

Al-Faruqi, Ismail "Rights of Non-Muslims Under Islam: social and cultural aspects" *Journal of the Institute of Muslim Minority Affairs* Vol. 1 No. 1 (1979)

Ali, F. letter published in *The Muslim* (25 March 1996).

Ali, Mayed "Pakistani religious leaders respond angrily to Carey's suggestion for rethink on blasphemy law" *The News* (8 December 1997)

Ali, Rafaqat "Government takes ambivalent position" *The Muslim* (9 February 1994)

Amjad-Ali, Charles "Islamisation and Christian-Muslim Relations in Pakistan" *Al-Mushir* Vol. 29 No. 3 (Autumn 1987)

Amjad-Ali, Christine "Opening the curtains: minorities and women in Pakistan" *Al-Mushir* Vol. 33 No. 4 (Autumn 1991)

Amjad-Ali, Christine "News from the country" *Al-Mushir* Vol. 35 No. 3 (Winter 1993)

An-Na'im, Abdullahi Ahmed "The Islamic Law of Apostasy and its Modern Applicability: a case from the Sudan" *Religion* Vol. 16 (1986)

Ansari, Athar Hasan "Minorities Contribution to Pakistan" *The Muslim* (9 July 1998)

Asad, Muhammad "What do we mean by Pakistan?" (May 1947) reproduced in abridged form in *Impact International* (September 2001)

Askari, Hussain "A departure from the past" *The News* (25 May 1997)

Baabar, Mariana "Apartheid at NA canteen" *The News* (6 November 1997)

Babar, Najma "Minorities want joint electorate" *Dawn* (30 September 1993)

Baig, Khalid "Moral World Order" *Impact International* (September 1998)

Balchin, Cassandra "Some are less equal than others" *Frontier Post* (27 December 1991)

Bhutto, Benazir "Minorities, Women and the Political Processes" *Al-Mushir* Vol. 33 No. 4 (Autumn 1991)

Blasphemy Laws Targeting Minorities: an inquiry" *Human Rights Commission of Pakistan Newsletter* Vol. 3 No. 2 (April 1992)

Bokhari, Sadia "More sinned against..." *The Nation (Sunday Review)* (25 May 1997)

Bouma, Cees "Ninth Amendment and Shariat Bill" *Al-Mushir* Vol. XXVIII No. 4 (Winter 1986)

Bouma, Cees "Pakistan's Islamization 1977-88: The Zia era in retrospect" *Al-Mushir* Vol. 31 No. 1 (Spring 1989)

Brown, Stephen "World Council of Churches urges Pakistan to repeal blasphemy law" *ENI Bulletin* No. 10 (27 May 1998)

Butler, Fr R.A. "Islamic Resurgence in Pakistan and the Church" – a lecture given to the pastoral workers of the Catholic Archdiocese of Karachi in September 1980, and reproduced in *Al-Mushir* Vol. XXIII No. 2 (Summer 1981)

Calendar of State Papers, Colonial Series, East Indies (1862) 1513-1616 No. 659

Calkins, Philip B. "A note on lawyers in Muslim India" *Law and Society Review* Vol. III No. 2 (1968/9)

Centre for Legal Aid Assistance and Settlement *Update* (1ˢᵗ January – 30ᵗʰ June 1996)

Centre for Legal Aid Assistance and Settlement *Update: Christians in Pakistan* (August 2000)

Changez, Justice (retd.) A.R. "The Qanune-Shahadat, 1984" *Pakistan Times* (8 November 1984)

Chaudhry, Gulzar Wafa "A prophetic kiss: self-sacrifice for liberation" *The Minorities' View* (September – October 1998)

Choudhury, G.W. "Religious Minorities in Pakistan" *The Muslim World* Vol. XLVI No. 4 (1956)

"The Christian Church in Pakistan: a vision for the 21ˢᵗ century" Final statement of a seminar held at the Pastoral Institute, Multan, 7 to 11 April 1997 published in *Al-Mushir* Vol. 39 no. 2 (1997)

Coutts, Joseph letter published in *Dawn* (28 May 1998)

Deedes, W.F. and Combe, Victoria "Christians and the Cross" *The Daily Telegraph* (29 March 1999)

Dil, S.F. "The myth of Islamic resurgence in South Asia" *Current History* (April 1980)

Faruqi, M.H. "Jinnah's Pakistan: Islamic or secular?" *Impact International* (August 1995)

Faruqi, M.H. "Integral to Islam" *Impact International* (February 1998)

Fazl-ud-Din, Joshua "Separate electorates: the Life-Blood of Pakistan" originally published in *Punjabi Darbar* (Lahore, date not given) and later reproduced in Grover, Verinder and Arora, Ranjana (eds.) *Pakistan Fifty Years of Independence* (New Delhi: Deep and Deep Publications, 1997)

Final statement of the National Seminar on Religious Minorities in Pakistan: struggle for identity (July 18-20, 1996, Rawalpindi) reproduced in *Al-Mushir* Vol. 38 No. 3 (1996)

Fleming, Fr James " One victim's ordeal" *The Herald* (September 1997)

Forte, David F. "Apostasy and Blasphemy in Pakistan" *Connecticut Journal of International Law* (Fall, 1994)

Geijbels, M. "Pakistan, Islamisation and The Christian Community. Part two: The Status and Calling of Christians" *Al-Mushir* Vol. XXII No. 3 (Autumn 1980)

Geijbels, M. "The Prophet Muhammad's Birthday Festival" *Al-Mushir* Vol. XXVIII No. 4 (Winter 1986)

George, Naseem "The role of religious minorities in Pakistan's politics and the future direction" – a paper given at a seminar on "Religious Minorities in Pakistan: struggle for identity" (July 1996) reproduced in a book of the same title ed. Moghal, Dominic and Jivan, Jennifer (Rawalpindi: Christian Study Centre, 1996)

Gibb, H.A.R. "The Fiscal Rescript of 'Umar II" *Arabica* Vol. II No. 1 (January 1955)

Goldenberg, Susan "Fear among reviled believers breeds Christian soldiers" *The Guardian* (11 June 1998)

Gul, Muhammad Shan "Christians versus Christians" *The Friday Times* (6-12 February 1998)

Gul, Muhammad Shan "Courting the Law" *The Friday Times* (29 May – 4 June 1998)

Haider, Ejaz "A live given to a worthy cause" *The Friday Times* (15-21 May 1998)

Hasan, Suhaib Letter published in *The Times* (27 May 1998) under the heading "Earthly vengeance for blasphemy"

Howard, Roger "Wrath of Islam: the HUA analysed" *Jane's Intelligence Review* (October 1997)

Huq, Mahfuzul "Some reflections on Islam and Constitution-Making in Pakistan 1947-56" *Islamic Studies*, Vol. V No. 2 (1966)

Hussain, Sheher Bano [title unknown] *Newsline* (August 1997)

Hussein, Akbar "The Silenced Minority" *The Herald* (January 1992)

Hyder, Khurshid "Pakistan under Bhutto" *Current History* Vol. 63 No. 375 (November 1972)

Hyman, Anthony "The Impact of the Taleban on Pakistan" *Dialogue* (published by the Public Affairs Committee for Shi'a Muslims, London) (May 1999)

"Interview with Mohan Lal Shahani" *Rutherford International* Vol. 2 Issue 8 (August 1998)

Iqbal, M.M. "Blasphemy law" *The News* (22 December 1997)

Irfan, Ahmad "47 years! Time to roll back Islam" *Impact International* (August 1994)

Ismail, Muhammad "Major electoral reforms approved" *The Frontier Post* (27 February 1996)

Jacob, Noshin "Stranger at home" *The News* (24 July 1997)

Jacob, Peter "The Question of Identity for Religious Minorities" – a paper given at a seminar on "Religious Minorities in Pakistan: struggle for identity" (July 1996) reproduced in a book of the same title ed. Moghal, Dominic and Jivan, Jennifer (Rawalpindi: Christian Study Centre, 1996)

Jamshaid, Arif "The people time forgot" *The News* (15 June 1997)

Jan, Matiullah "Dual voting right: a constitutional discovery?" *The Frontier Post* (29 February 1996)

Jardine, Kenneth W.S. "Church and State in Pakistan" *The East and West Review* Vol. XV No. 4 (October 1949)

Jehangir, Asma "Minorities and Women in Pakistan" Paper presented at a seminar on the Constitutional Rights of Minorities and Women in Pakistan, Lahore, 21 October 1991, reproduced in *Al-Mushir* Vol. 33 No. 4 (Autumn 1991)

Jehangir, Asma "Submission of report the Hon'ble Supreme Court in the matter of bounded *(sic)* labour A.R. (L)/88-S.C.J. *All Pakistan Legal Decisions* Vol. XLII SC 583-588 (1990)

Jillani, Anees "Blasphemy laws and the minorities" *The News* (14 May 1998)

Jillani, Shahzeb "Choosing to stay with his people" *The News* (21 December 1997)

Khair Ullah, F.S. "The future of Christians in Pakistan" *Al-Mushir* Vol. XV No. 1 (1973)

Khan, Aamer Ahmed "Bearing Their Cross" *The Herald Annual* (January 1993)

Khan, Aamer Ahmed "The blasphemy law: the bigot's charter?" *The Herald* (May 1994)

Khan, Aamir *(sic)* Ahmed "Protest resignations are a family trait" *The Herald* (November 1992)

Khan, Justice Gul Muhammad "Islamization of the Laws in Pakistan" Presidential address at 5th Pakistan Jurists Conference, Karachi, reprinted in *All Pak. Legal Decisions* Vol. XXXVIII (1986) Journal 249

Khel, Muhammad Nazeer Kaka "The role of ideology in constitutional development in Pakistan" *Journal of Law and Society* Vol. I No. 1 (1982)

Khwaja, Imrana "Guilty even if proven innocent" *The Friday Times* (27 Feb – 4 Mar 1992)

Korson, J. Henry "Islamization and Social Policy in Pakistan" *Journal South Asian and Middle East Studies* Vol. 71 (1982)

Kraan, J.D. "Education in Pakistan: developments in 1984-1985" *Al-Mushir* Vol. XXVII No.1 (Spring 1985)

Kraan, J.D. "Muslim-Christian relations and Christian Study Centres" *Al-Mushir* Vol. XXVI Nos. 3 & 4 (1984)

Kraan, J.D. "News from the country" *Al-Mushir* Vol. XXVII No. 1 (Spring 1985)

Kraemer, Joel L. "Apostates, rebels and brigands" *Israel Oriental Studies* Vol. 10 (1980)

Lau, Martin "Islam and Fundamental Rights in Pakistan: the case of Zaheer-ud-Din v. The State and its impact on the fundamental right to freedom of religion" *Centre of Islamic and Middle Eastern Law Yearbook* Vol. 1 (1996)

Laville, Sandra "Christians massacred at prayer" *The Daily Telegraph* (29 October 2001)

Levrat, Jacques *Une Expérience de Dialogue. Les Centres d'Etude Chrétiens en Pays Musulmans* (Thèse de Doctorat présentée à la Faculté de Théologie de Lyon, 1984)

Lewis, Bernard "Behind the Rushdie Affair" *American Scholar* (1991)

Lewis, P. "The Shrine Cult in Historical Perspective" *Al-Mushir*, Vol. XXVI No. 2 (Summer 1984)

Lodhi, Justice Zakaullah "Ijtehad in the process of Islamization of laws" address at the seminar on the "Application of the Shari'ah" held at Islamabad 9-11 October 1979, reprinted in *All Pakistan Legal Decisions*, Vol. XXXII (1980) Journal 21-29

Malick, Mohammad "Minorities large and small" *Horizons* (The *Frontier Post* magazine) (7 January 1992)

Malick, Nasir "Religious Minorities provided protection, says Niazi" *Dawn* (6 January 1991)

Mangha, Raphael "Iqbal and the Reinterperation of Islam: a ground and guide for the theological task" *Al-Mushir* Vol. 38 No. 2 (1996)

Manyon, Julian "Blood and Fundamentalism" *The Spectator* (22 September 2001)

Masih, Shaukat letter to Benazir Bhutto, published in *Jaudat International* Vol. 5 no. 40 (April 1995)

Maudoodi, Syed Abul A'la "Psychological Basis of Separate Electorates" originally published in *The Punjabi Darbar* (Lahore, date not given) and later reproduced in Grover, Verinder and Arora, Ranjana (eds.) *Pakistan Fifty Years of Independence* (New Delhi: Deep and Deep Publications, 1997)

Mawdudi, S. Abul A'la "Twenty-nine years of the Jamaat-e-Islami" *The Criterion* (Karachi) Vol. 6 No. 1 (Jan-Feb 1971)

McClintock, Wayne "A sociological profile of the Christian minority in Pakistan" *Missiology : An International Review* Vol. XX No. 3 (July 1992)

Mehdi, Tabir "Polls Apart" *Newsline* (January 1997)

Mendes, Bonnie "Looking back at the ID card issue" *Focus* Vol. 13 supplement (1993)

Mendes, Bonnie "The Separate Electorate: Election 90" *Focus* Vol. 12 No. 4 (1990)

Mingana, A. "The Early Spread of Christianity in India" *Bulletin of the John Rylands Library*, Vol. X No. 2 (Manchester, 1926)

Mir, Anita "That way madness lies..." *The Frontier Post* (29 January 1994)

Mir, Anita "Citadels of difference?" *The Frontier Post* (16 February 1994)

Moghal, Dominic "Alienation of the Local People: the future of religious minorities in Pakistan" *Al-Mushir* Vol. 37 No. 2 (1995)

Moghal, Dominic "The status of non-Muslims in the Islamic Republic of Pakistan: a confused identity" – a paper given at a seminar on "Religious Minorities in Pakistan: struggle for identity" (July 1996) reproduced in a book of the same title ed. Moghal, Dominic and Jivan, Jennifer (Rawalpindi: Christian Study Centre, 1996)

Moghal, Dominic "The right of dual vote for non-Muslim Pakistanis and the anxieties of the religious groups: A moment of reflection for inter-faith harmony in Pakistan" Urdu version in *Al-Mushir* Vol. 38 No.2 (1996), English version in *Al-Mushir* Vol. 39 No. 2 (1997)

Mughal, Aftab Alexander "Freedom Without Fear" *Newsline* (December 1994)

Nazir, Noreen "The Concept of Ummah in the Medina Pact and its Implications on Pakistani non-Muslims" *Al-Mushir* Vol. 41 No. 4 (1999)

Niazi, M.A. "In the name of Islam" *The News International* (25 August 1996)

Paul, David "Recruitment policy and minorities" *The Frontier Post* (24 January 1992)

Paul, David "Do minorities enjoy equal rights" *The Frontier Post* (2 March 1992)

Peters, Rudolph and DeVries, Gert J.J. "Apostasy in Islam" *Die Welt des Islams* Vol. XVII Nos. 1-4 (1976-7)

Pirzada, Sayyid A.S. "The oppositional role of ulama in Pakistani politics" *Monthly Current Affairs Digest* 49 (September 1998)

Popham, Peter "Pakistan prepares to kill for blasphemy as Musharraf surrenders grip to the mullahs" *The Independent* (8 September 2001)

Powell, Avril "Contested Gods and Prophets: Discourse among minorities in late nineteenth-century Punjab" *Renaissance and Modern Studies* (December 1995)

Rahman, Fazlur "Islam and the constitutional problem of Pakistan" *Studia Islamica* Vol. XXXII No. 4 (December 1970)

Rahman, Fazlur "Non-Muslim minorities in an Islamic State" *Journal of the Institute of Muslim Minority Affairs* Vol. 7 (1986)

Rahman, Hafizur "Minorities in our midst" *Dawn* (23 September 1998)

Raja, Salman Akram "A blow to the federal structure of the state" *The News International* (12 September 1998)

Ramdey, Khalil report submitted to a meeting held under the direction of the Supreme Court of Pakistan (31 August 1998) *All Pakistan Legal Decisions* Vol. XLII SC 549-556 (1990)

Rashid, Ahmed "Pakistan backs down over blasphemy laws" *The Daily Telegraph* (18 May 2000)

Rehman, I.A. "UN advice on minorities" *The News* (12 July 1996)

Research staff of the Christian Study Centre "Country Focus" *Al-Mushir* Vol. 41 No. 2 (1999)

Richter, W.L. "Political Dynamics of Islamic Resurgence in Pakistan" *Asian Survey* (June 1979)

Rooney, John "Exploring St Thomas" *Al-Mushir* Vol. XXV Nos. 1&2 (1983)

Rumalshah, Munawar "Contemporary Challenges to the Religious World in Pakistan" *Al-Mushir* Vol. 39 No. 2 (1997)

Rumalshah, Munawar "Being a Christian in Pakistan" the testimony of Bishop Munawar (Mano) Rumalshah of the Diocese of Peshawar, Pakistan before the Senate Foreign Relations Committee on 17 June 1998, reproduced in Sheridan, Sharon *Hear the cry! Standing in solidarity with the suffering Church* Report of a consultation organised by the Episcopal Council for Global Mission, New York, April 1998 (New York: Anglican and Global Relations, 1998)

Rumalshah, Munawar "Hear the cry – of the voiceless: being a Christian in Pakistan" in Sheridan, Sharon *Hear the cry! Standing in solidarity with the suffering Church* Report of a consultation organised by the Episcopal Council for Global Mission, New York, April 1998 (New York: Anglican and Global Relations, 1998)

Ruxton, F.H. "Convert's Status in Maliki Law" *Moslem World* Vol. 3 No. 1 (1913)

Sada, Mehboob "The cheating of history" *Al-Mushir* Vol. 38 No. 3 (1996)

Sadeque, Najma "Leaving some issues to God" *The News* (26 May 1998)

Sadiq, Shanzay "Christians protest discrimination, victimisation" *Frontier Post* (15 April 1991)

Sadullah, Shahed "From Raiwind to Rochester" *Daily Jang* (26 August 1994)

Samdani, Zafar "Cornelius, a man always at peace with himself" *Dawn* (22 December 1991)

Sardar, Asawal "Test of faith" *Newsline* (September 1995)

Sarwar, Beena "God forbid..." *Frontier Post* (25 March 1993)

Sarwar, Beena "Pakistan: Blasphemy Law to Stay, Minor Modifications" *Inter Press Service* (19 July 1994)

Scott-Clark, Cathy and Levy, Adrian "Beyond Belief" *The Sunday Times Magazine* (24 January 1999)

Shahani, Mohan Lal interviewed in *Rutherford International* Vol. 2 Issue 8 (August 1998)

Shakir, Chaudhry Naeem "Fundamentalism, Enforcement of Shariah and the Law on Blasphemy in Pakistan" *Al-Mushir* Vol. 34 No. 4 (1992)

Shakoore, S. "Pakistan for All?" *Frontier Post* (date unknown, probably December 1993 or January 1994)

Shazad, W. "Revival of Liaquat-Nehru Pact and establisment of Minority Commission in Pakistan demanded" *Pakistan Christian Post* (7ᵗʰ August 2001)

Shehab, Rafi Ullah "Status of Non-Muslims under Holy Prophet's administration" *Pakistan Times* (12 April 1979)

Shirazi, Saj "Meet your sweeper" *The News* (22 June 1997)

Shirvanee, Imran "Crisis of identity" *The News International* (27 December 1997)

"Special Report of CLAAS" *Human Rights Today* (May-June 1996)

Stacey, V. "Of whom the world was not worthy" *Missionary Fellowship* (quarterly magazine of the Bible and Medical Missionary Fellowship, June 1960)

Suleri, Z.A. "Counter-revolution in Pakistan" *The News International* (14 August 1996)

Syrjänen, Seppo "Bradri – Millat – Ecclesia: the interrelationship of faith and community" *Al-Mushir* Vol. XV Nos. 11-12 (Nov-Dec 1973)

Tanzil-ur-Rahman "Some Aspects of the Islamic Law of Evidence" *All Pakistan Legal Decisions* Vol. XXXV (1983)

Tebbe, James "Interviews with Christian Members of the National Assembly" *Al-Mushir* Vol. XXVII No. 2 (Summer 1985)

Tebbe, J.A. "Separate Curriculum in Religious Education for Christians" in "News from the Country: the Christian community" *Al-Mushir* Vol. XXVII No. 2 (Summer 1985)

Tebbe, R.F. "Education in Pakistan: a minority perspective, 1982" *Al-Mushir* Vol. XXV No. 3 & 4 (Autumn and Winter 1983)

uz-Zahman, Waheed "Editor's Note" in *The Quest for Identity* (Proceedings of the First Congress on the History and Culture of Pakistani held at the Unviersity of Islamabad, April 1973. Islamabad: University of Islamabad Press, 1974)

Vemmelund, Laurits "The Christian Minority in the North West Frontier Province of Pakistan" *Al-Mushir* Vol XV Nos. 4-6 (April-June 1973)

Weaver, Mary Anne, "The CIA poured billions into a jihad …" reproduced in *Pakistan Christian Post* (7th September 2001)

Werge, Fiona "Analysis: Pakistan's Christian Minority" BBC World News website www.news.bbc.co.uk/hi/english/world/south_asia/newsid_1624000/1624617.stm (28 October 2001)

Wijoyo, Alex Soesilo "The Christians as religious community according to the hadit" *Islamochristiana* Vol. 8 (1982)

William, Javed "What role have the political parties played regarding the identity of religious minorities in Pakistan?" – a paper given at a seminar on "Religious Minorities in Pakistan: struggle for identity" (July 1996) reproduced in a book of the same title ed. Moghal, Dominic and Jivan, Jennifer (Rawalpindi: Christian Study Centre, 1996)

Wynne-Jones, Jonathan "Bishops stand 'shoulder to shoulder' with Muslims" *The Church of England Newspaper* (21 September 2001)

Yusuf, Zohra "The apartheid card" *The Herald* (November 1992)

Zaidi, Mazhar "Doomed by Faith" in *Newsline* (May 1994)

Zebiri, Kate "Relations between Muslims and Non-Muslims in the Thought of Western-Educated Muslim Intellectuals" *Islam and Christian-Muslim Relations* Vol. 6 No. 2 (1995)

Zia ul-Haq, interview in the *Pakistan Times* (5 March 1985)

United Nations Papers

Report by the Special Rapporteur, Mr Bacre Waly Ndiaye, submitted pursuant to commission on human rights resolution 1993/71, Commission on Human Rights, 50th session (1994), E/CN.4/1994/7 (7 December 1993)

Report by the Special Rapporteur, Mr Bacre Waly Ndiaye, submitted pursuant to Commission on Human Rights resolution 1994/82, Commission on Human Rights 51st session (1995), E/CN.4/1995/61 (14 December 1994)
Statement by Representative David Littman on 6 February 1995 to the United Nations Commission on Human Rights, Geneva (30 January – 10 March 1995)

Fourteenth Periodic Report of States parties due in 1996, Addendum Pakistan, submitted to the Committee on the Elimination of Racial Discrimination of the United Nations (International Convention on the Elimination of all Forms of Racial Discrimination) CERD/C/299/Add.6 (13 June 1996)

Littman, David and Wadlow, René, Association for World Education, letter to Mary Robinson (8 May 1998)

Unpublished Papers (including legal papers)

Ahmad, Qazi Hussain letter to Rt Reverend Mano Rumalshah, Bishop of Peshawar (undated but replying to the bishop's letter of 18 March 1997)

Allen, Trevor "Report on the death of Tahir Iqbal" (undated MS reporting information he received on 7 October 1992 in Lahore)

Anglican Communion News Service "Pakistan: WCC urge repeal of blasphemy law" circular (22 May 1998)

Arinze, Cardinal Francis, president of the Pontifical Council for Religious Dialogue, letter to Mr A.H. Zameer Ahmed, chief executive of the Group of Liberal Muslims, Lahore (undated but received 18 February 1998)

Barnabas Fund "Pakistan Blasphemy Petition Update No. 3" (19 March 1999)

Bhutto, Benazir, letter to Chairman of the Nobel Peace Prize Committee (10 April 1996)

Binyamin, A.H. Zameer Ahmed convener / chief executive of the Group of Liberal Muslims, on behalf of the Central Organising Council of the Muslim-Christian Solidarity Council Letter to the Bishop of Peshawar (8 April 1998)

Brutal murder of Christian teacher Naimat Ahmer under the garb of the blasphemy law (Lahore: National Affairs Commission of the National Council of Churches in Pakistan, no date but probably late January 1992)

Carey, George, *The human family and the duty of religion* Address by the Archbishop of Canterbury at the International Islamic University, Islamabad, Pakistan, visit to Pakistan 4-7 December 1998

Choudhury, Cecil interviewed in a radio report on *The World Tonight* (BBC Radio 4, 10 June 1998)

Christian Study Centre Rawalpindi *Annual Report 1997*

Christian Study Centre Rawalpindi – introductory leaflet describing their work (1996)

Christian Study Centre – leaflet "Study Islam in Pakistan" (undated but not earlier than 1995)

David, Dr P.J. and Shams, Qamar, president and general secretary respectively of the Pakistan Christian Welfare Organisation, letter to Mr Elahi Bux Sumro, speaker of the National Assembly of Pakistan and Mian Riaz Samee, High Commissioner of Pakistan (13 May 1998)

Dean, Dr George, fax letter to Patrick Sukhdeo *(sic)* (undated, but some time between 7 and 13 May 1998)

Fatchett, Derek, Secretary of State for Foreign and Commonwealth Affairs, House of Commons written answers for 23 June 1998 column 470

First Information Report No. 297/90 Police Station South Cantonment, Lahore (7 December 1990)

Francis, Joseph M. of the Centre for Legal Aid Assistance and Settlement *Christian massacre in Nowshera* CLAAS (30 November 1998)

Francis, M. Joseph "Statement of Protest" issued by the Pakistan Christian National Party (undated, but shortly after 9 Dec 1990)

Francis, Joseph *Update on Pastor Salim and Saleema Case* (Centre for Legal Aid Assistance and Development, undated but probably soon after 7 August 1997)

Ghauri, Sardar Hassan (Diocesan Treasurer) *Diocese of Peshawar Church of Pakistan Budget for 1996*

Horner, S. Horner of the South Asian Department of the Foreign and Commonwealth Office Letter to Shaheen Zar, secretary of the Asian Christian Church, Walthamstow (25 March 1997)

House of Commons Hansard debates (available on the Internet http://www.parliament.the-stationery-office.co.uk)

Human Rights Watch *Press Release* (10 July 1993)

Ismail, Zafar "Report on the Tahir Iqbal case" (5 August 1992, unpublished)

Ismail, Zafar *Pakistan: the Islamic state and the Christian community* unpublished paper presented at a consultation held at Glen Eyrie, Colorado Springs, 8-12 November 1992

Joseph, John Bishop of Faisalabad "The final step against 295-C" Open Letter (5 May 1998)

Joseph, John Bishop of Faisalabad *Vienna rally against death sentence in blasphemy law* (unpublished paper, 11 August 1998)

Judgement of additional sessions judge, Faisalabad, in Muhammad Yousaf vs. The State, 12 November 1991

Judgement sheet in the Lahore High Court at Lahore, Judicial Department on appeal no. 4385-B/ of 1991 arising from a hearing dated 2 March 1991

Judgement in the Court of Khan Talib Hussain Baloch, Additional Sessions Judge, Sargodha, Sessions Case No. 6 of 1992, Sessions Trial No. 6 of 1992, The State vs. Gul Masih s/o Dolat Masih caste Christian r/o Chak No. 46 N.B. City Sargodha

Khan, Sardar Feroze *An overview of Pakistan and socio-economic-political and religious issues facing the Christian community* (unpublished paper, probably 1991)

Malik, Alexander J. untitled paper given at Christian consultation, Lahore (September 1988)

Malik, Alexander John (Bishop of Lahore) Welcoming speech at the 31st session of the Church of Pakistan Lahore Diocesan Council (24 October 1991)

"Observations, comments and reactions to the Shariat Bill submitted by the Christian group, meeting with the Shariat Bill Committee on 27th December 1990" signed by Bishop Alexander John Malik of Lahore Diocese of the Church of Pakistan and Rev. Dr Charles Amjad-Ali, director of the Christian Study Centre, Rawalpindi

Mall, Gerald, address at St Thomas' Theological Seminary, Gujranwala (28 January 1999)

Nazir-Ali, Michael "Pakistani Christians" (21 October 1991)

"Pakistan: time to take human rights seriously" Amnesty International Index ASA 33/12/97 (1 June 1997)

Paul, David *The Untold and Unknown Christian Sufferings in Pakistan* (Lahore: Pakistan Christian Community Council, probably 1992)

Press conference on the desecration of churches, the Holy Bibles and the houses of Christian (sic) *in Khanewal and Shantinagar,* a statement addressed to journalists and signed by Bishop Samuel Azariah, of the Church of Pakistan Diocese of Raiwind, Mr Joseph Francis of the Centre for Legal Aid, Assistance and Settlement, Hina Jilani of the Human Action Forum, I.A. Rehman, director of Human Right of Pakistan, Group Capt (retd.) Cecil Chaudhury of St Anthony's School, Robert Taylor, territorial commander of the Salvation Army, Amjad Saleem Mehnaz of Punjab Nojawan, Younas Rahi of the Pakistan Christian National Party, Chaudhury Naeem Shakir of the Committee for Justice and Peace, and Shahtaj Qasilbash of the Joint Action Committee

The Role of Minorities in National Development – papers from a seminar held 27-29 April 1978 under the auspices of the Institute of Political and Social Studies of Forman Christian College, Lahore

Rumalshah, Mano *A New Paradigm: the Future of the Christian Community in Pakistan* (unpublished paper produced by Diocese of Peshawar, Lent 1996)

Scot, Daniel Personal testimony (July 1996)

Shahani, M.L. *Constitution, Law and Status of Minorities* (unpublished paper, 26 April 1992)

Sharif, Nawaz, speech to the National Assembly, 28 August 1998, quoted in *Dawn* 29 August 1998

Sialkot Diocesan Council, Minutes of the 24th annual meeting held on May 06 and 07, 1996
Letter dated 19 February 1997 to Mr Moin Jan Naim, Acting High Commissioner for Pakistan, signed by Rt Rev. David Smith, the Bishop of Bradford and Rev. Canon Peter Maguire, representing the Catholic Bishop of Leeds, Councillor Mohammed Ajeeb, ex-Lord Mayor of Bradford, Rev. Geoff Reid, representing the Rev. Peter Whittaker, Chairman of the Methodist Church West Yorkshire District, Sher Azam, ex-president of the Bradford Council for Mosques, Mr Andrayas Khan, Pakistan Christian Action Group, Faqir Mohammed, general secretary of the Bradford Council for Mosques, Khadim Hussain, President of the Bradford Council for Mosques, and Ishtiaq Ahmed, director of Bradford's Racial Equality Council

Stone, Rev. Christopher *Feedback from meeting on 13 May 1998 – Pakistani High Commission* notes taken by Stone, Rev. Christopher, communications officer of the Diocese of Rochester (representing the Bishop of Rochester at the meeting)

Letter to Prime Minister Nawaz Sharif on the subject of "Problems arising for Christians from the Shariat Bill" from Bishops Trinidade, Malik, Lobo, Pereira, Joseph and Azariah (4th December 1990)

Vaugh, Mr and Mrs Mason *A study of Economic Development in West Pakistan, Report and Recommendations* (unpublished paper, 1956)

Victor, Rajan – statement addressed to the Station Officer, Lakhidar Police Station, District Shikarpur (22 May 1993)

Zar, Shaheen, secretary of the Asian Christian Church (London) Letter to Rt Hon. John Major (17 February 1997)

Papers on Shanti Nagar incident, February 1997

Azariah, Bishop Samuel and nine other Christian leaders *Press Conference on the Desecration of Churches, the Holy Bibles, and the Houses of Christian in Khanewal and Shantinagar* (8 February 1997)

Dean, George "Incident at Shanti Nagar, Pakistan, Feb 5th and 6th 1997" (8 February 1997)

Fazal, Asghar, teacher at St Joseph's Catholic School, Khanewal (11 February 1997)

George, Sister Naseem and Mughal, Aftab Alexander *Shantinagar's Incident: special report* (Justice and Peace Commission of the Conference of Major Religious Superiors in Pakistan, 13 February 1997)

Ismail, Zafar (14 February 1997)

Ismail, Zafar *Pakistan: Violence in Shanti Nagar – Khanewal February 5 and 6, 1997* (17 March 1997)

Wafa, Gulzar (14 February 1997)

Yusaf, Patras, Catholic Bishop of Multan in press release
of 8 February 1997 issued by Caritas Pakistan
"Muslims blaming Christians burning Holy Qur'an"
(unidentified Catholic source)

Pakistani newspapers and periodicals cited

The Christian Voice – a Roman Catholic newsletter,
published irregularly

The Daily Jang – the most reputable national and
international Urdu daily, it has the largest circulation of all
Urdu dailies in Pakistan and internationally

The Daily Nawa-i-Waqat, Rawalpindi – this takes an
extreme right wing stance and supports the Jama'at-i-Islami

The Daily Khabren – a tabloid Urdu daily, particularly
popular in cities of the Punjab

Dawn – a liberal, balanced, reliable daily

Focus – an occasional publication of the Roman Catholic
Church in Pakistan

The Friday Times – an ultra-secular weekly, sometimes
unreliable in its reporting of facts

The Frontier Post – a daily with accurate reporting which
supports the Awami National Party (formerly Communist)
and is very much against the extremist Muslims.

The Herald – a very reliable, secularist, feminist monthly

Human Rights Today – a publication of the Pakistan Christian National Party

Jaudat International – a monthly edited and owned by a reputable Catholic journalist, an organ for the Christian minority

The Minorities' View – an occasional periodical of the Pakistani Masihi League, very critical of state policies towards minorities

The Mirror – newsletter of the National Commission for Justice and Peace

The Muslim – a daily which takes a moderate Muslim stance and supports the Pakistan Muslim League of Nawaz Sharif.

The News – a moderate daily paper, which backs the party of the Pakistan Muslim League of Nawaz Sharif. It is very careful and cautious in its factual reporting, and has the highest circulation in Pakistan. There is also a London edition, called the *News International*, which puts a different slant on what it reports.

News Letter of the Justice and Peace Commission (of Major Superiors of Pakistan)

Newsline – a secular monthly, serious and well respected.

Pakistan Christian Post – the news website of the Pakistan Christian Congress, a Pakistani Christian political party based in New York

The Pakistan Observer – a long established and reputable monthly, with well researched, balanced analyses of national affairs

The Pakistan Times – a state organ published daily

Punjabi Darbar – a monthly edited by Joshua Fazl-ud-Din, which flourished in the 1960s but has now ceased publication

Raiwind Diocesan Newsletter – produced by the Church of Pakistan Diocese of Raiwind

Update – six-monthly reports from the Centre for Legal Aid Assistance and Settlement on human rights cases

INDEX

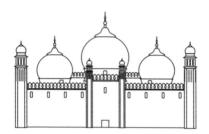

Other books from
Christian Focus Publications
and Isaac Publishing

A
CHRISTIAN'S
POCKET GUIDE
TO

PATRICK SOOKHDEO

'This little book is a helpful mine of factual information and
practical advice.'
Rt Rev. Colin Bennetts,
Bishop of Coventry

A Christian's Pocket Guide To Islam
Patrick Sookhdeo

Have you ever watched a T.V. programme or read a newspaper article where a commentator clumsily illustrates his complete ignorance of Christianity and it's claims? How often have you rolled your eyes and immediately discounted what is being said, saying to yourself "Well, why should I listen to them when they obviously haven't got a clue!" How, then, can we expect to witness effectively to those of the Muslim faith if all that we know of Islam is picked up from passing references in the media?

This fascinating book provides Christians with a simple description of the origins of Islam, what Muslims believe and how it affects their attitudes, worldview, everyday life and culture. Practical guidelines are given for relating to Muslims in a culturally appropriate way, as well as for witnessing effectively and caring for converts.

If you long to reach Muslim friends but are wondering where to start then this is the book for you.

'...clearly and concisely describes the major facets of that faith and is punctuated with helpful insights for those seeking positive ways to relate as Christian witnesses to Muslims.'
Rev. Dr Bill Musk, former missionary in the Middle East, author of three books on Christians relating to Muslims

'Written for those with no prior knowledge of Islam, this book gives all the basic facts which will help a Christian to be more effective in their witness, as well as helpful guidance on how to approach Muslims lovingly and appropriately.'
Zafar Ismail, chairman of Interserve's Ministry Among Asians in Britain

Patrick Sookhdeo is Director of the Institute for the Study of Islam and Christianity, a Christian research institute specialising in the status of Christian minorities in the Muslim world. Dr Sookhdeo is a well known lecturer and author who holds a Ph.D. from London University's School of Oriental and African Studies and a D.D. from Western Seminary, Oregon, USA.

ISBN 1 85792 699 4   96pp trade format

Coming soon from Isaac Publications and Christian Focus
Publications

World Of Islam

This major work comes in a three volume set,
comprehensively covering Islam, from it's origins through
to it's theology and practice. The world's fastest growing
religion is explained, analysed and revealed, helping you
to thoroughly grasp what motivates the hundreds of millions
who profess the muslim faith.

Volume 1 History of Islam

Volume 2 Islamic Theology

Volume 3 Living Islam